This book belongs to the collection of

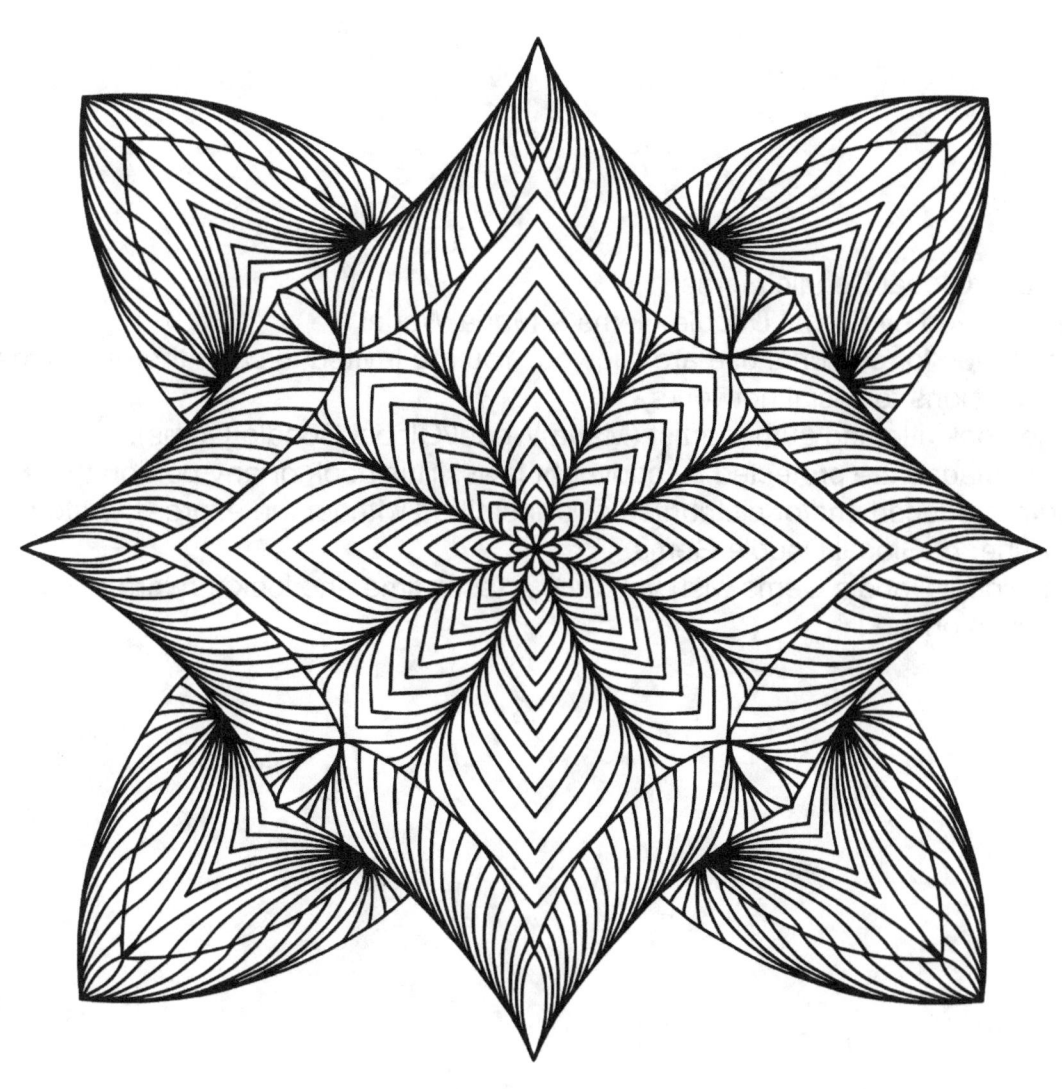

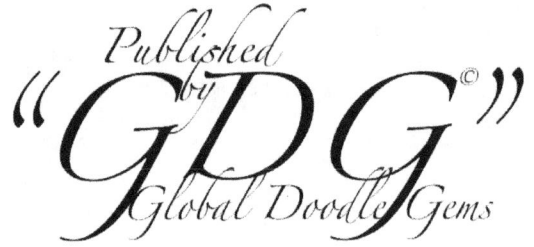

Copyright © 2019 Global Doodle Gems
All rights are reserved by Global Doodle Gems & Maria Wedel
Duplication of pages for personal use are allowed. You are invited to color the pages then scan/post your coloured versions to social networks,
mentioning the book title and author/artist (Maria Wedel/Global Doodle Gems).
All artwork and images are protected by copyright laws. This book or any portion thereof may not, otherwise, be reproduced and/or distributed or transmitted without the express written permission of the artist/publisher of Global Doodle Gems.
All of us from Global Doodle Gems wish you a colortastic time and look forward to seeing your wonderful color results online !

Kaleido 1

125 Kaleido drawings, intricate drawings to color and make great visual effects with !
These are sets of 25, where the first drawing is the template and starting point of the next 24 drawings,
to explore the different possibilities in the basic first drawing !

"This book is dedicated to the love of my life, my daughter Victoria Panthera. I make these books in hopes that your life as an adult will be everything you want It to be! I love you more than words can say!"

Maria Wedel

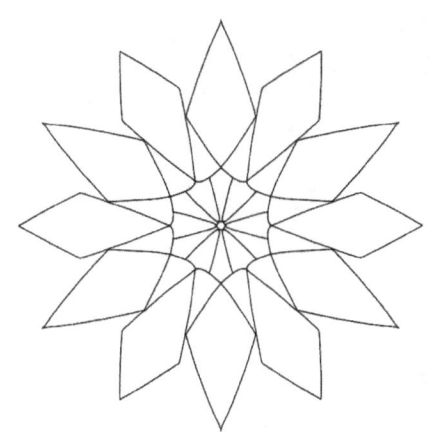
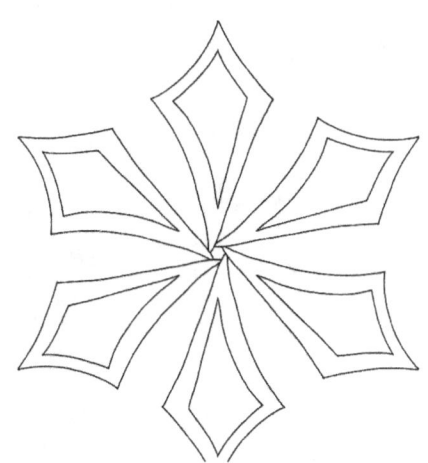
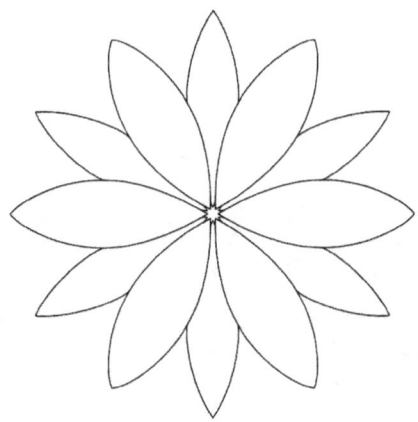
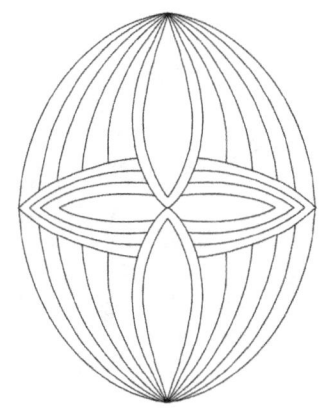
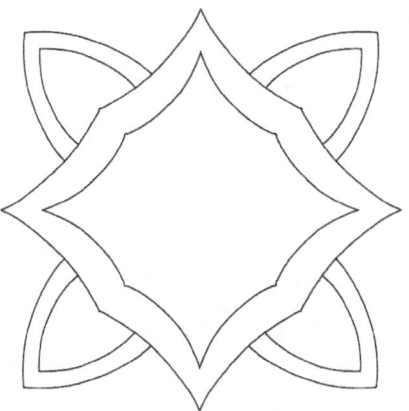

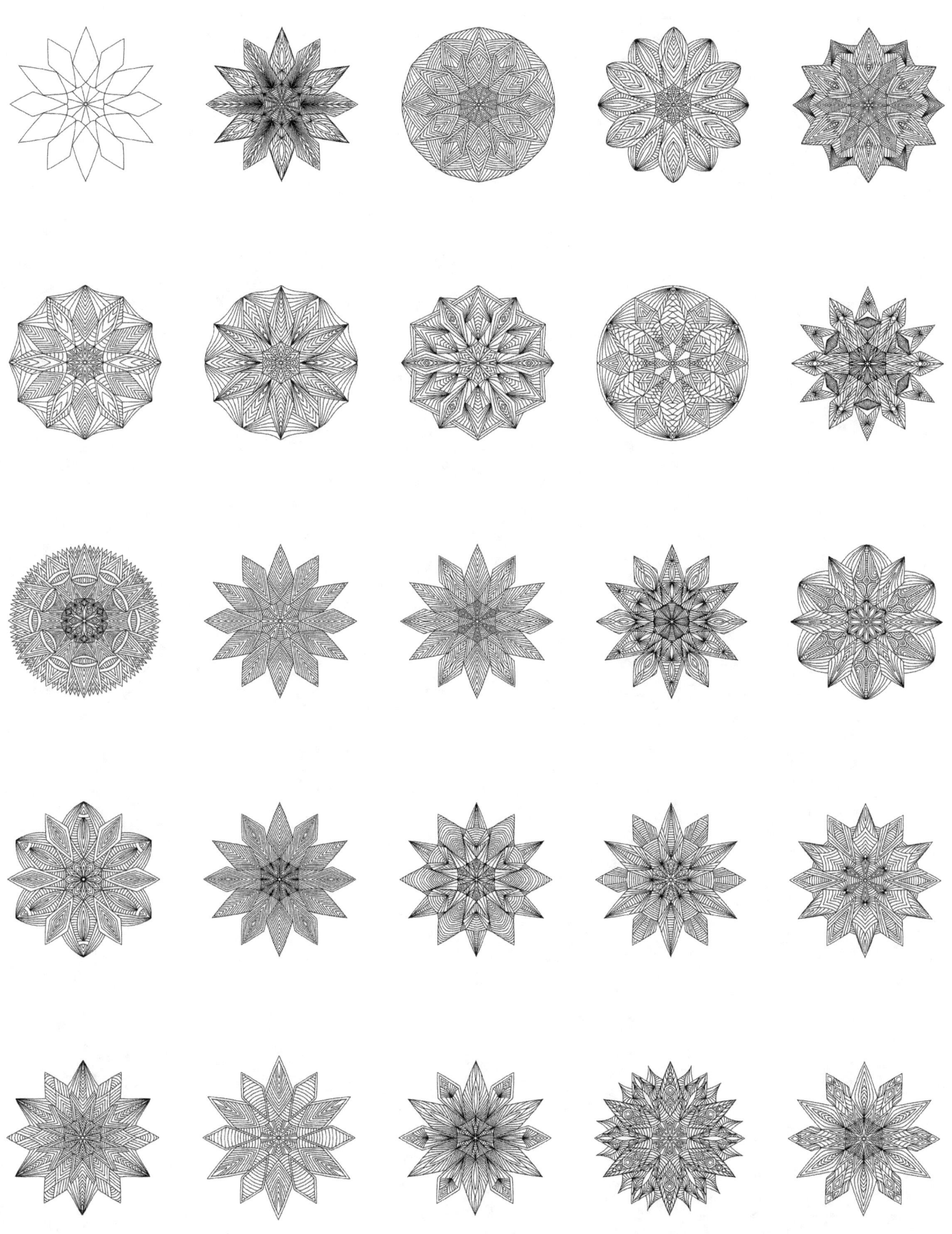

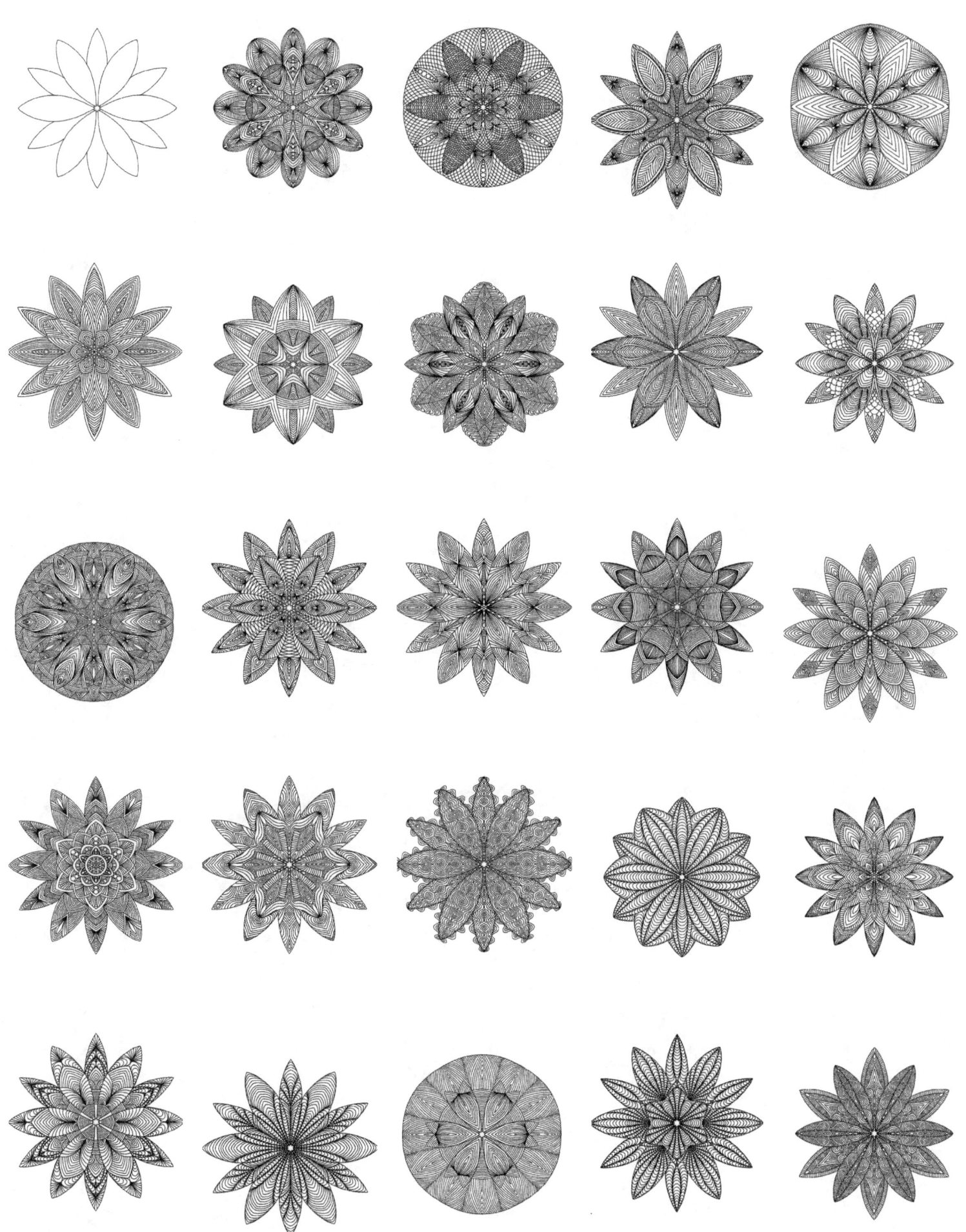

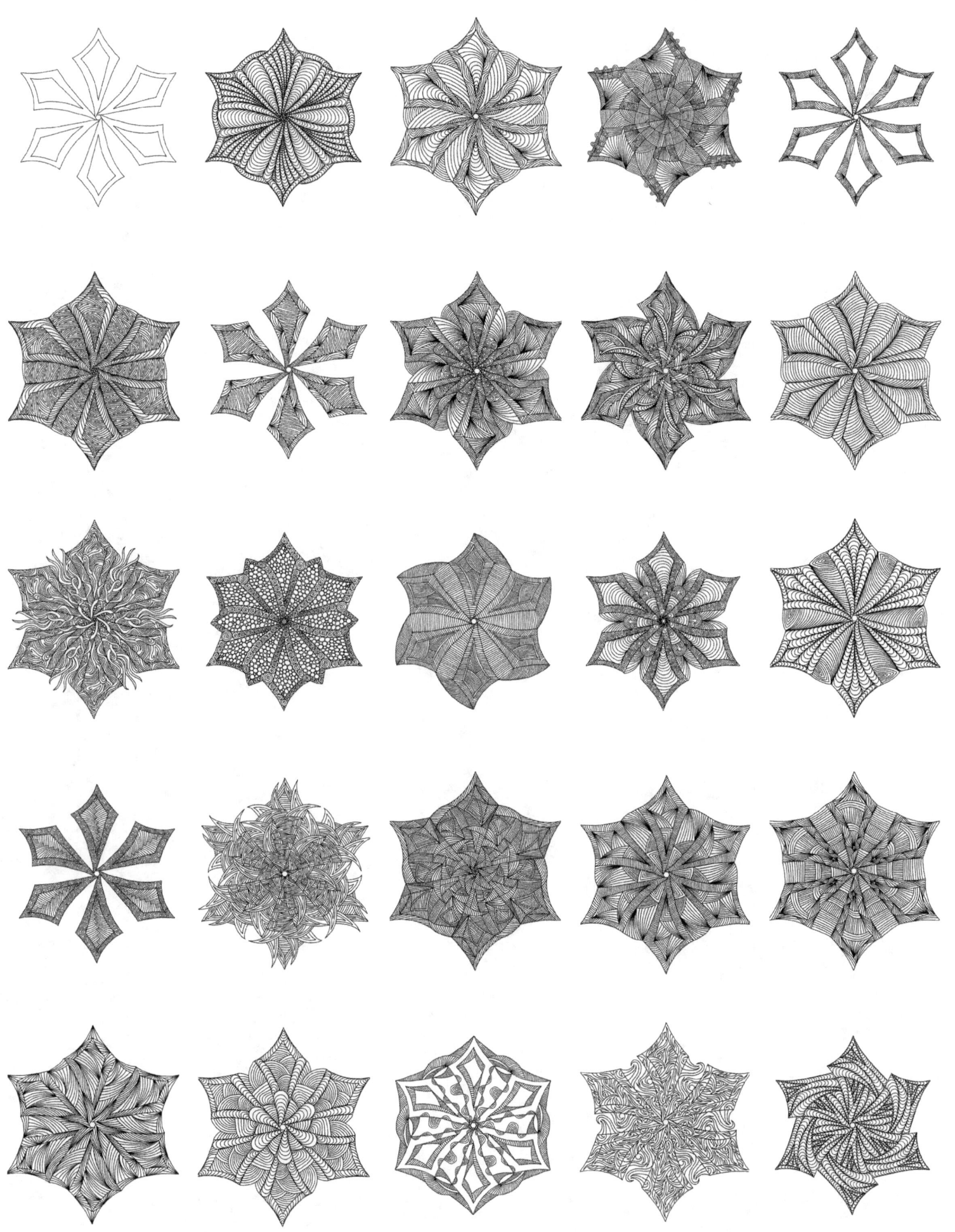

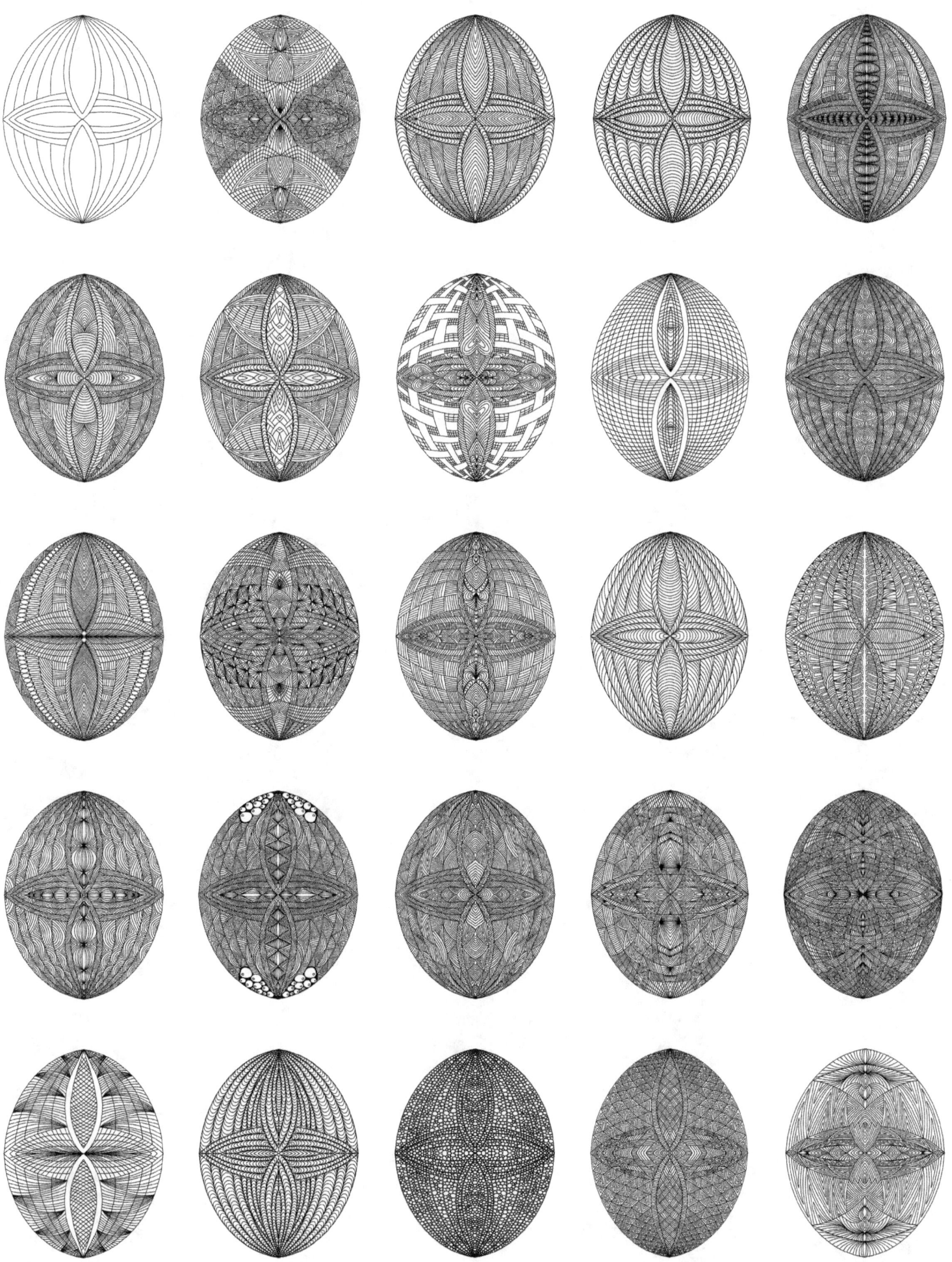

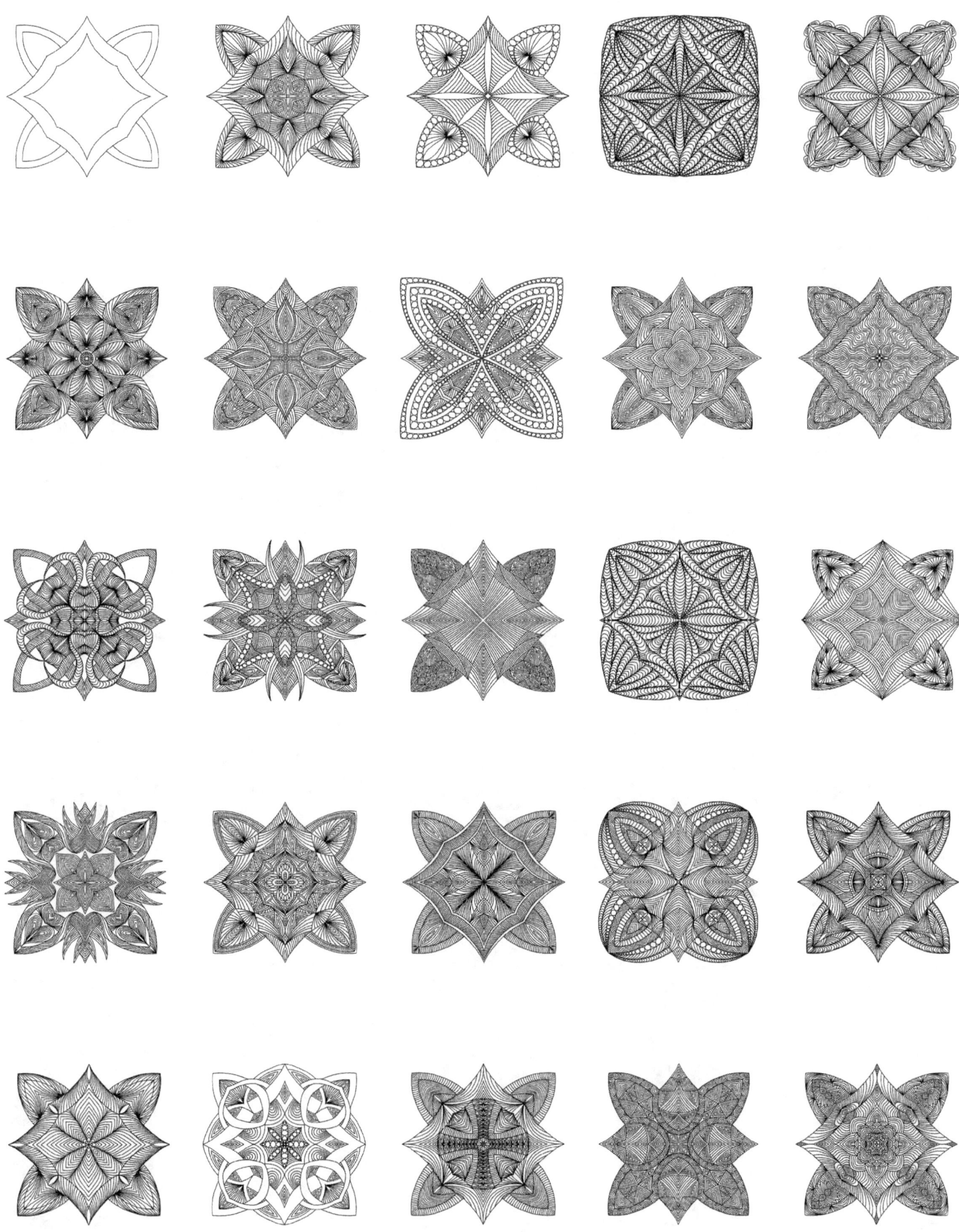

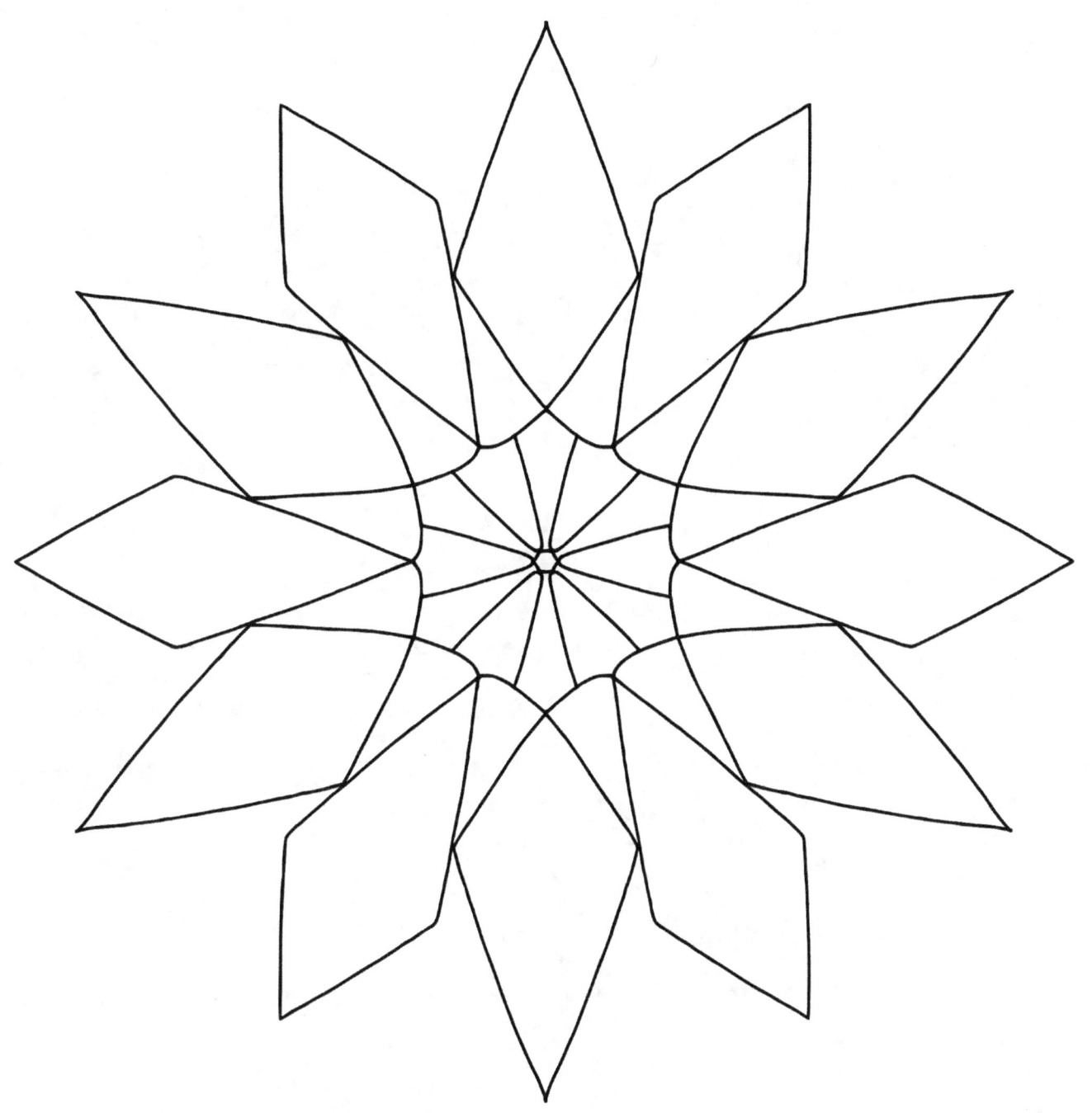

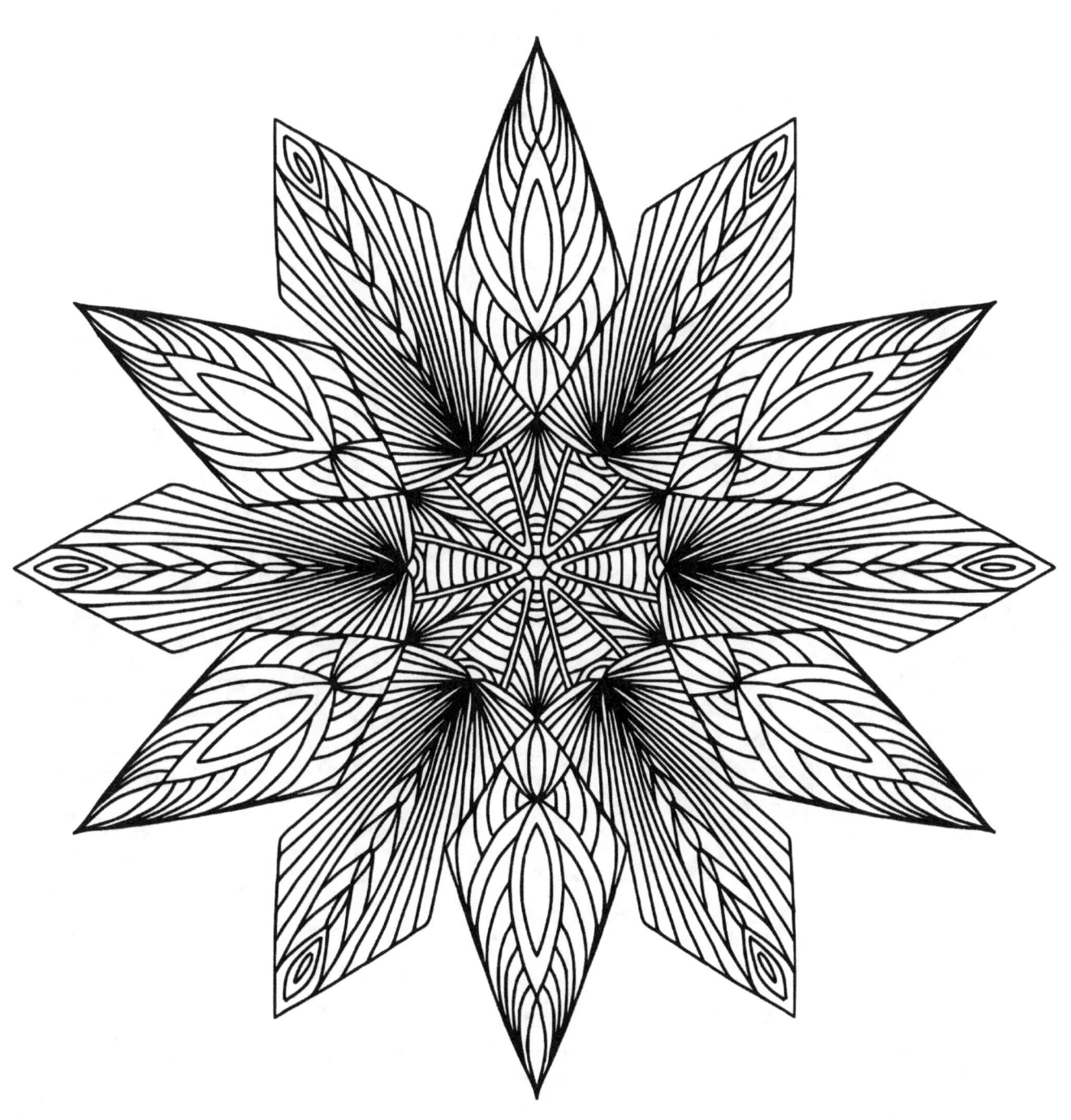

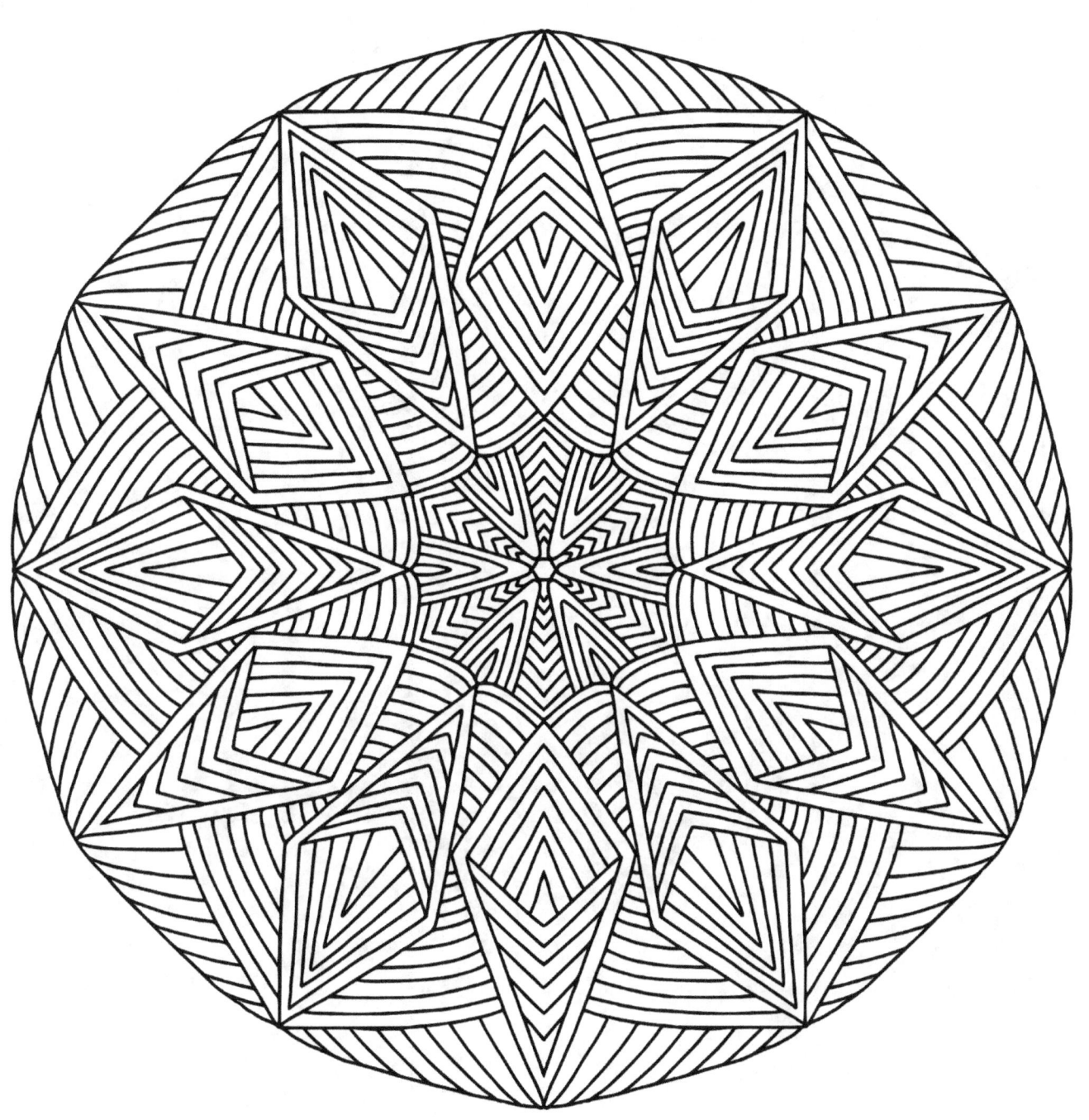

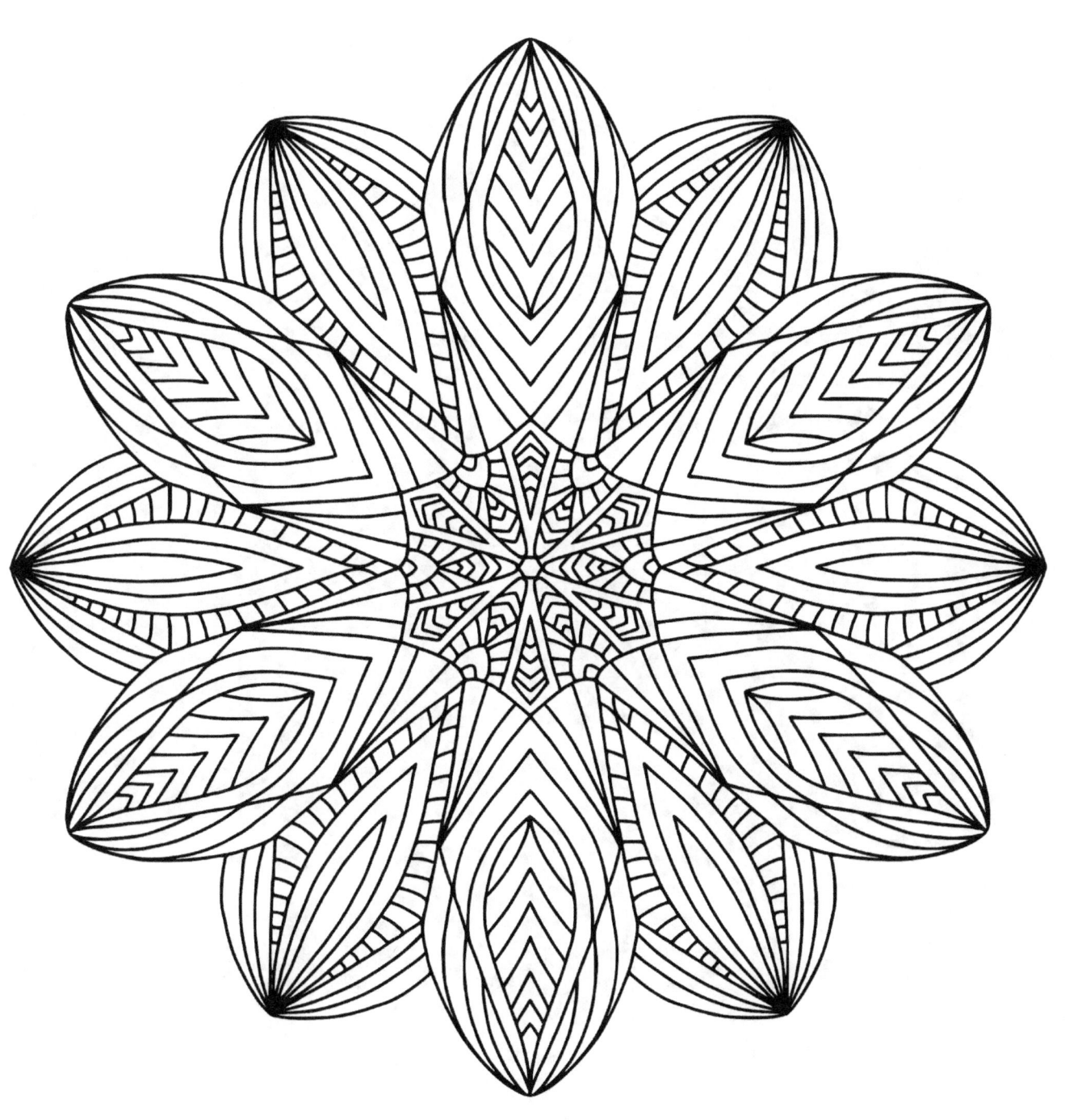

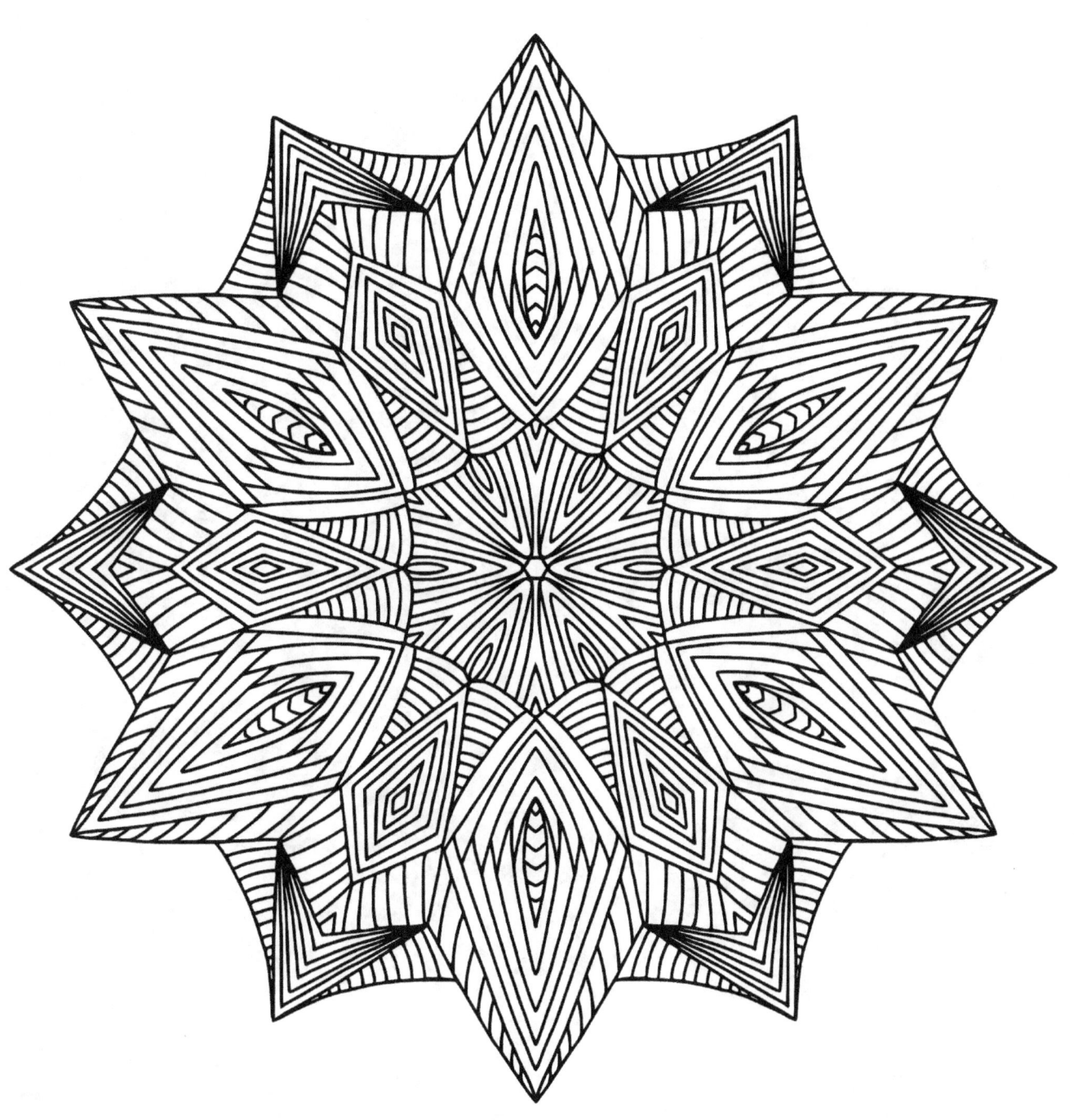

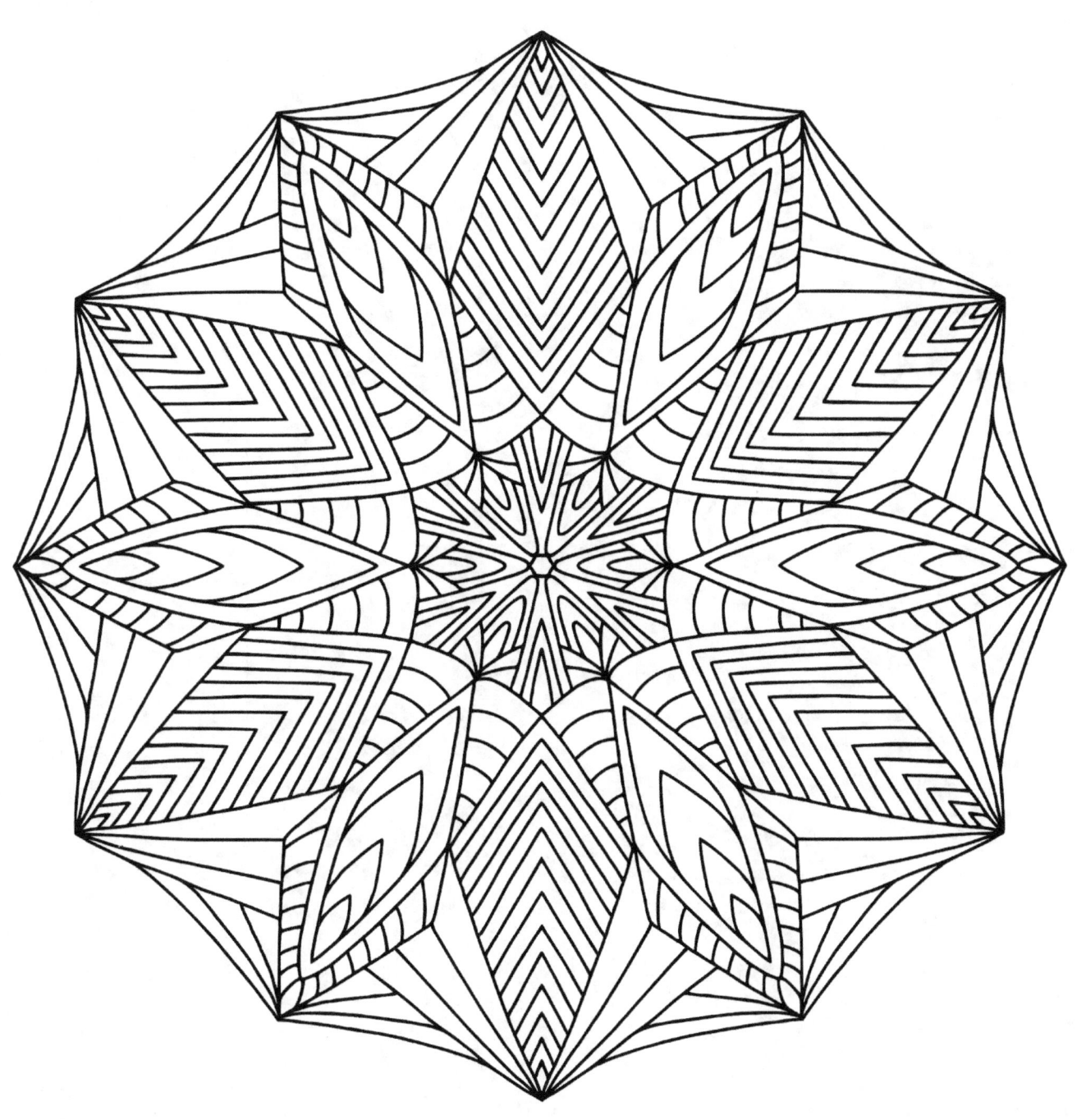

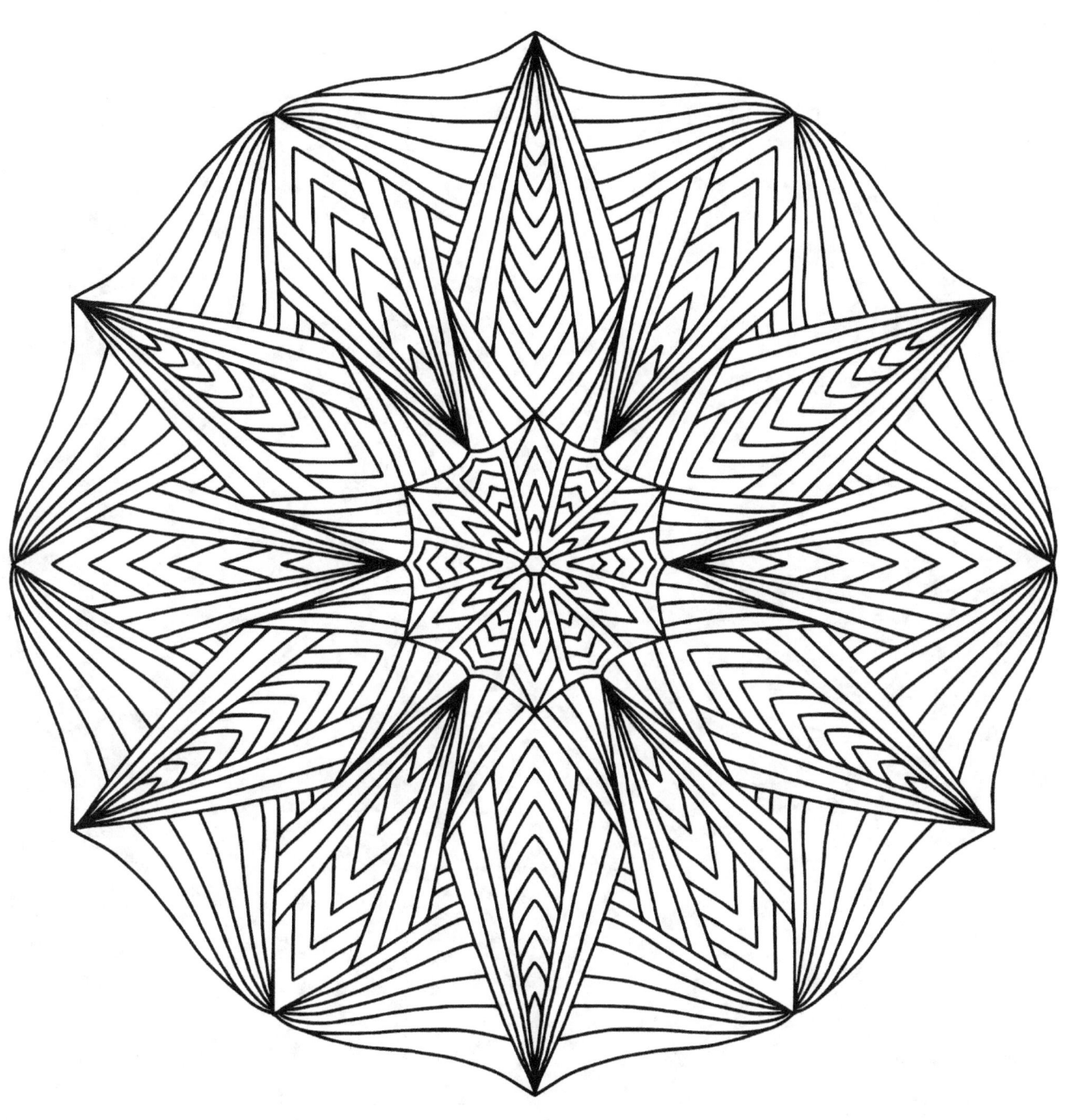

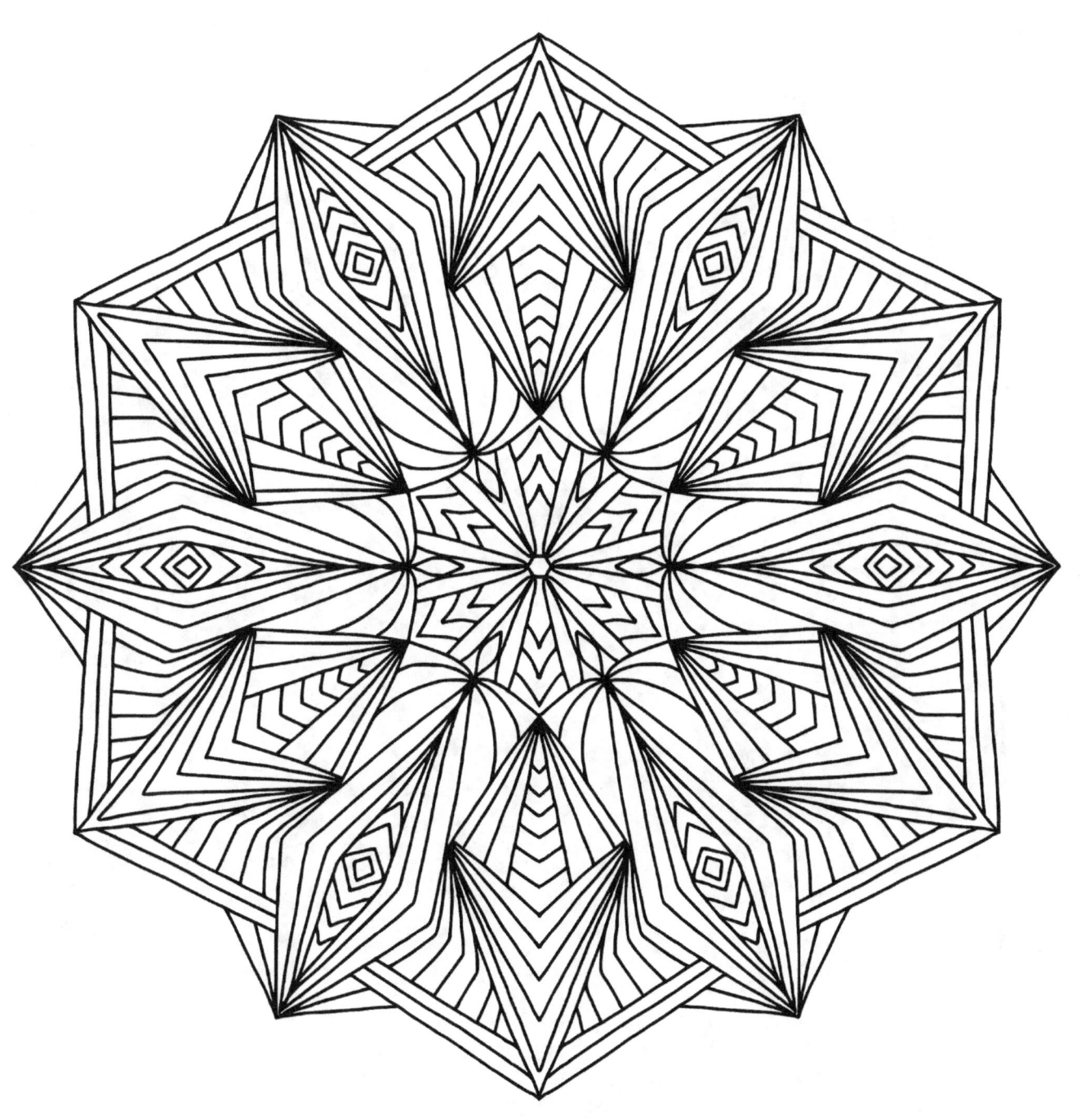

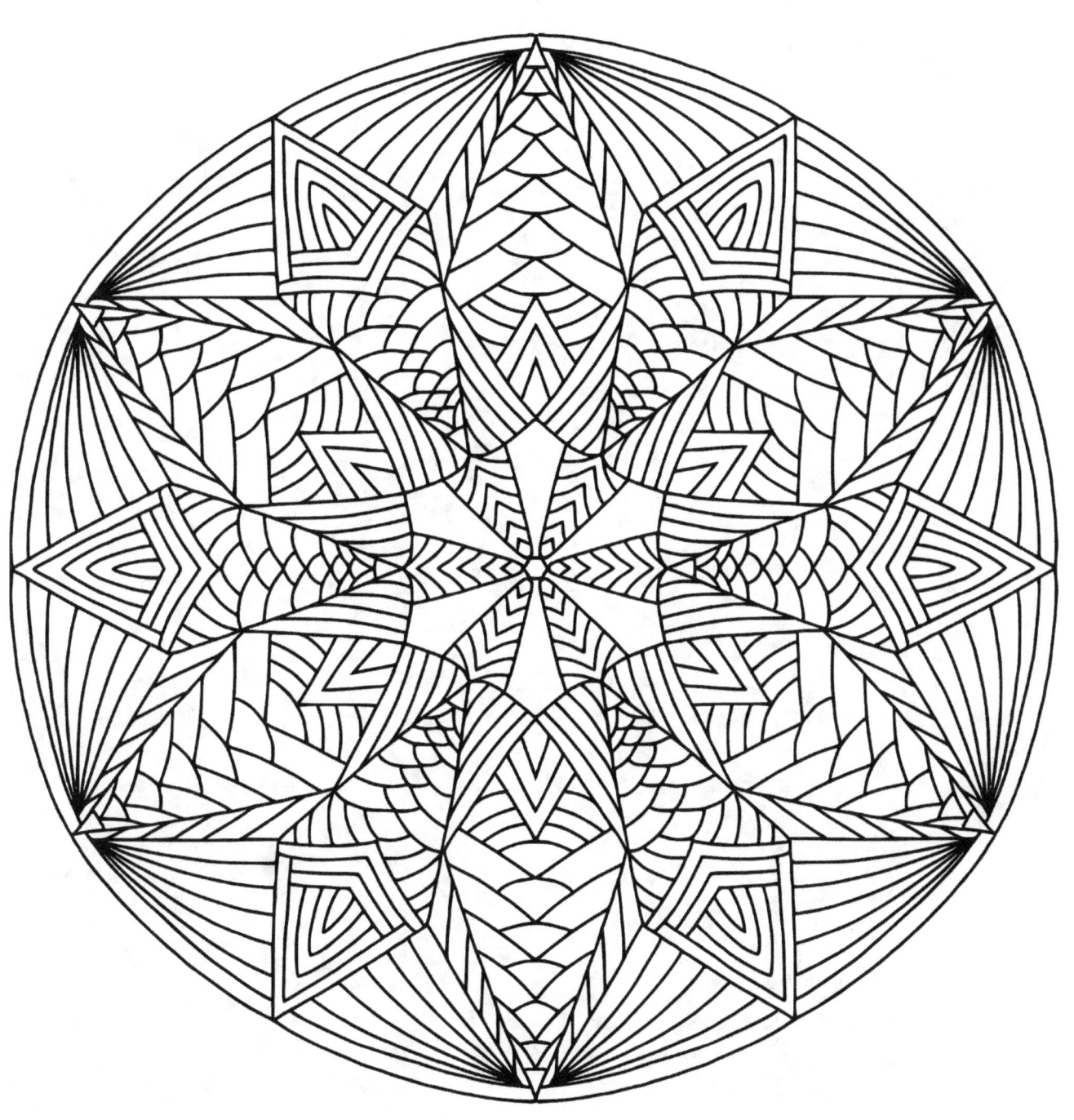

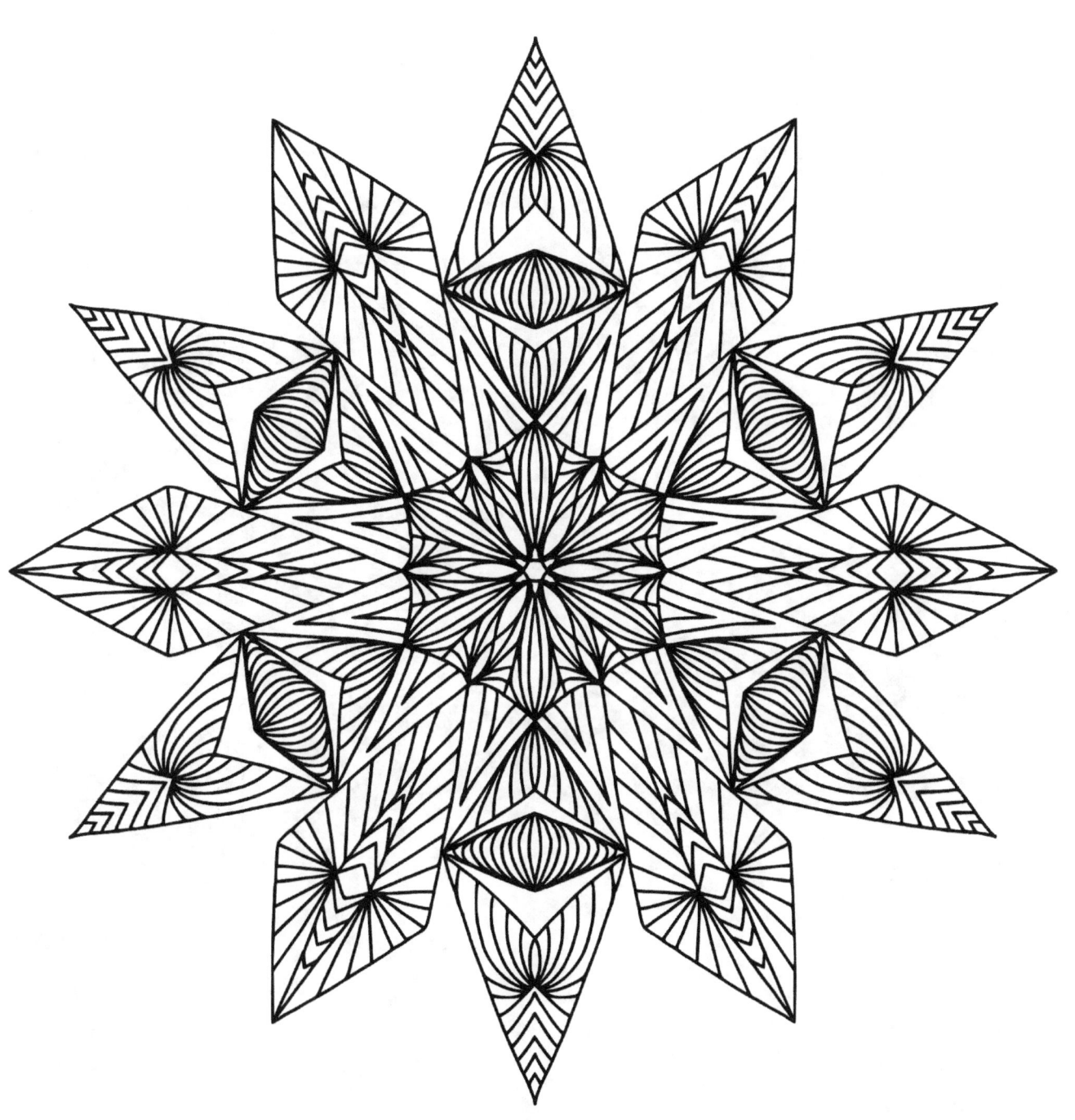

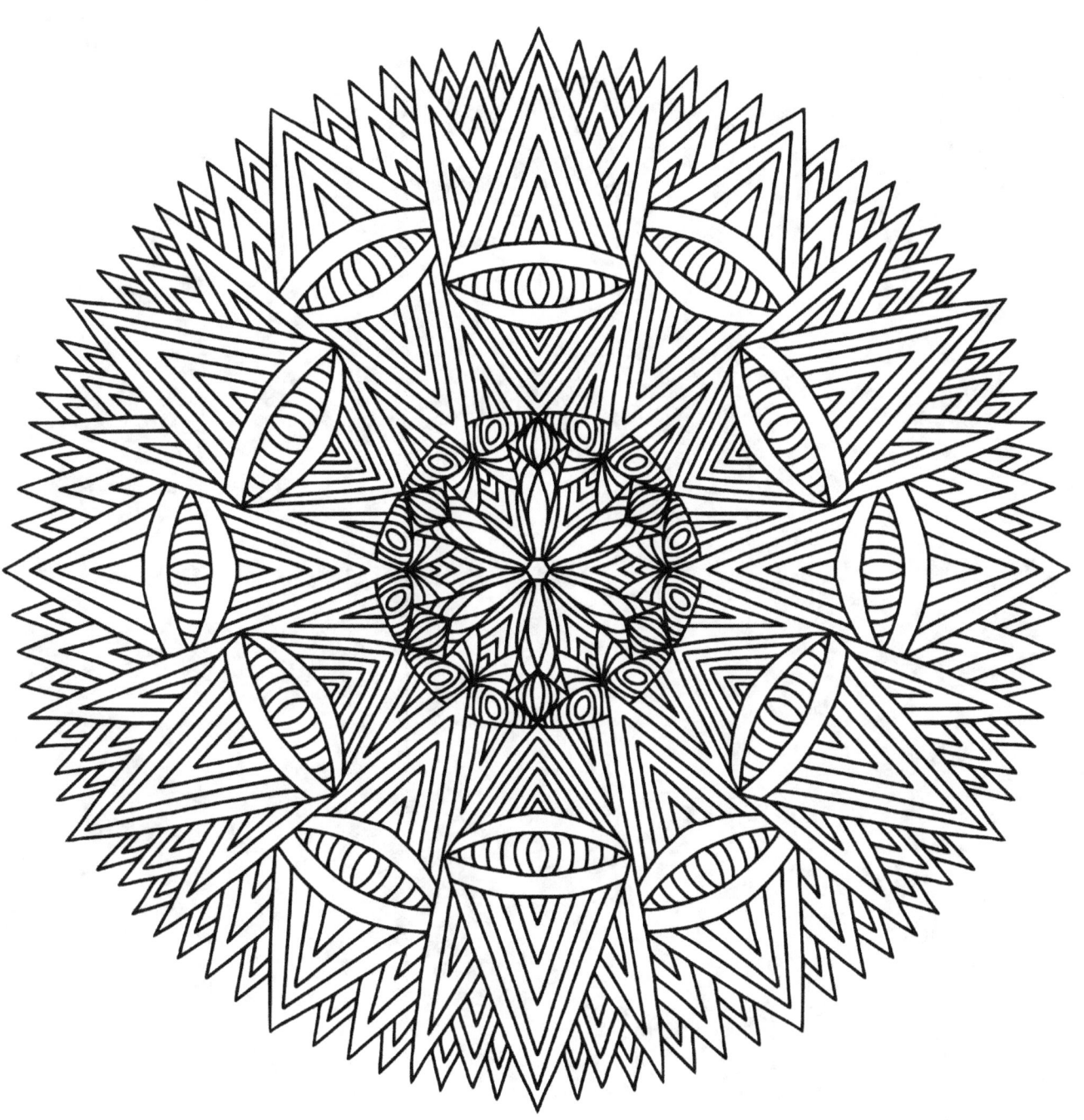

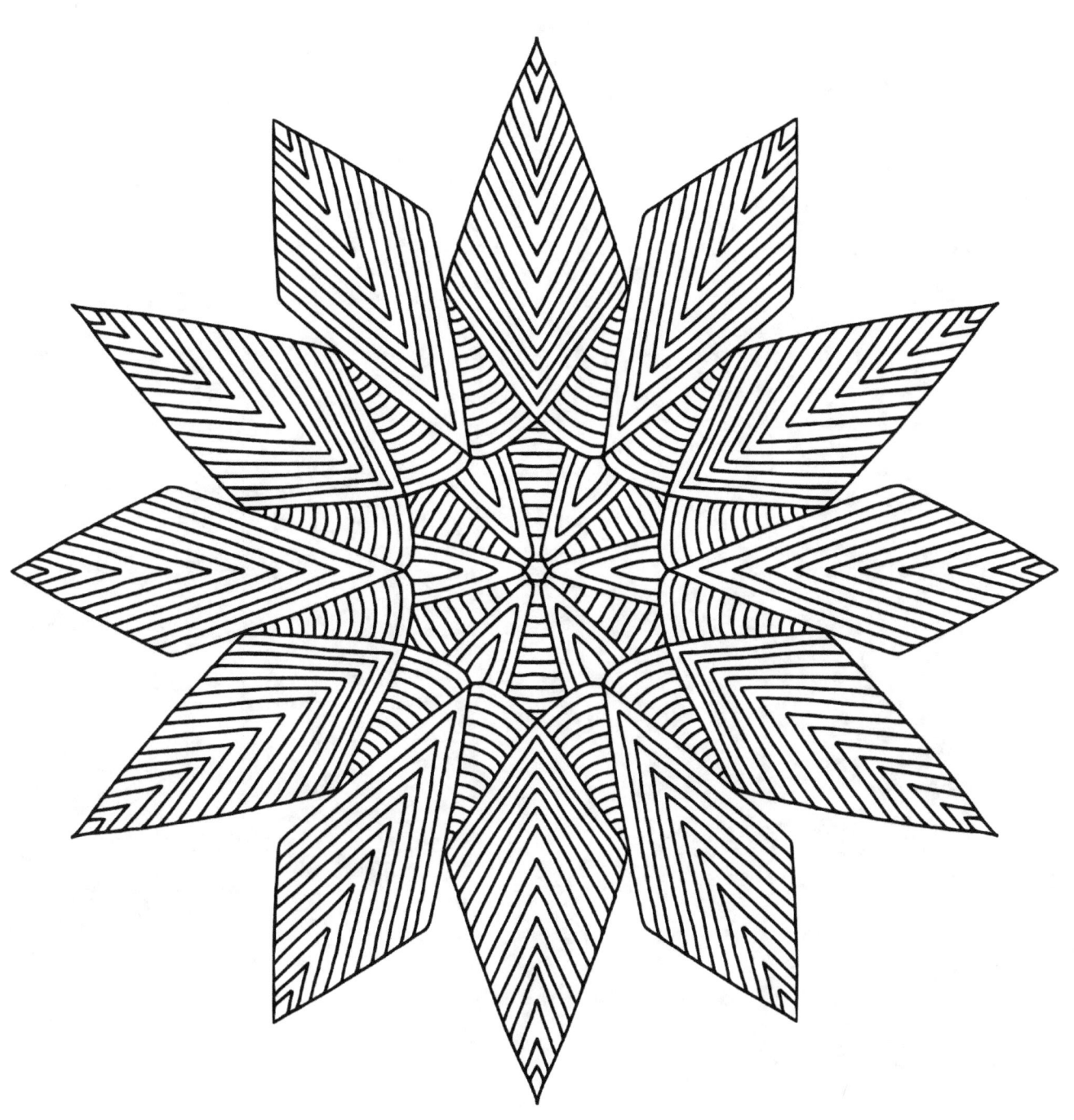

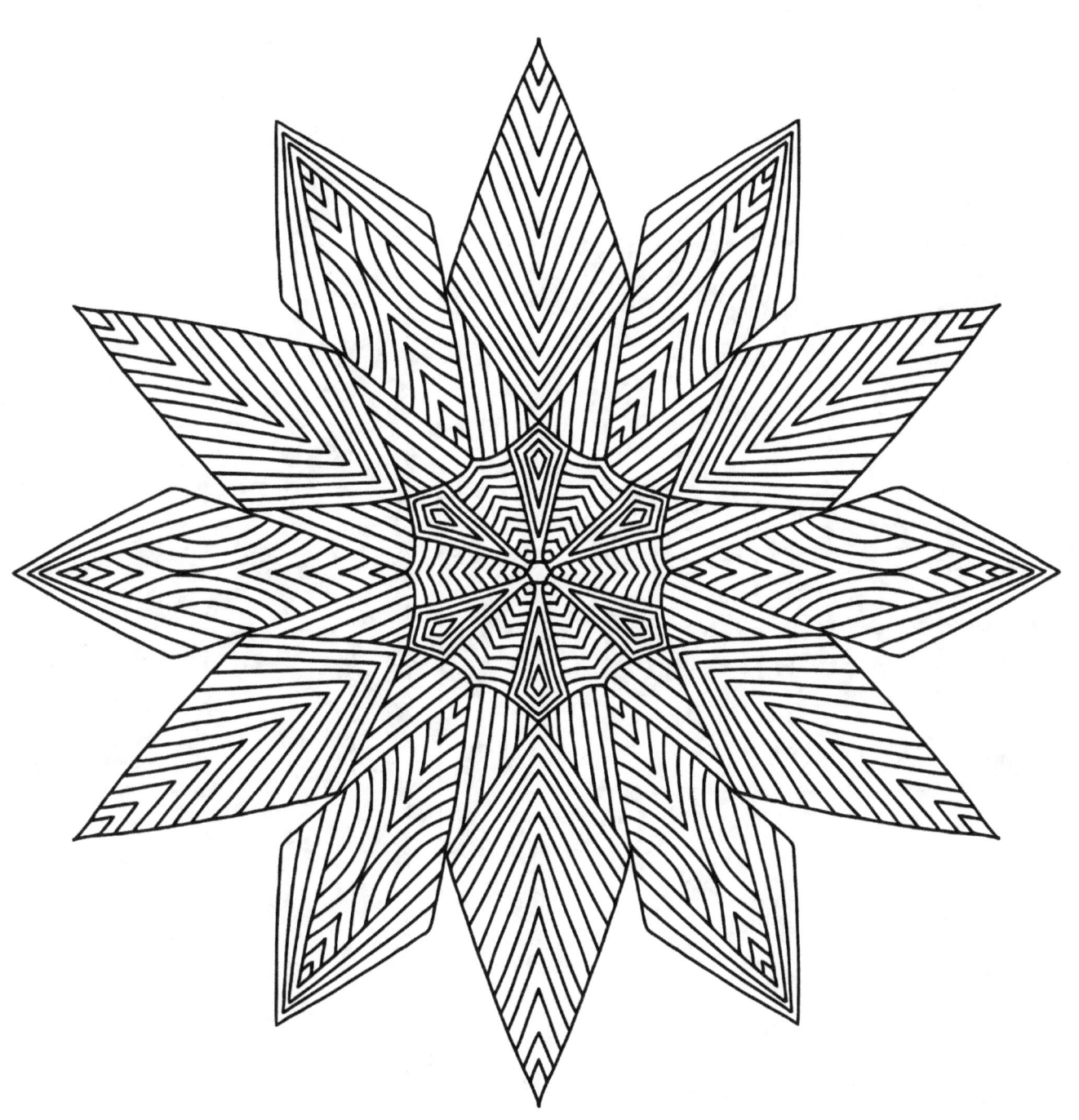

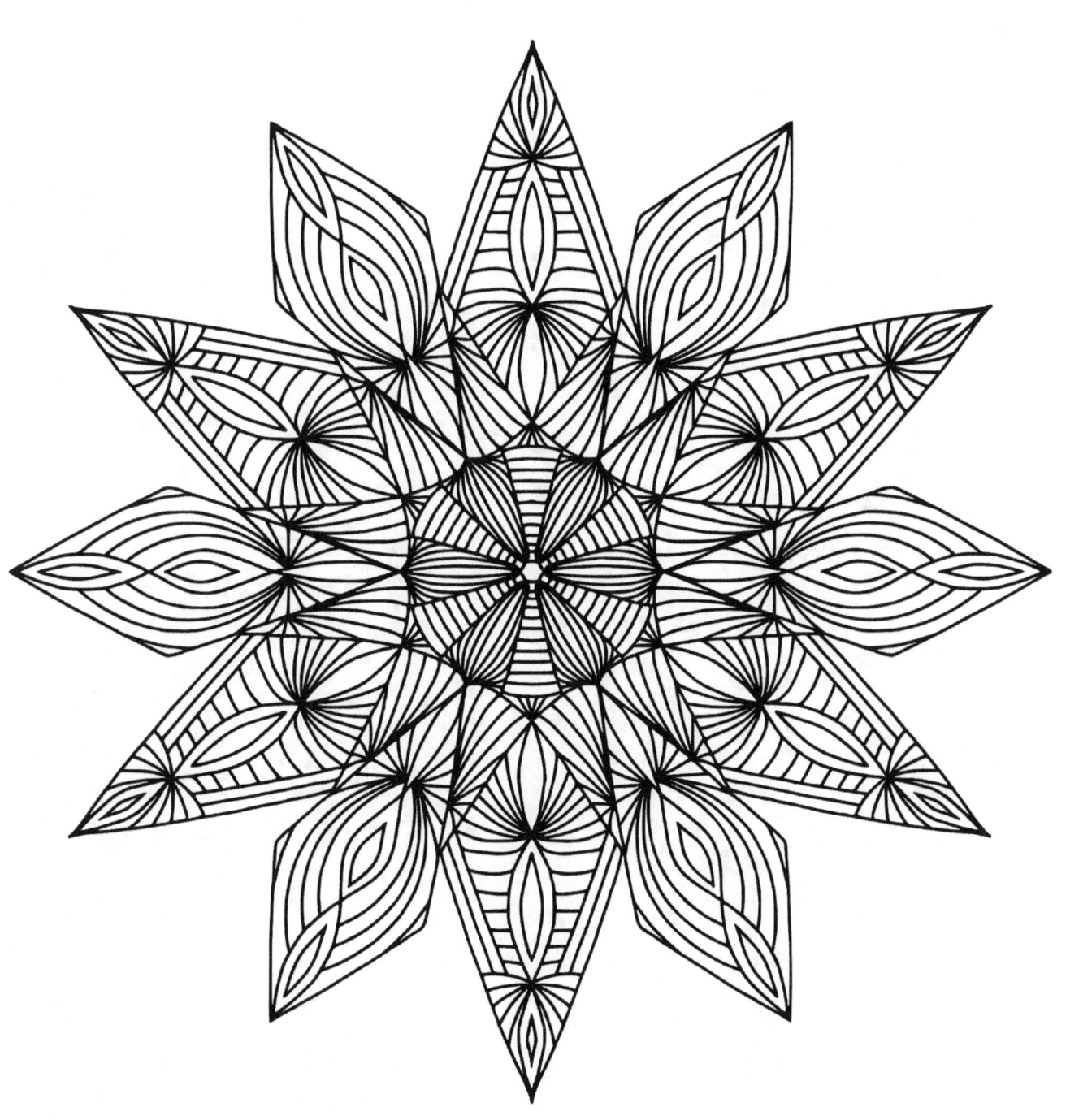

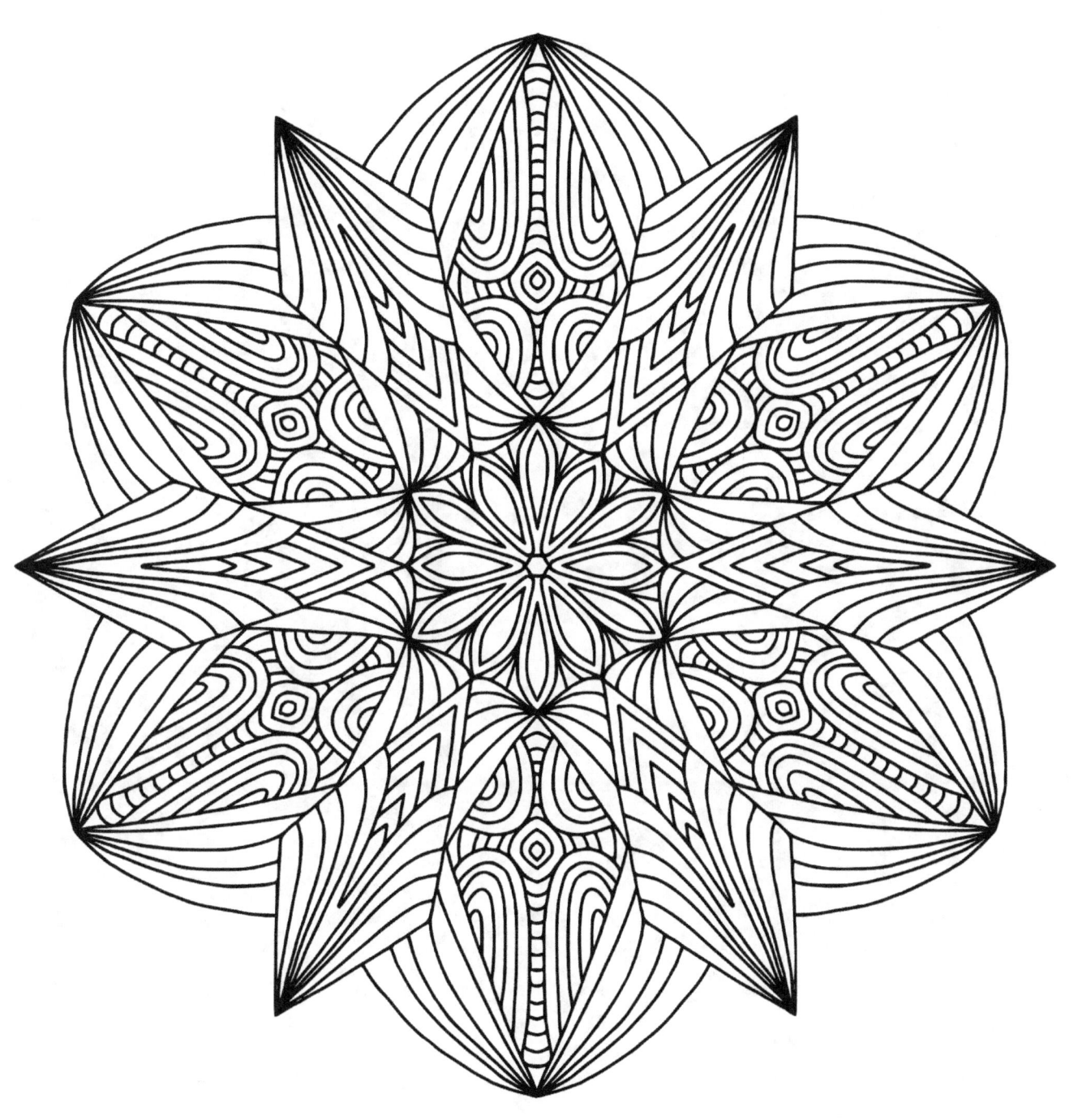

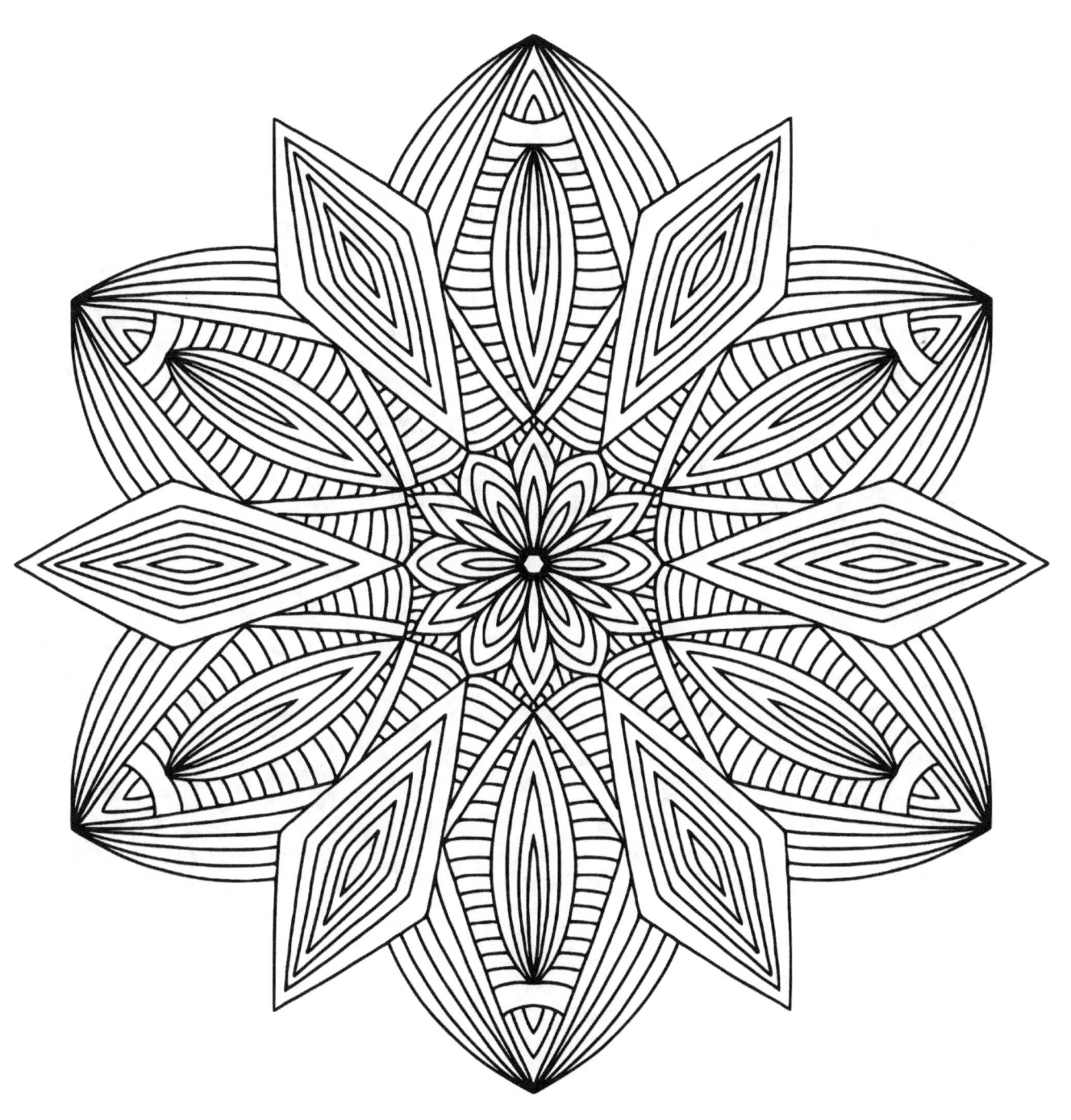

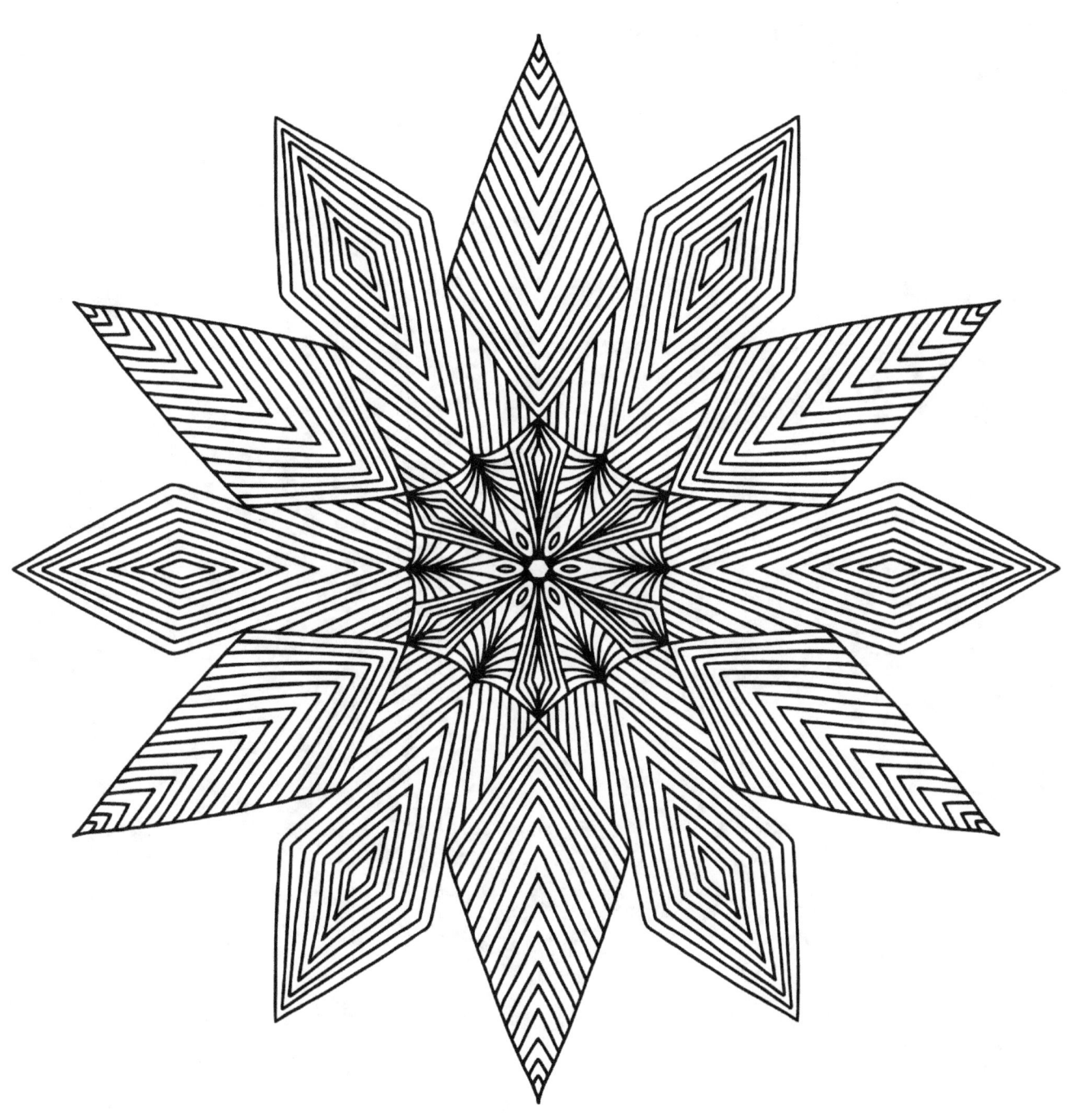

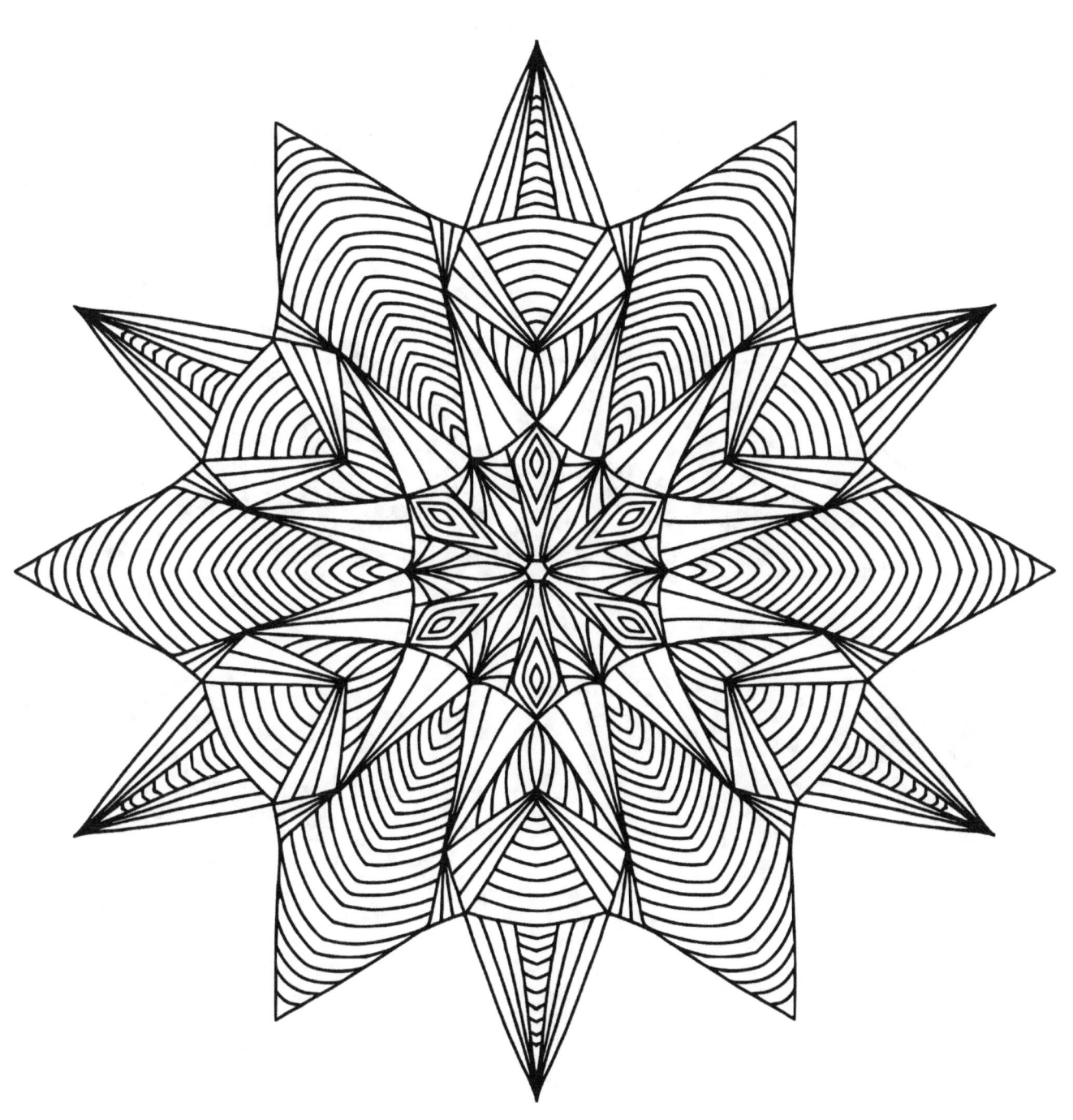

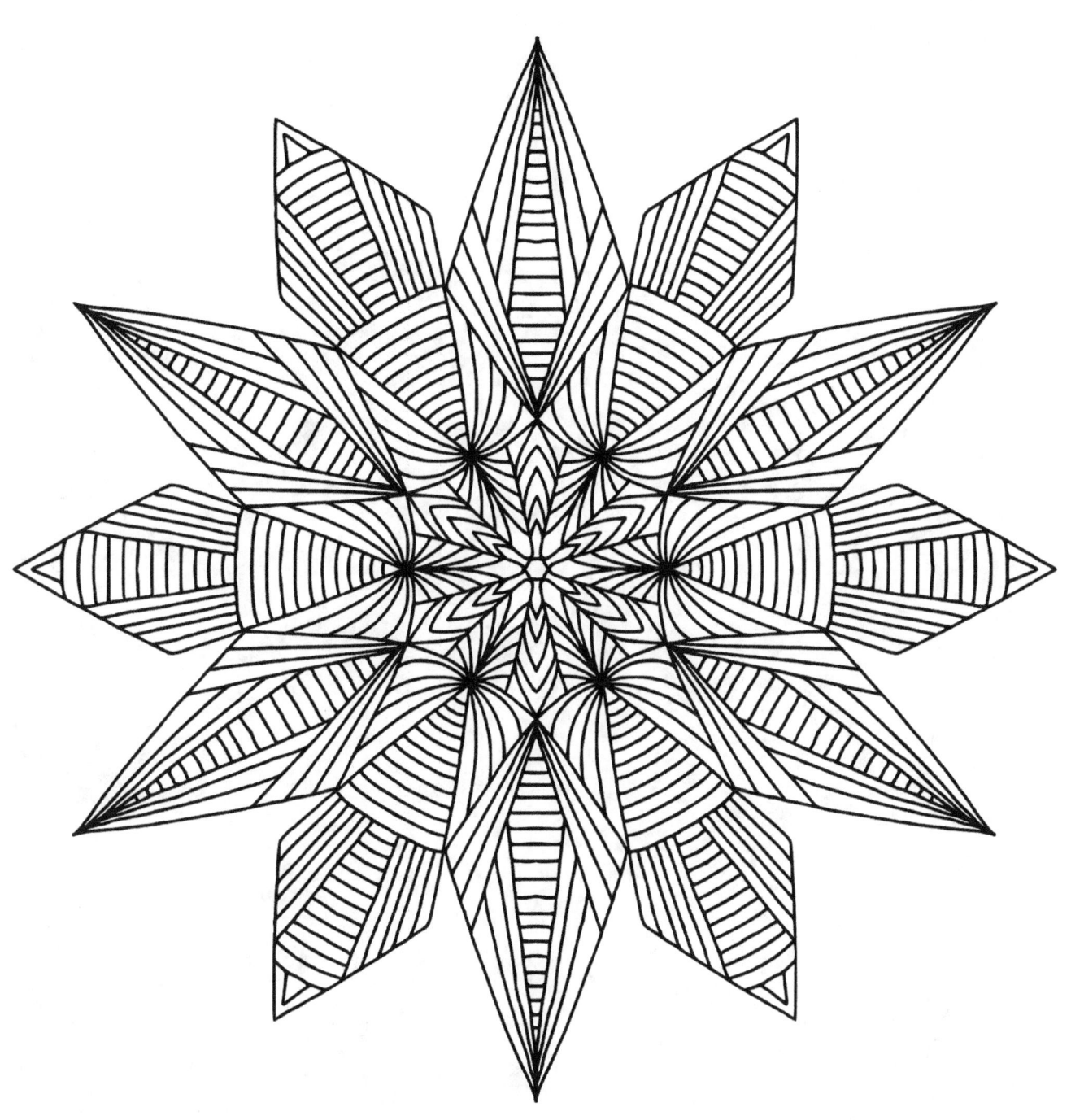

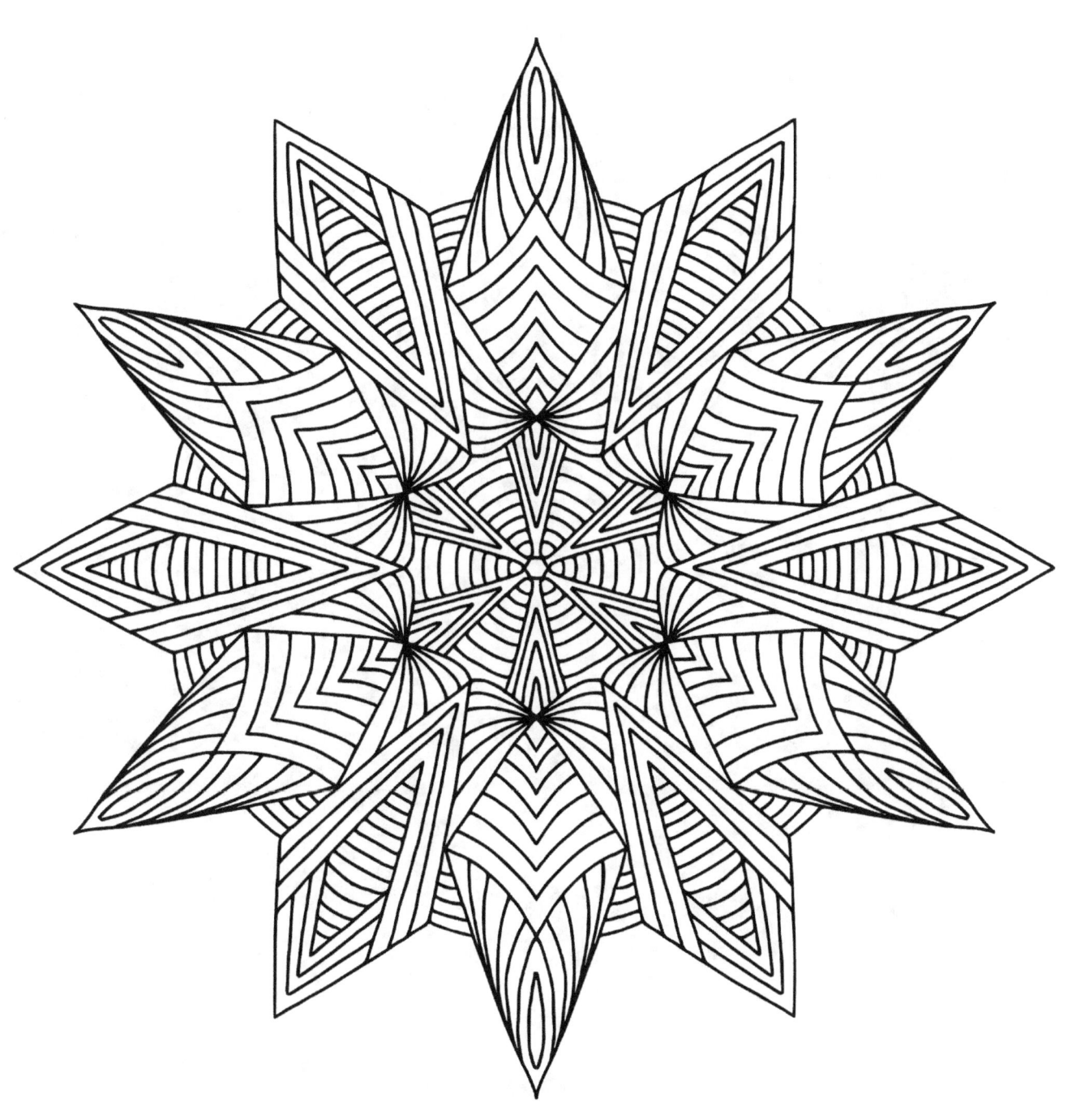

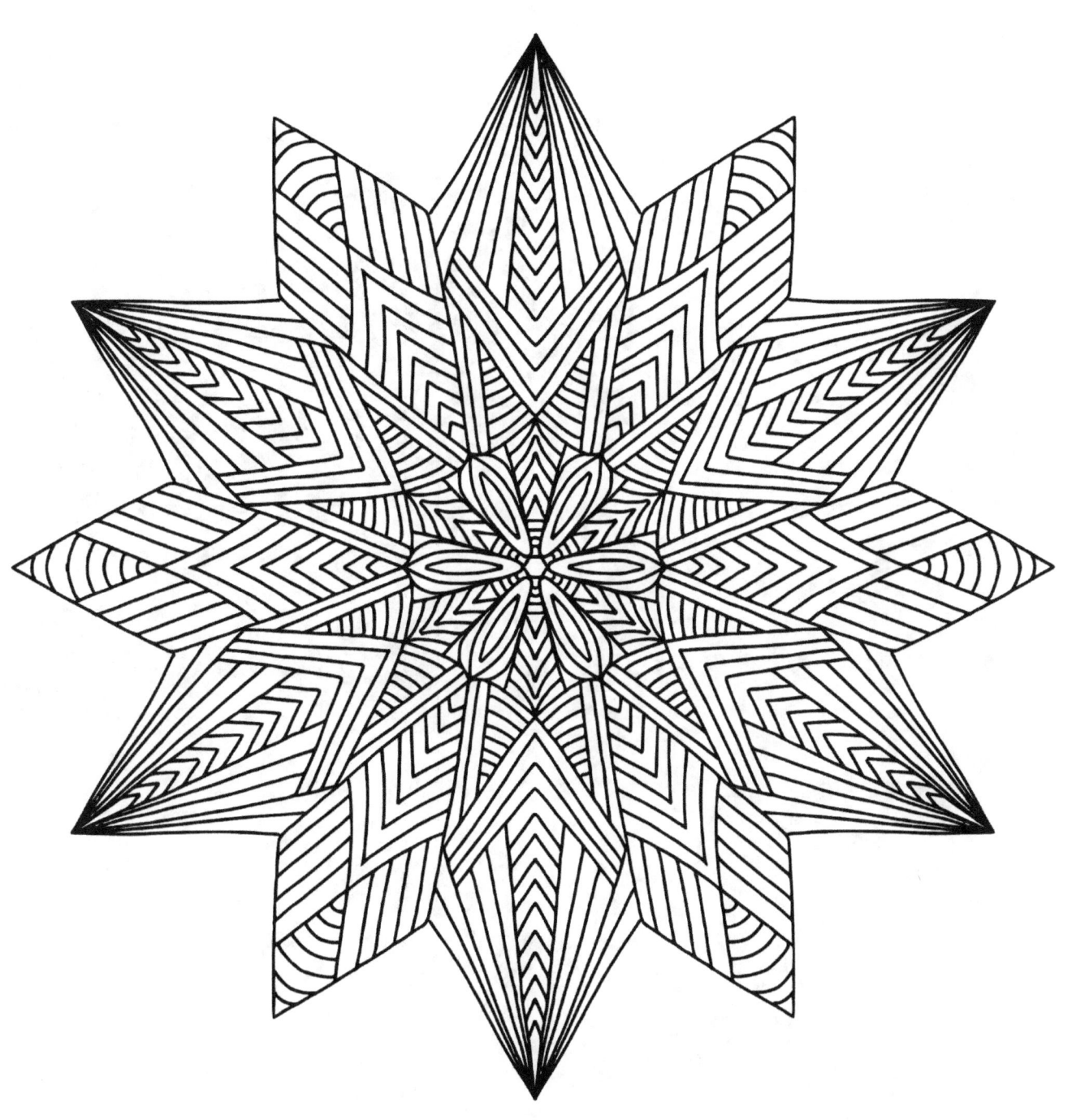

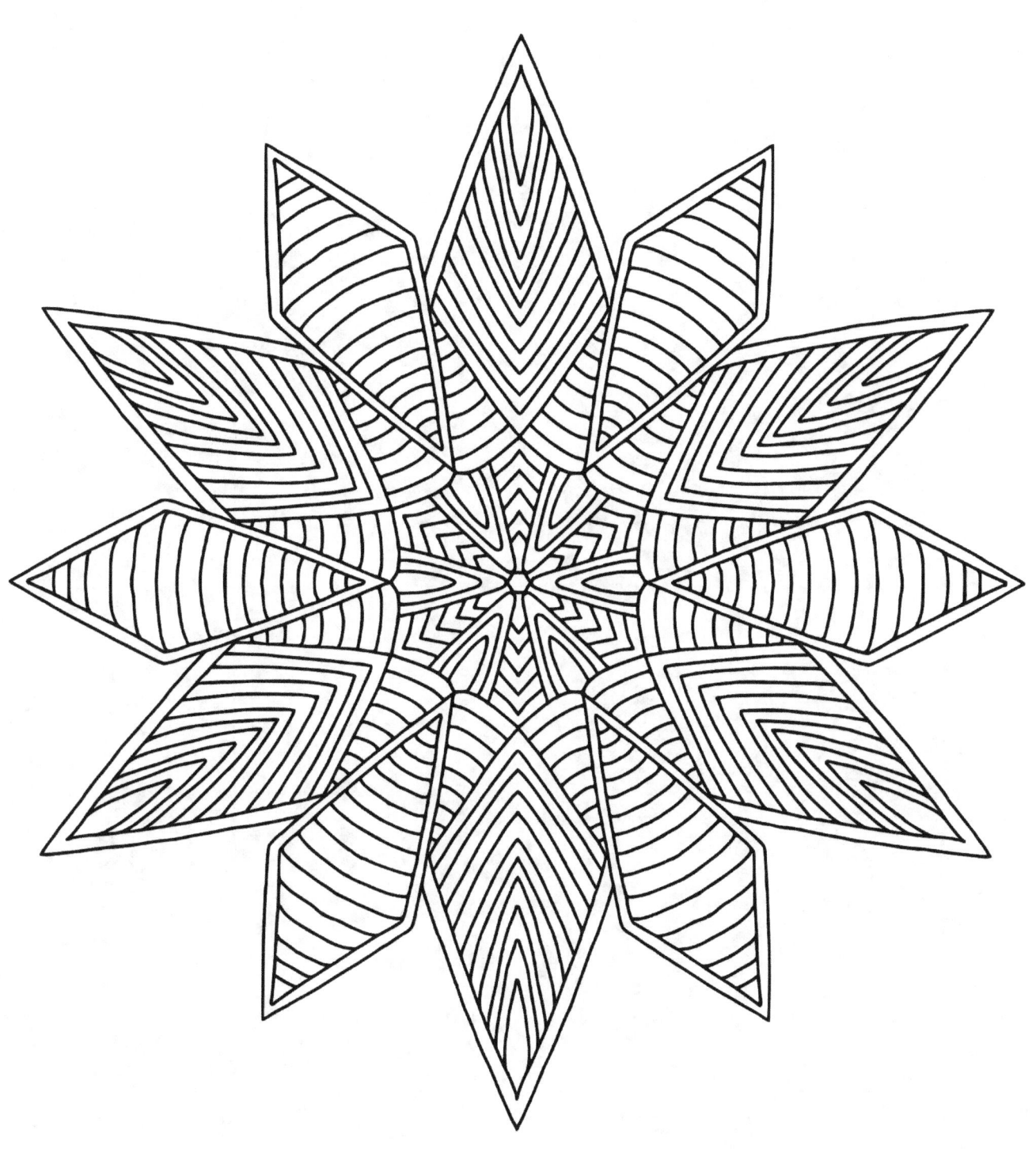

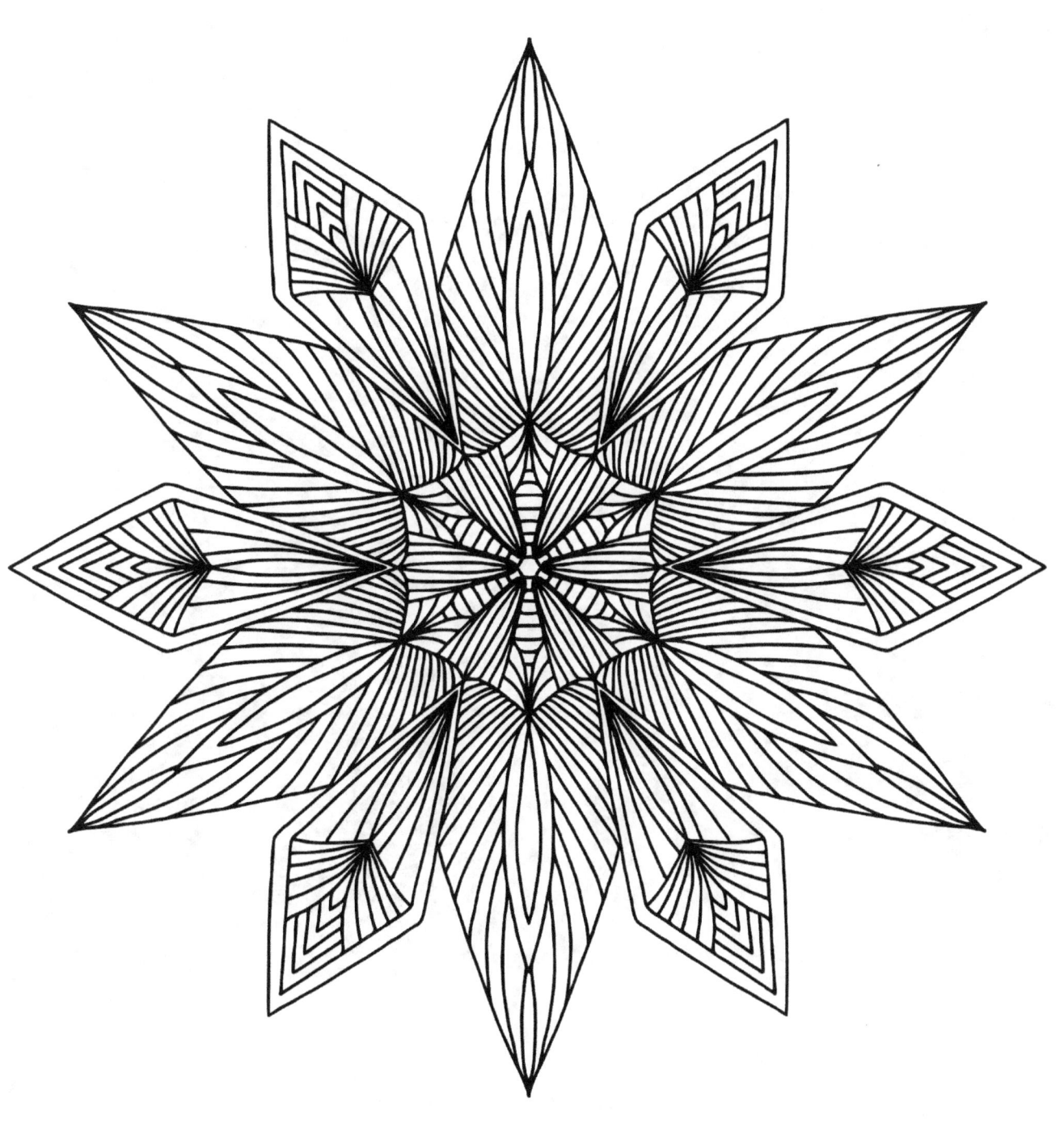

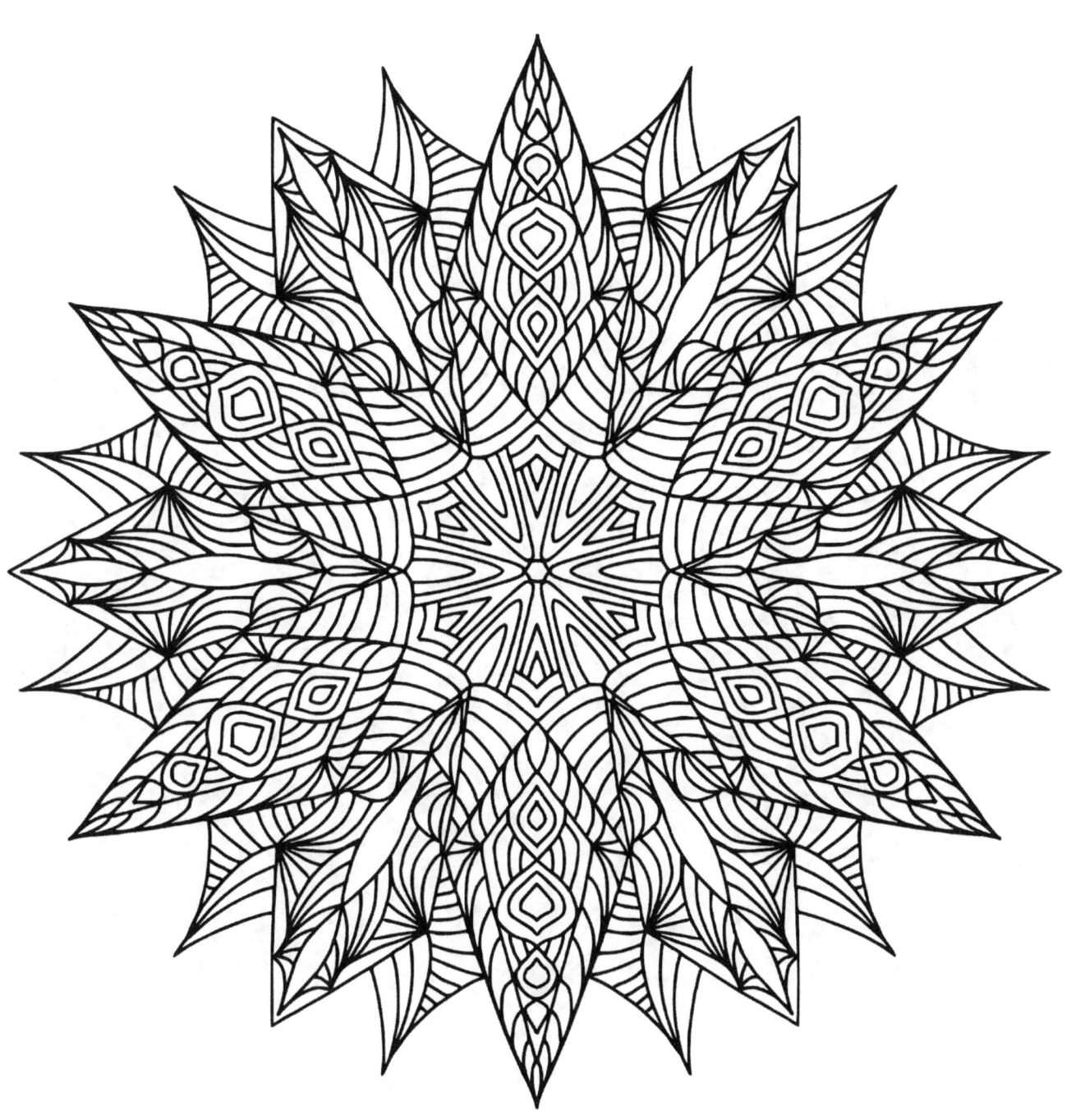

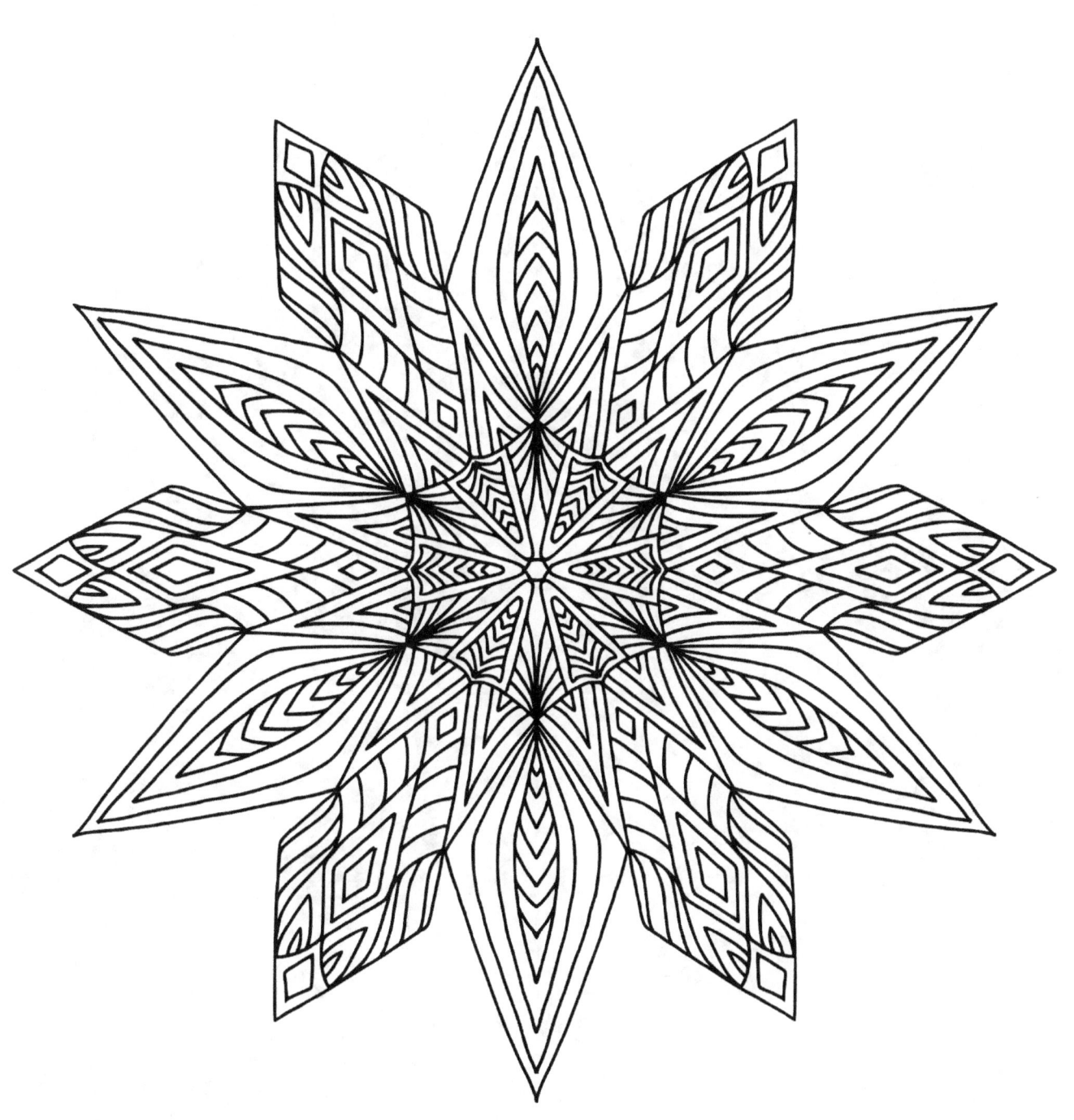

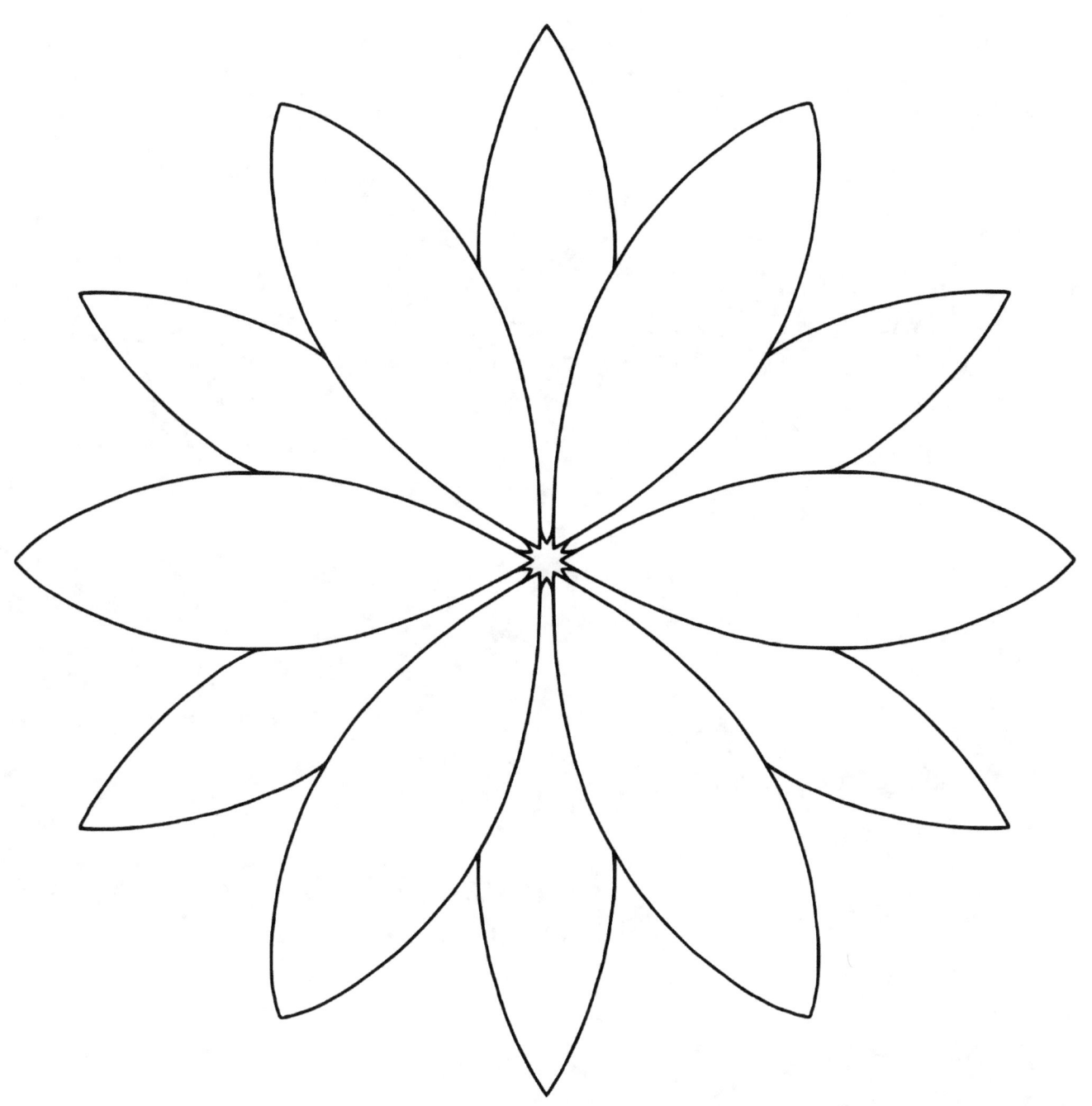

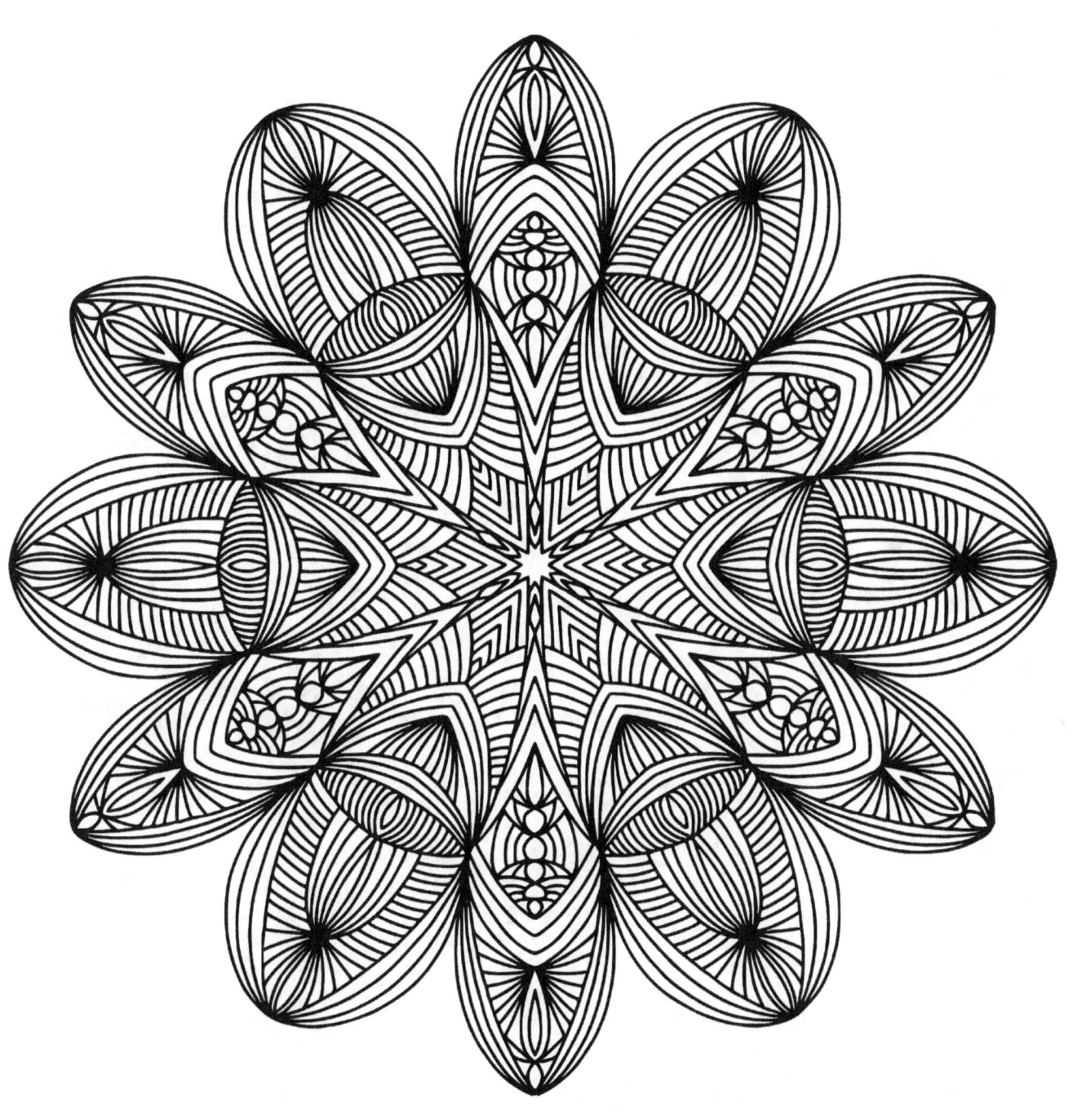

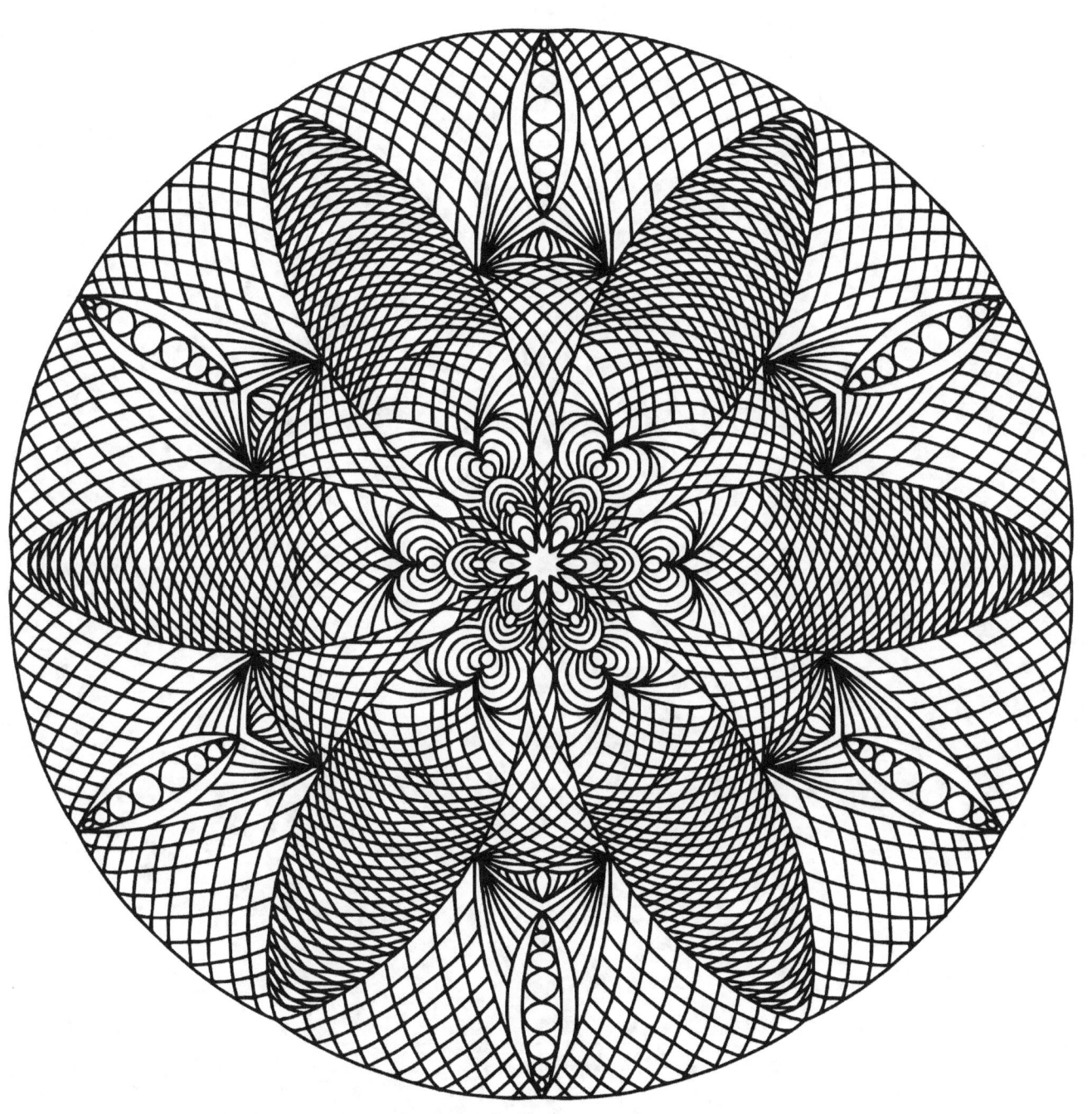

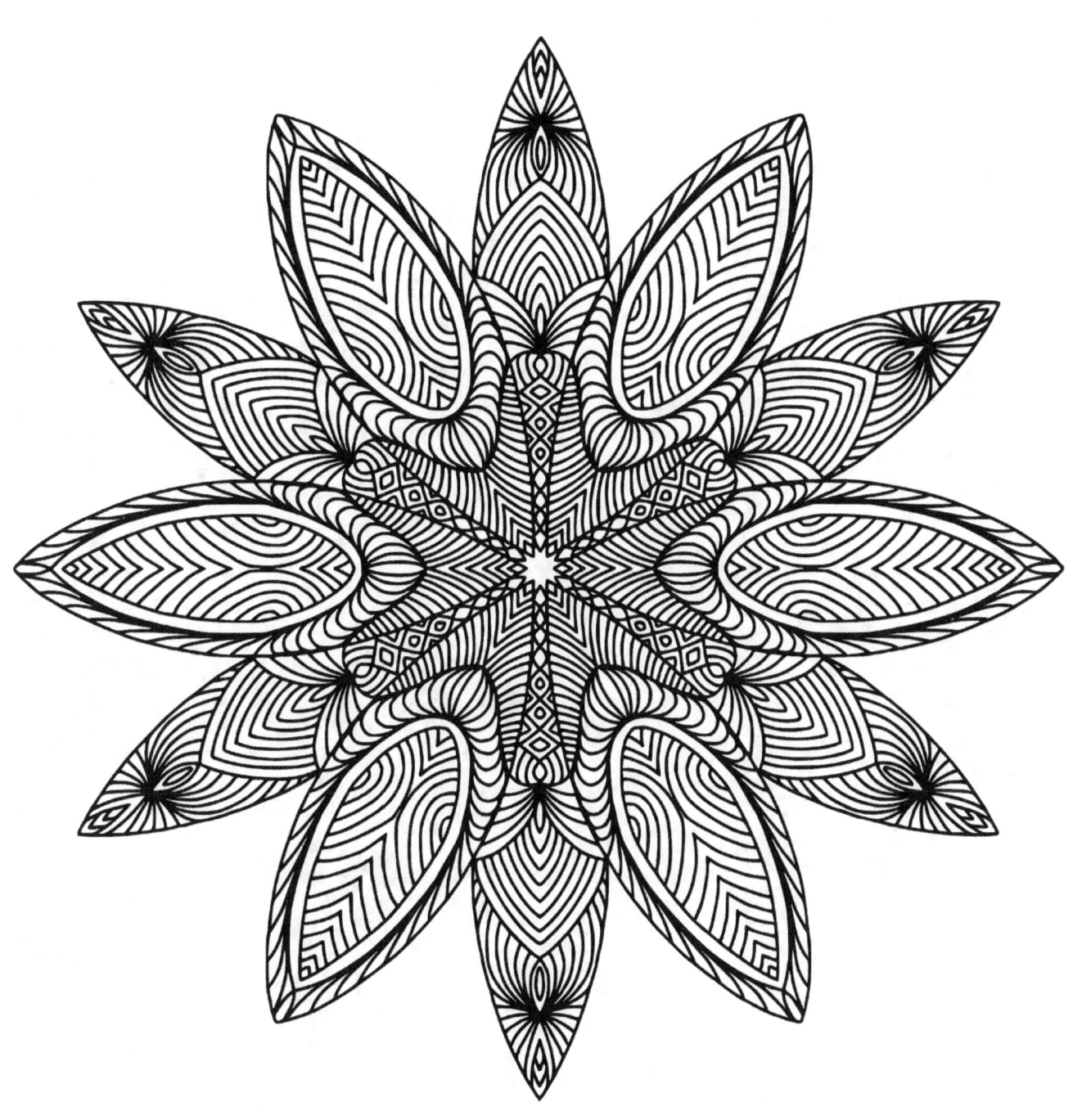

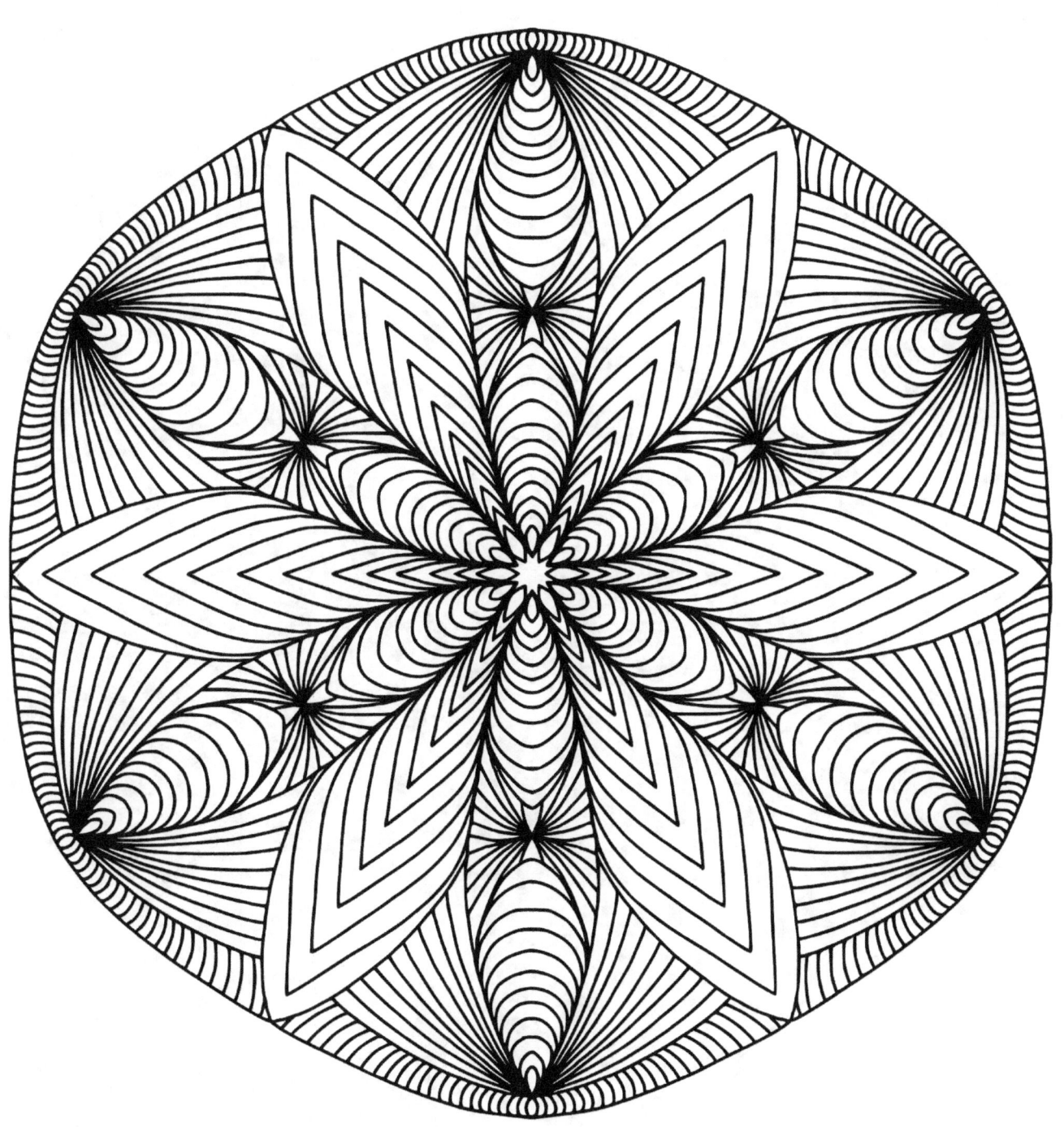

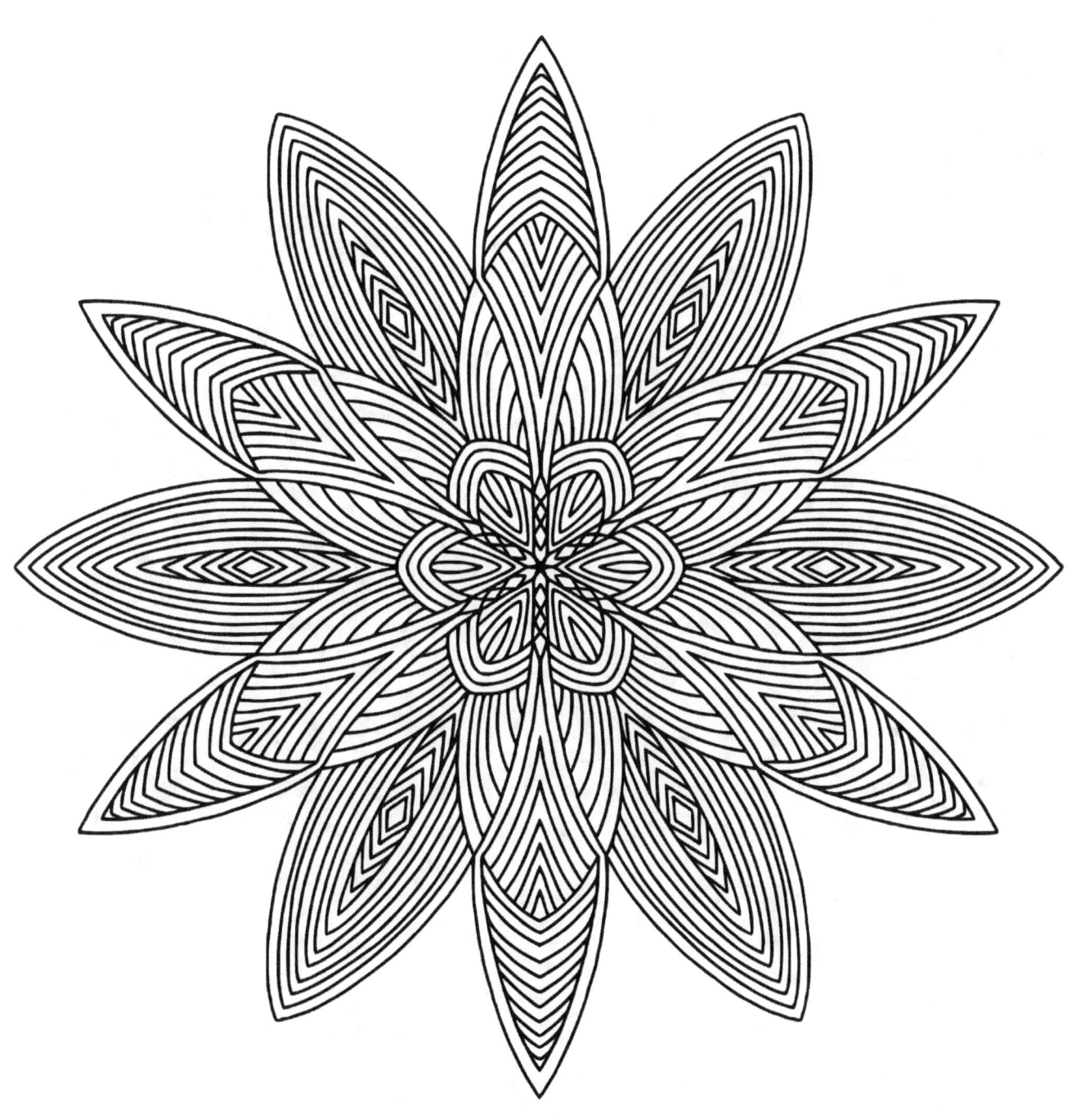

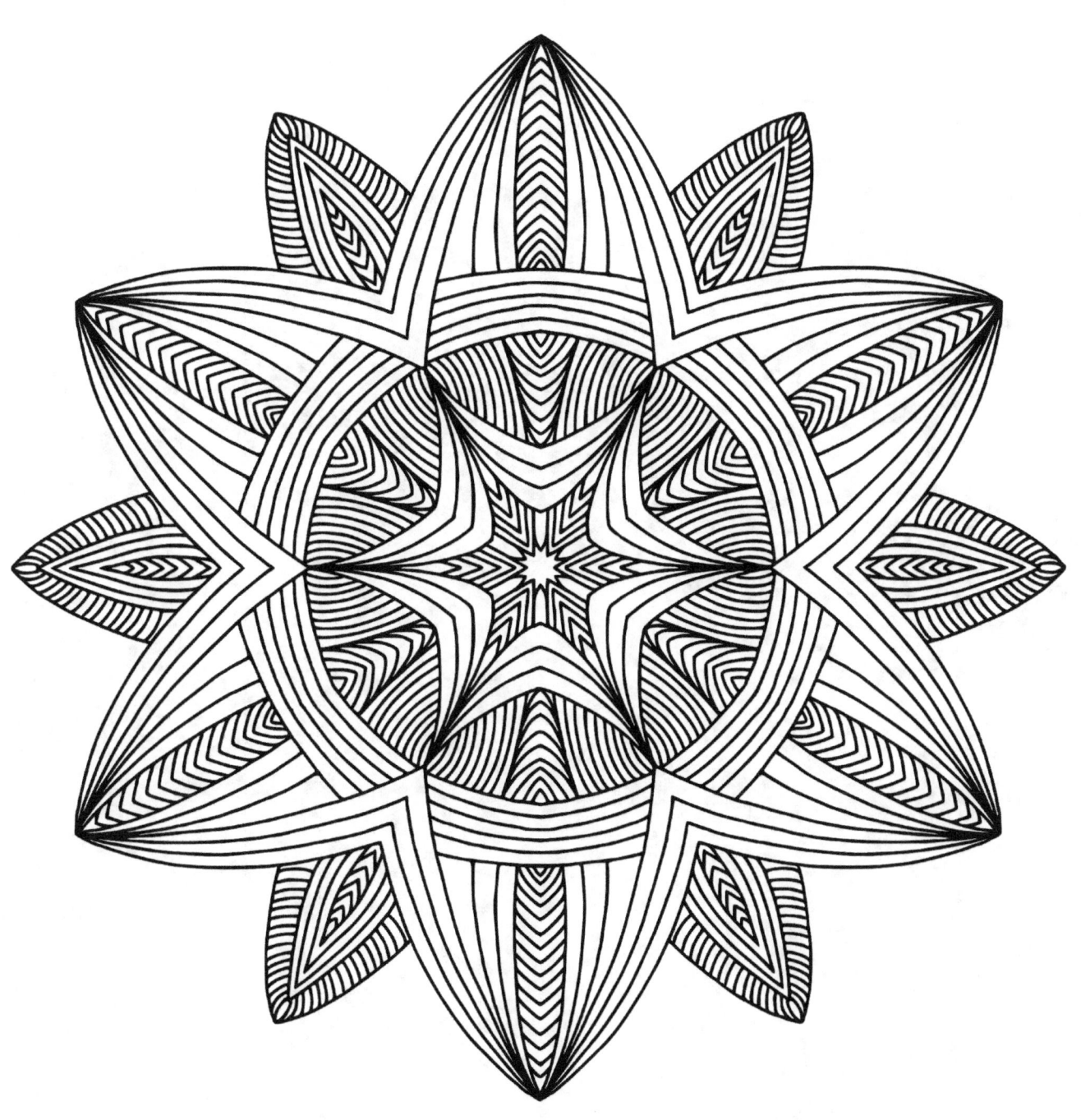

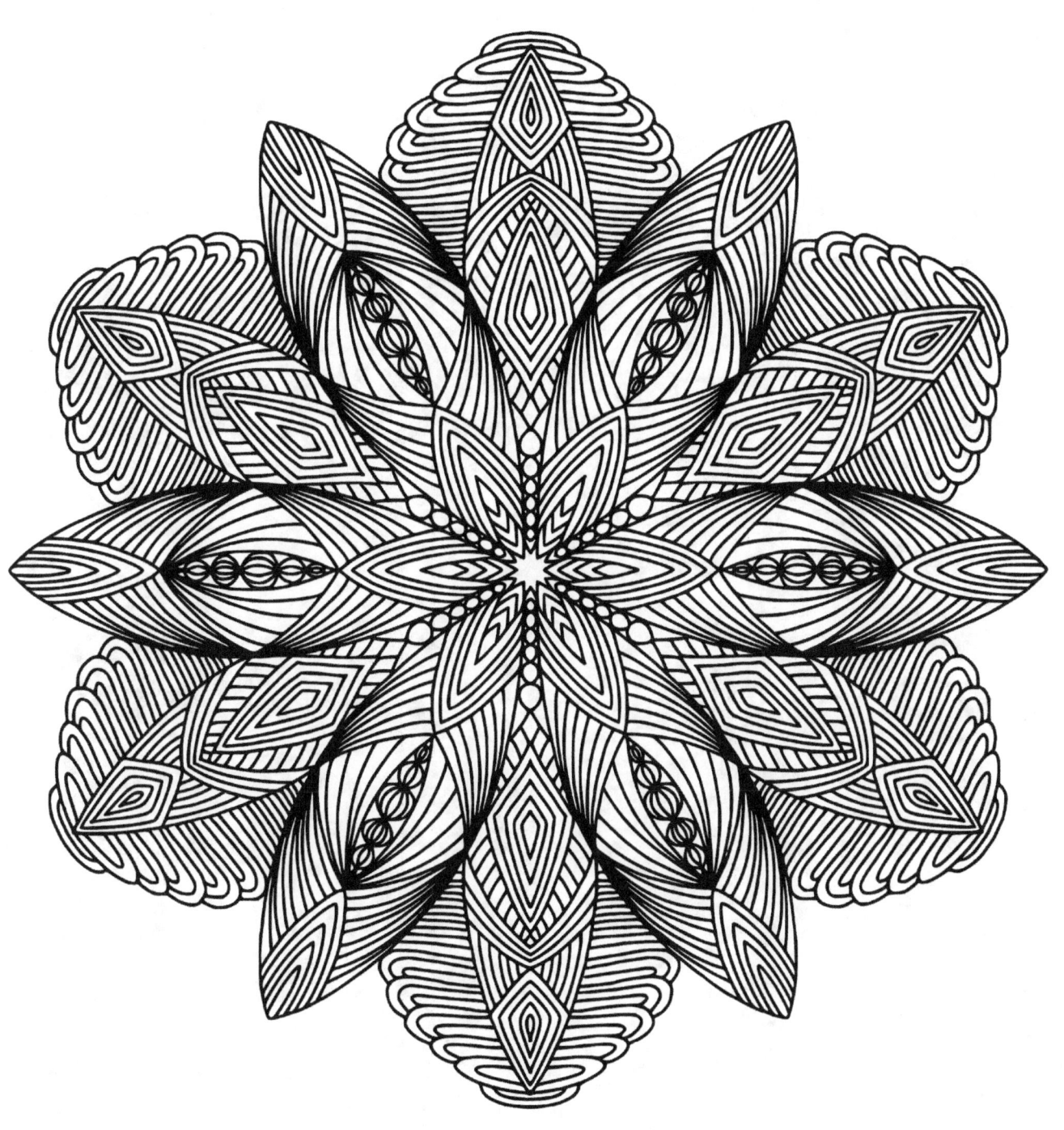

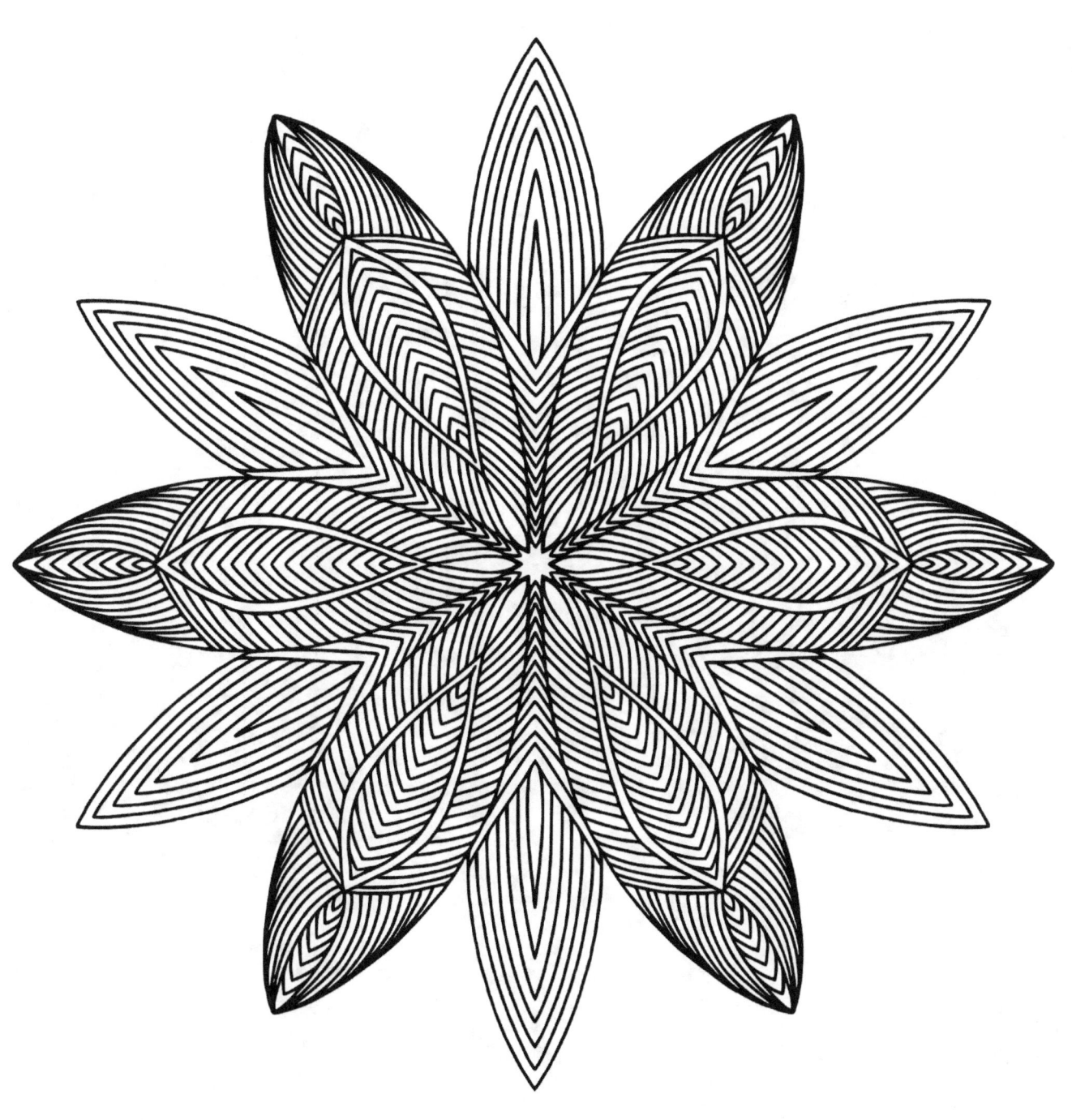

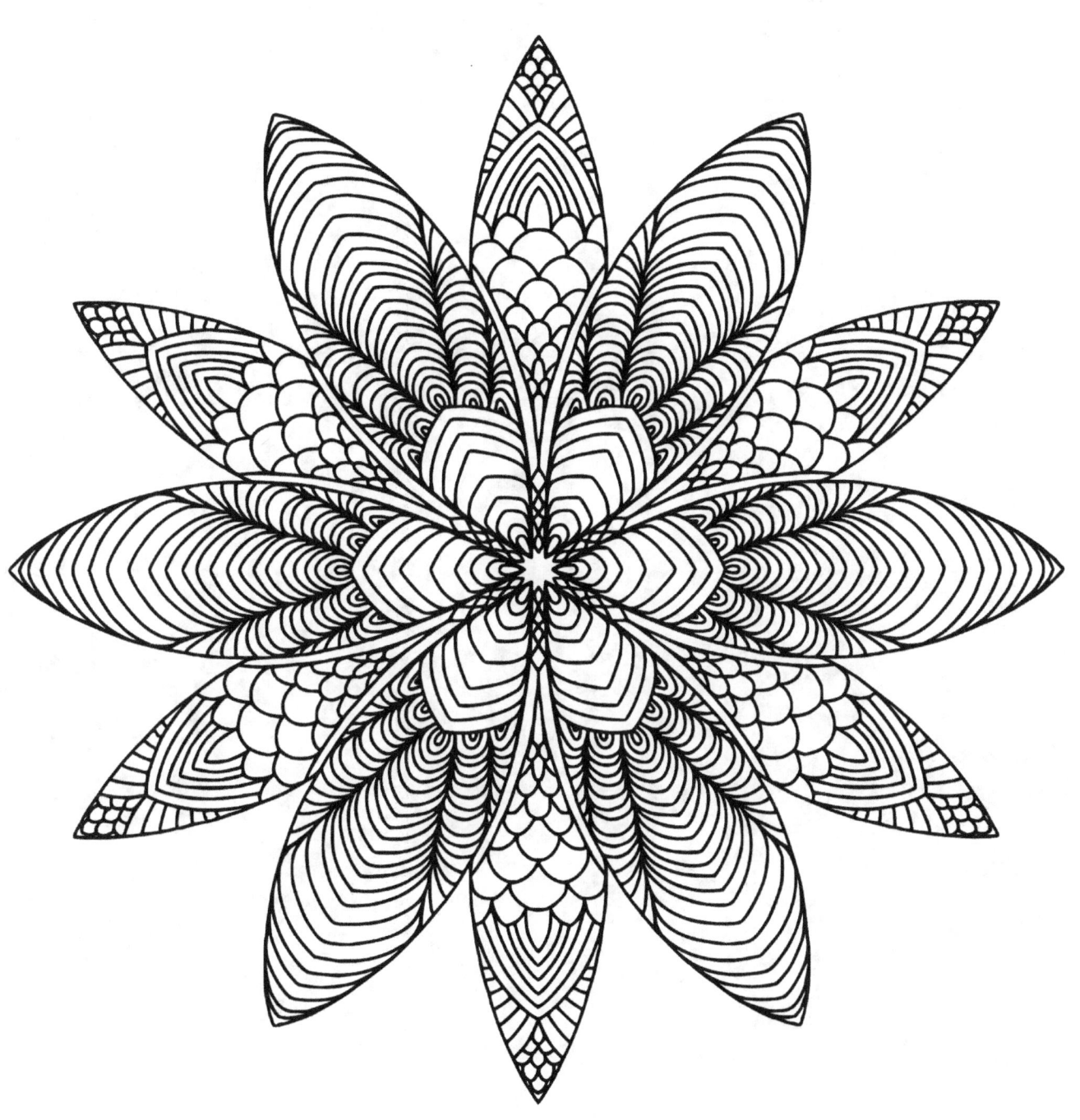

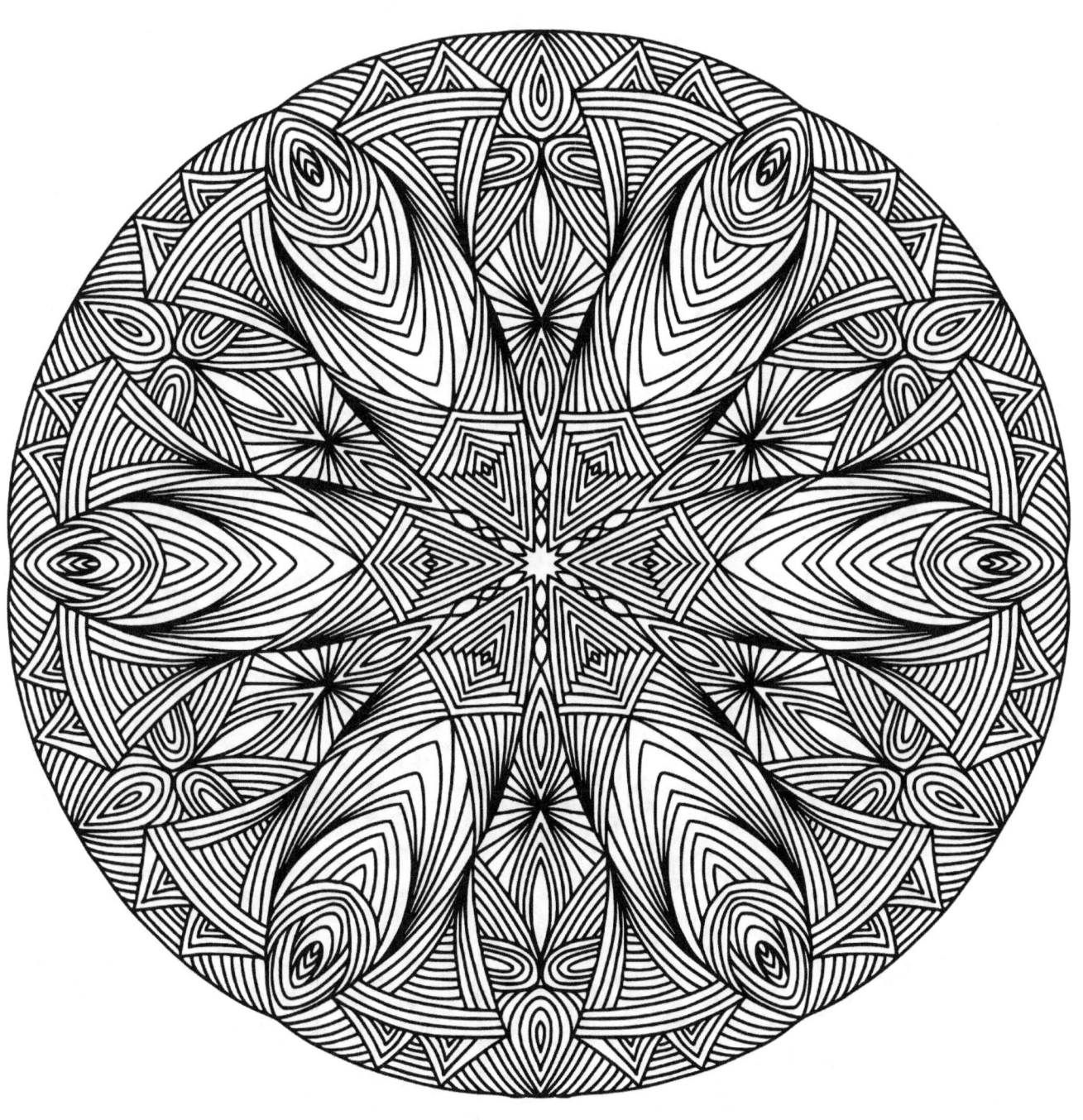

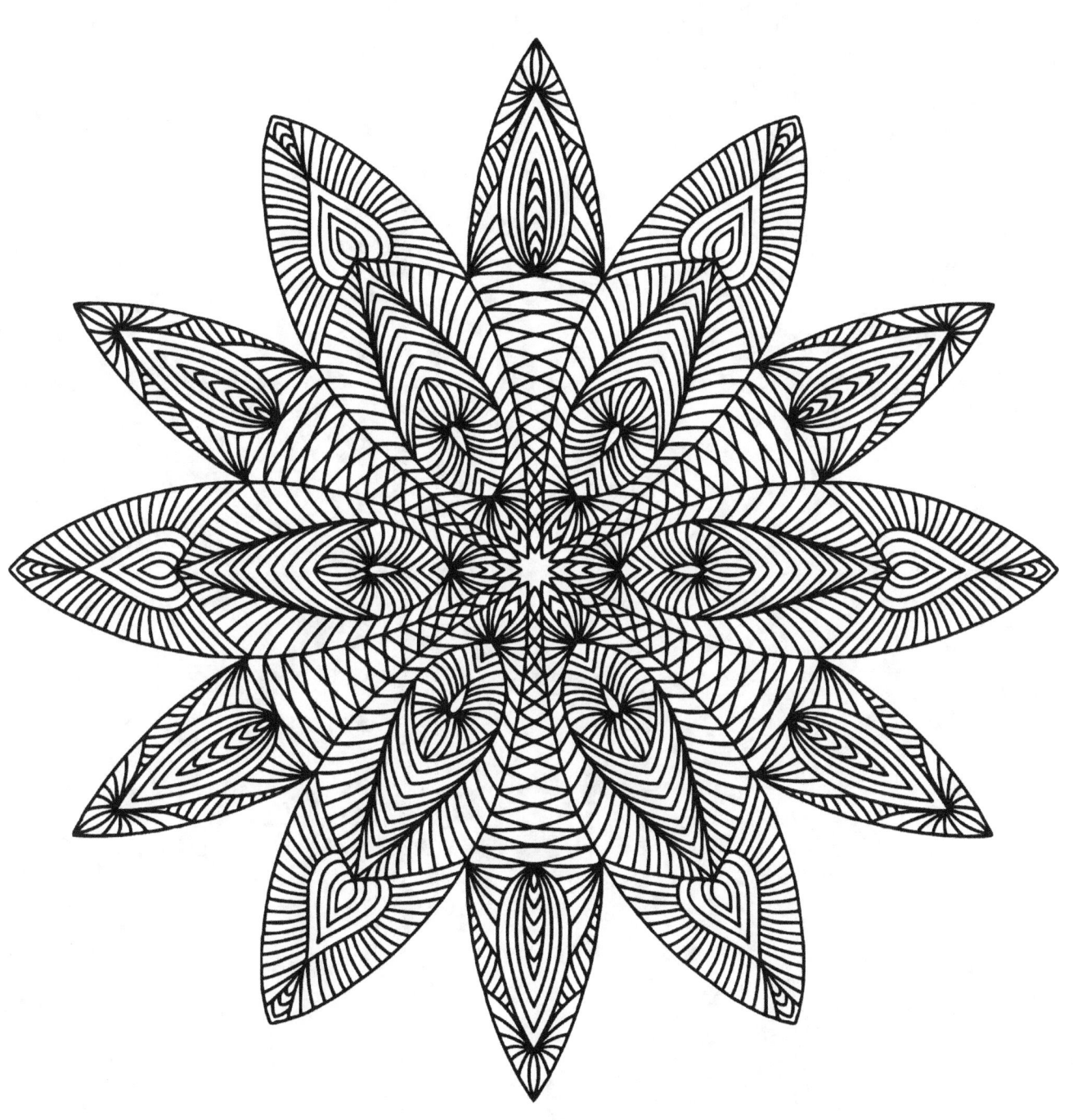

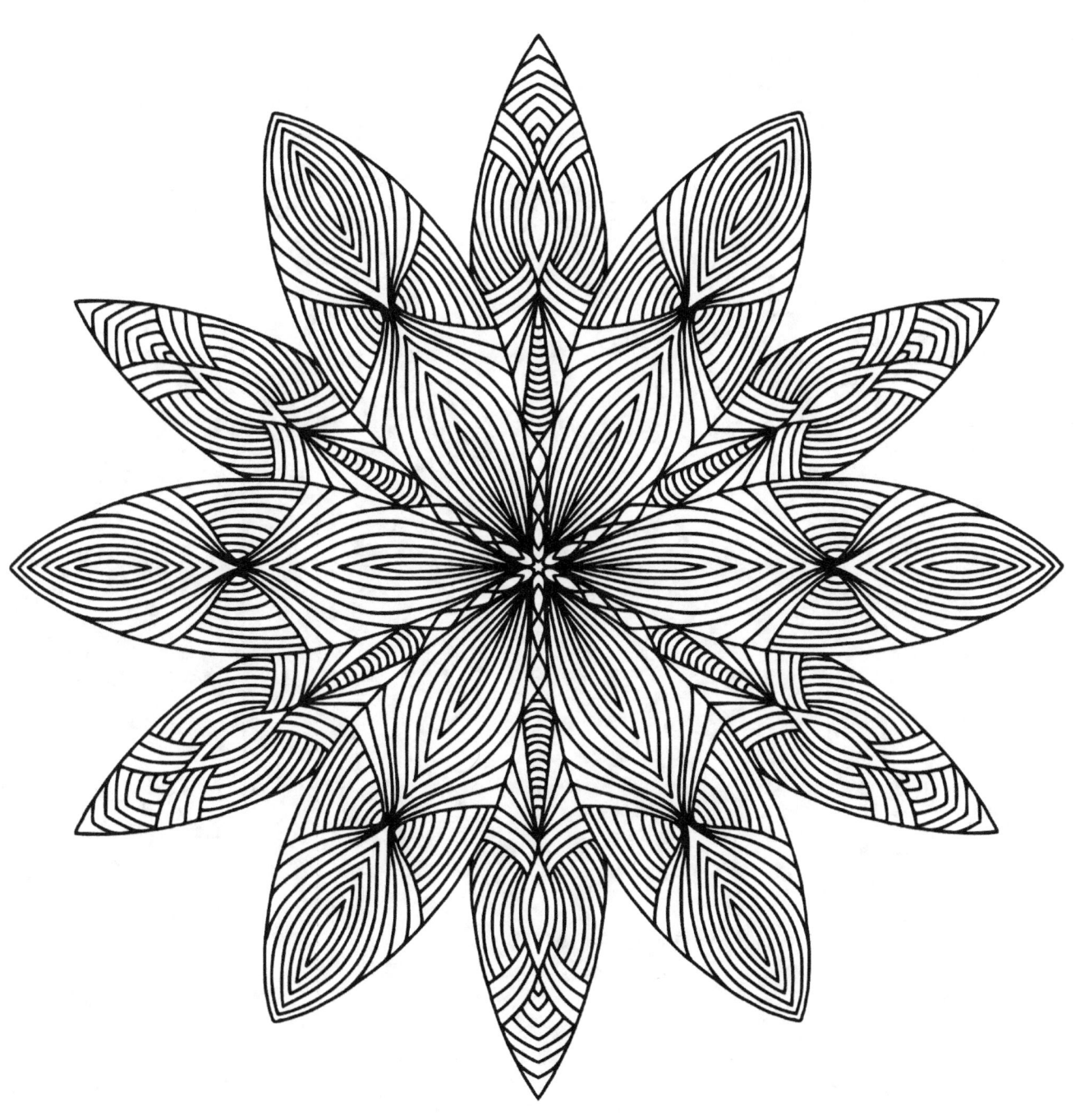

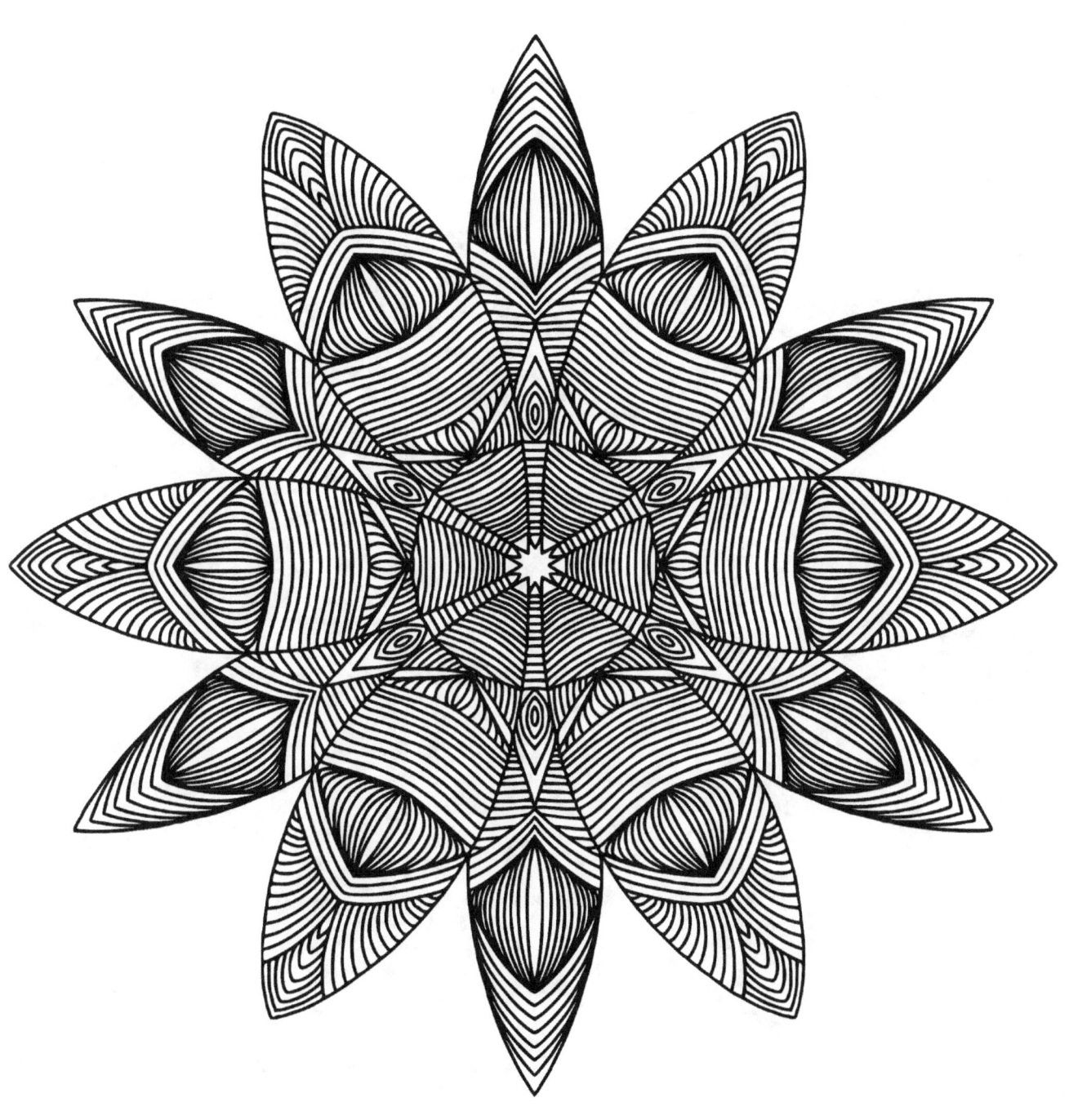

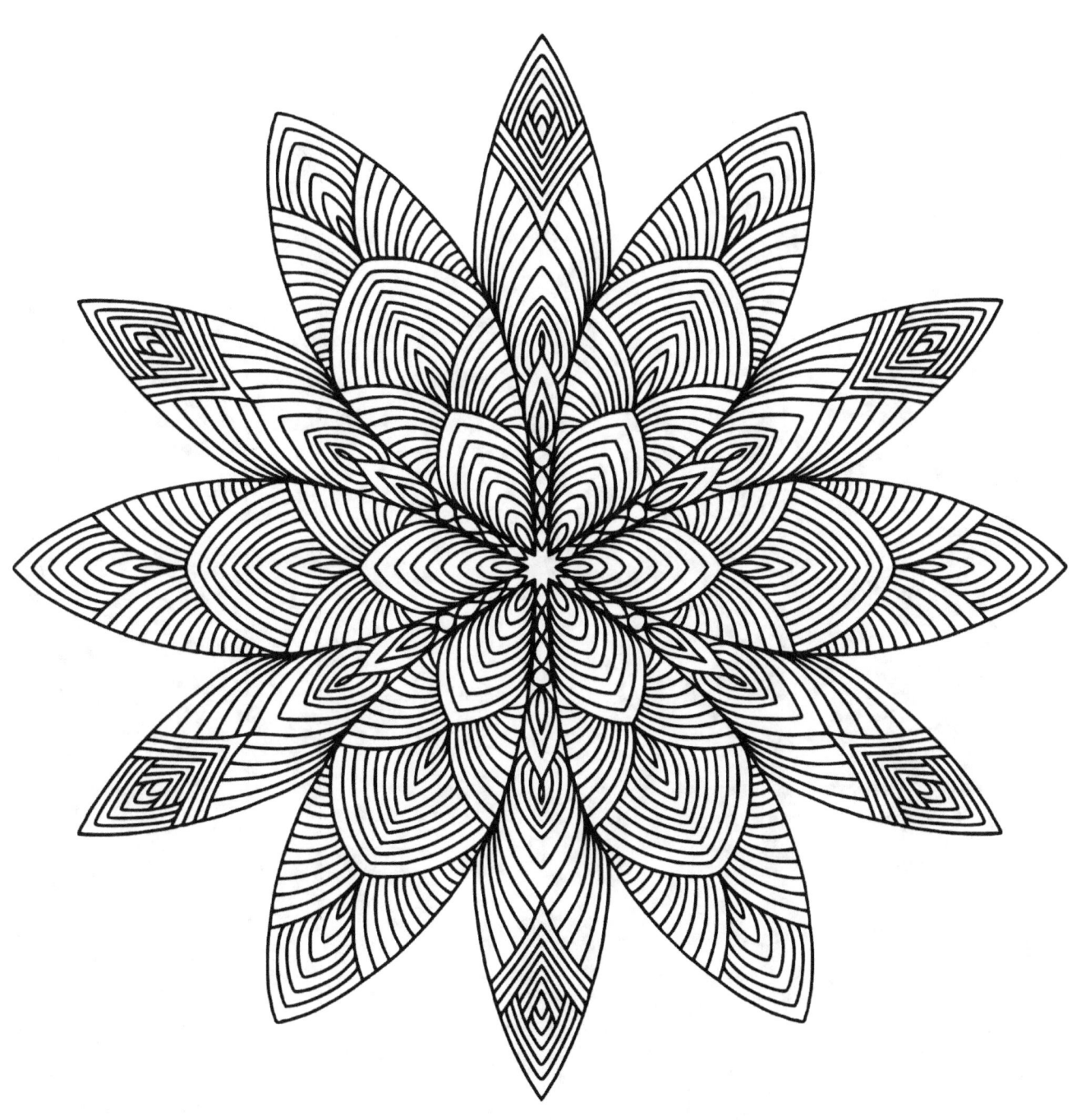

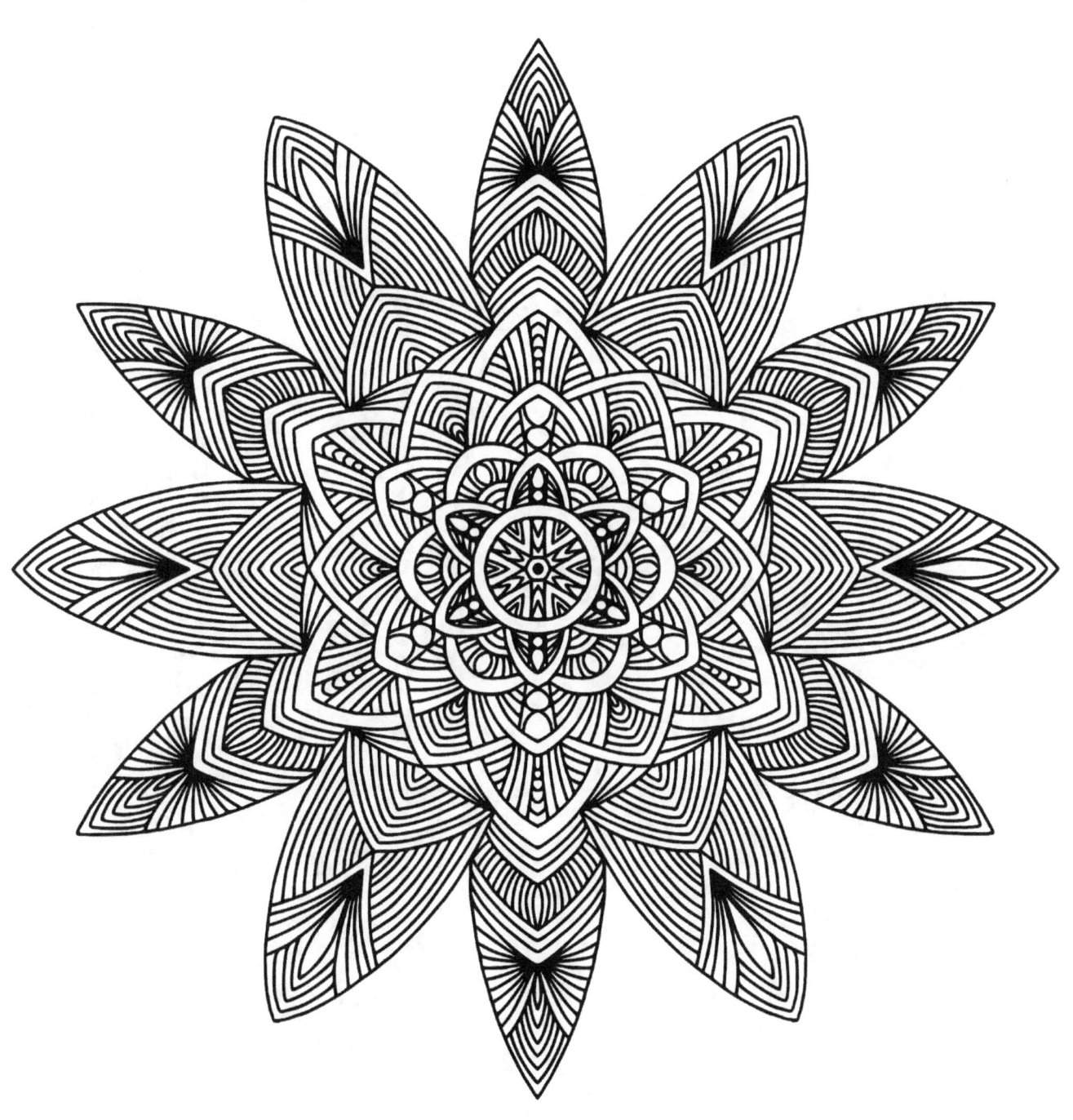

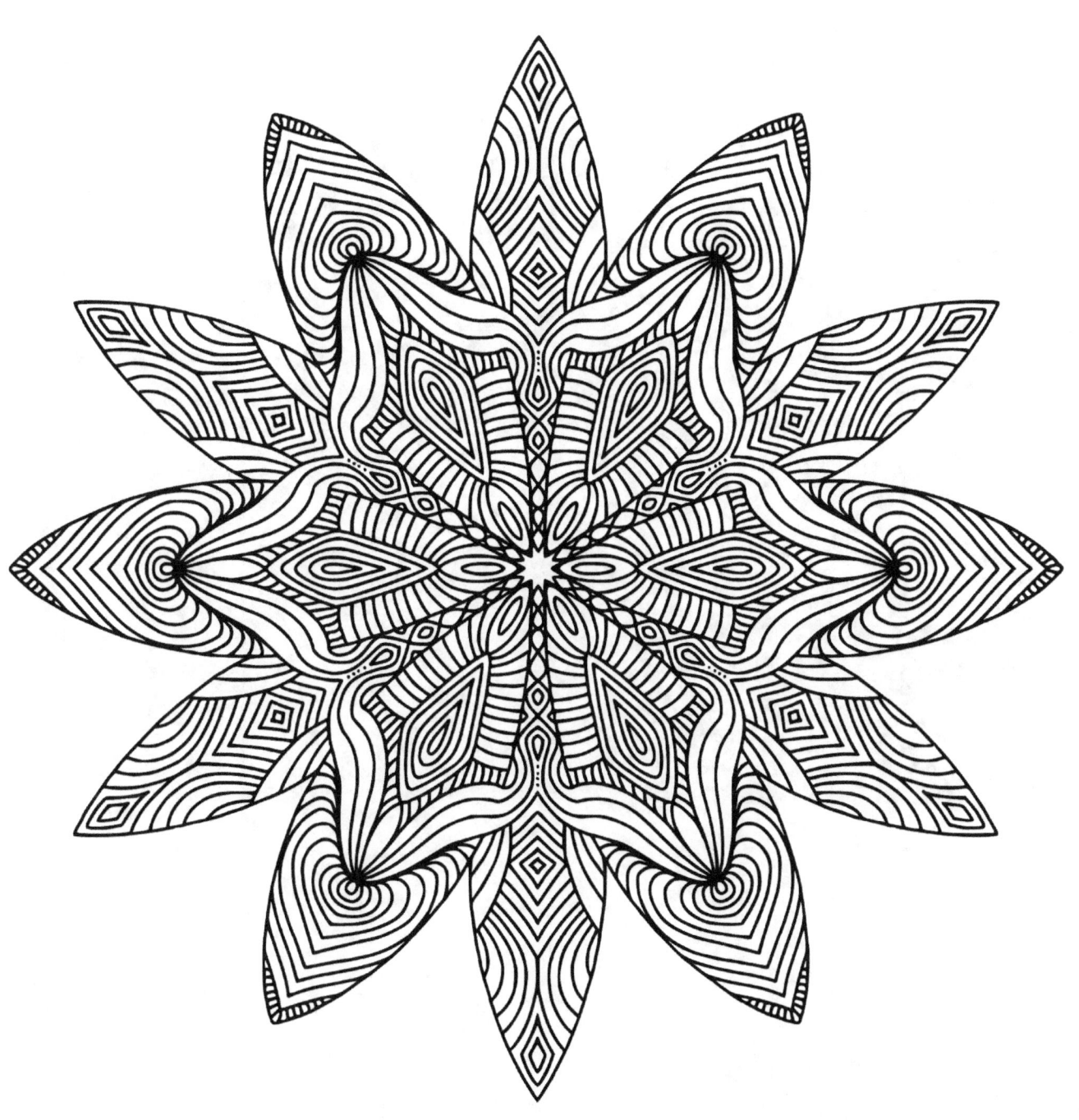

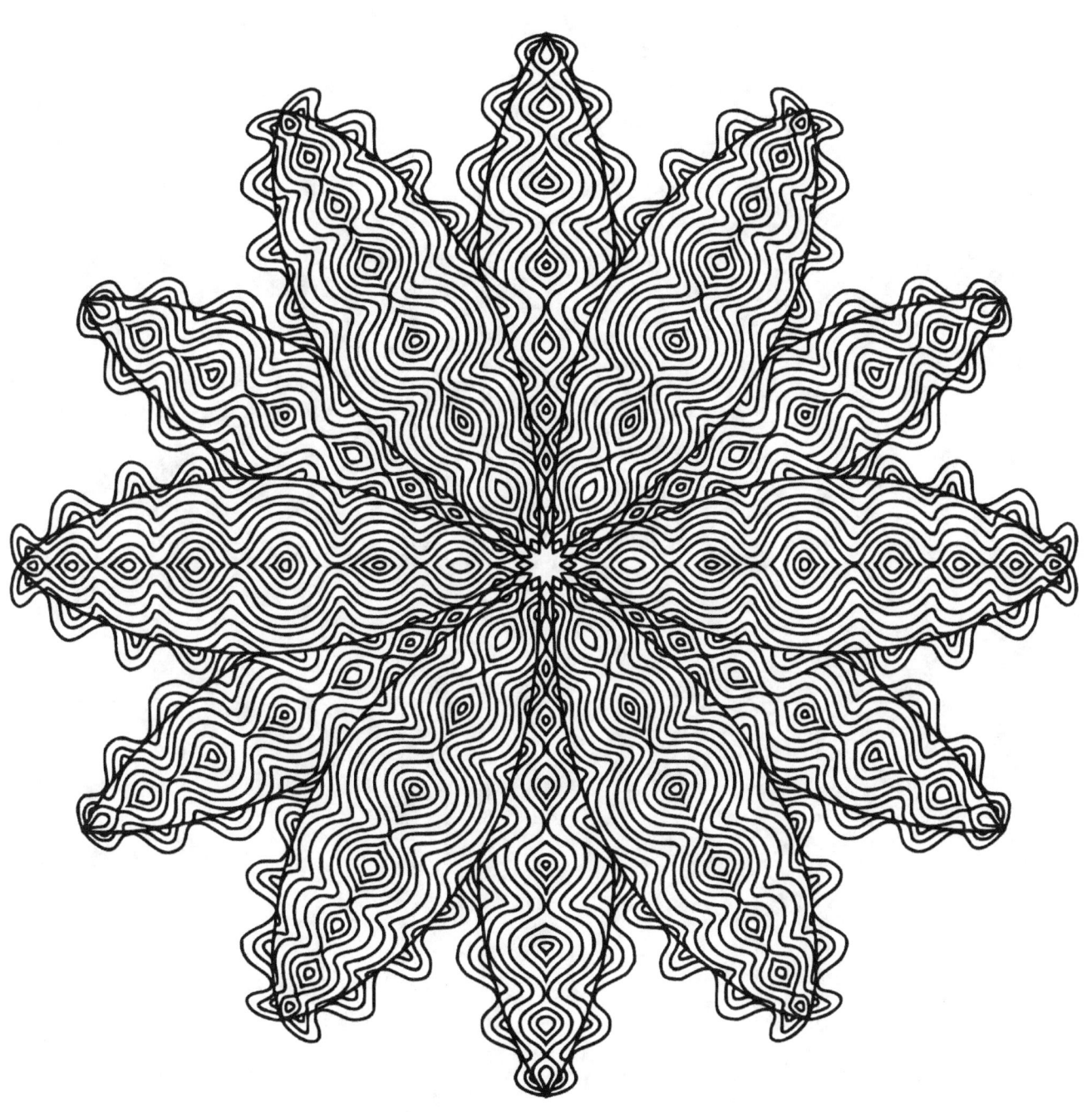

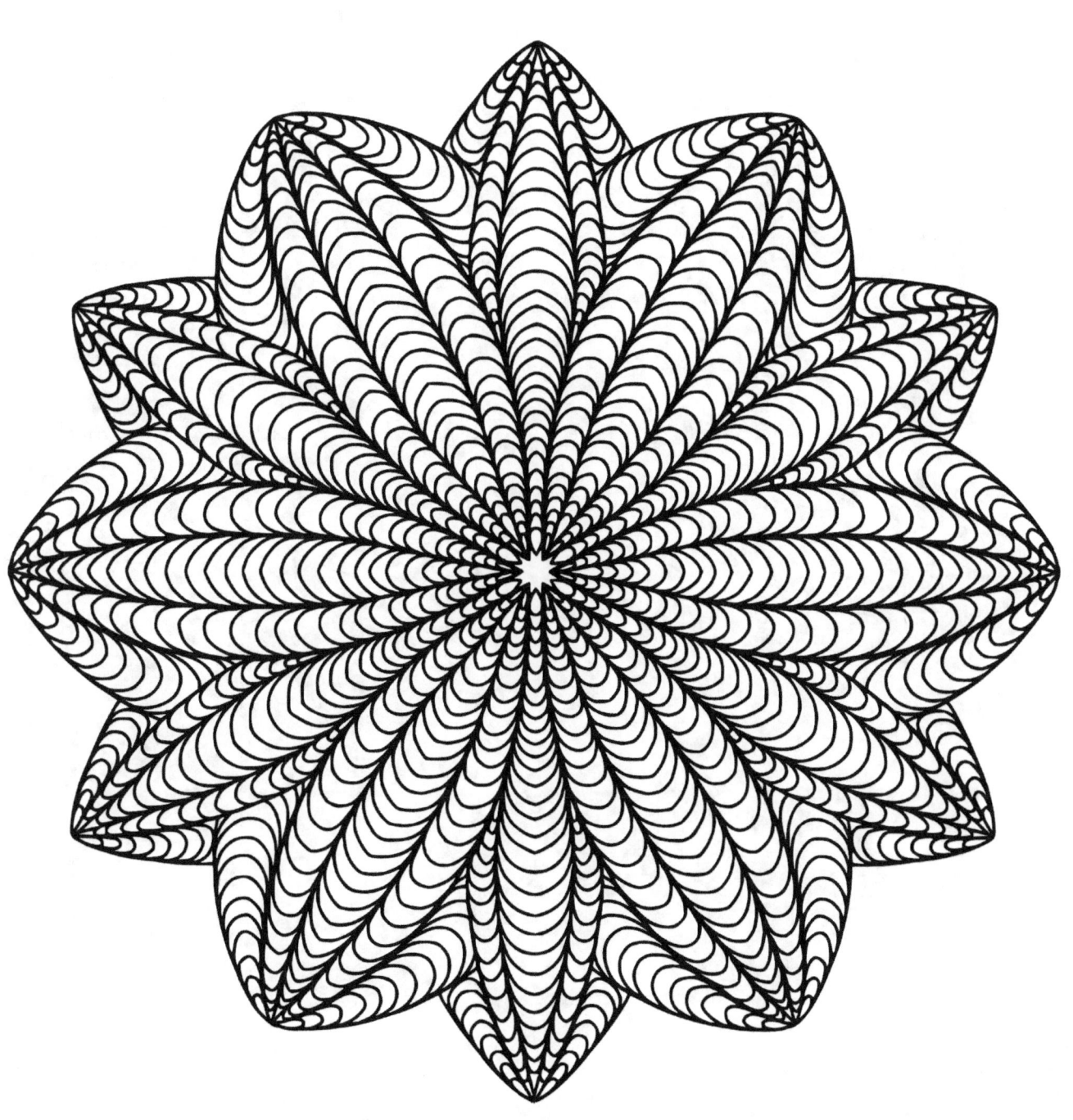

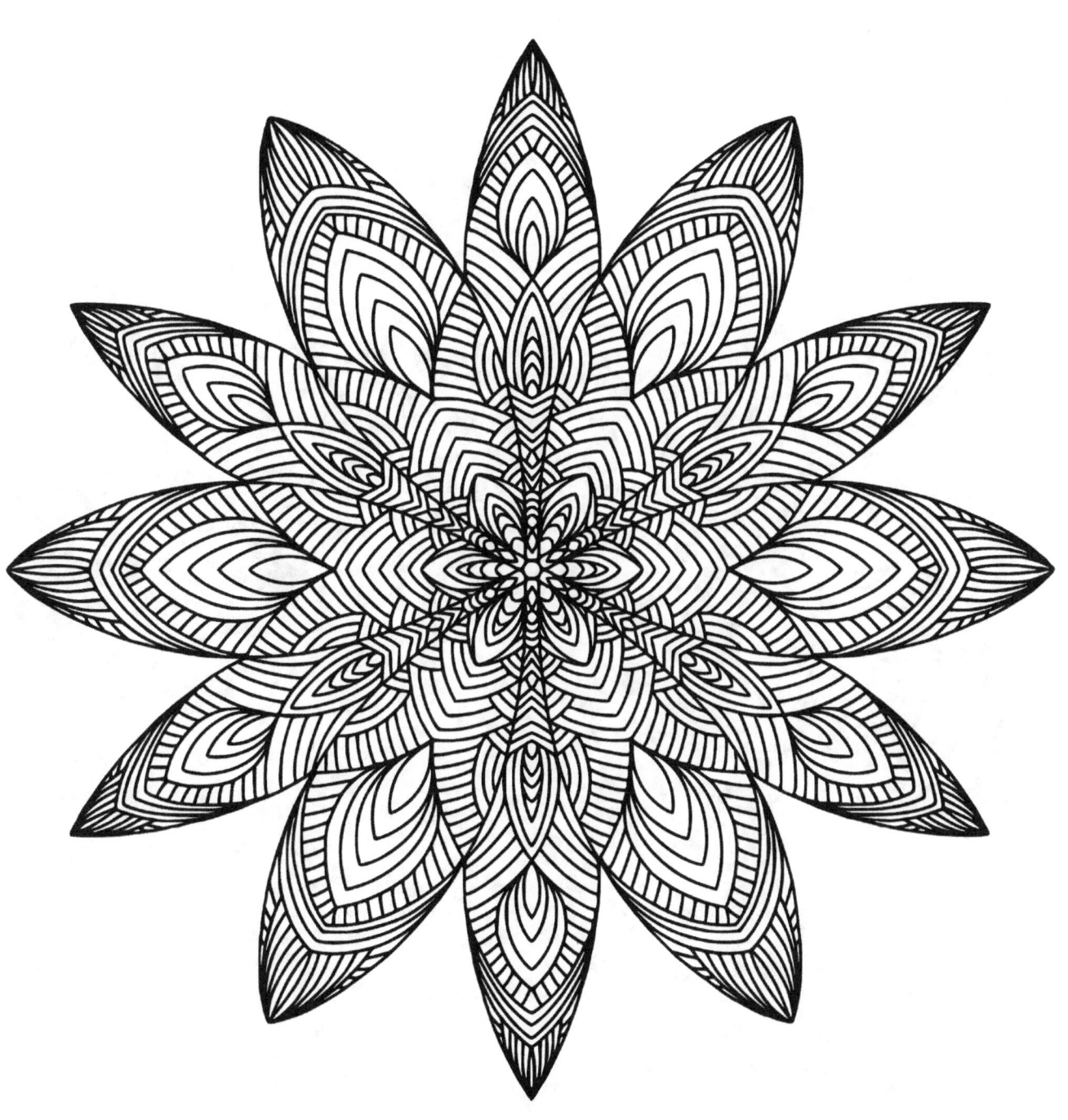

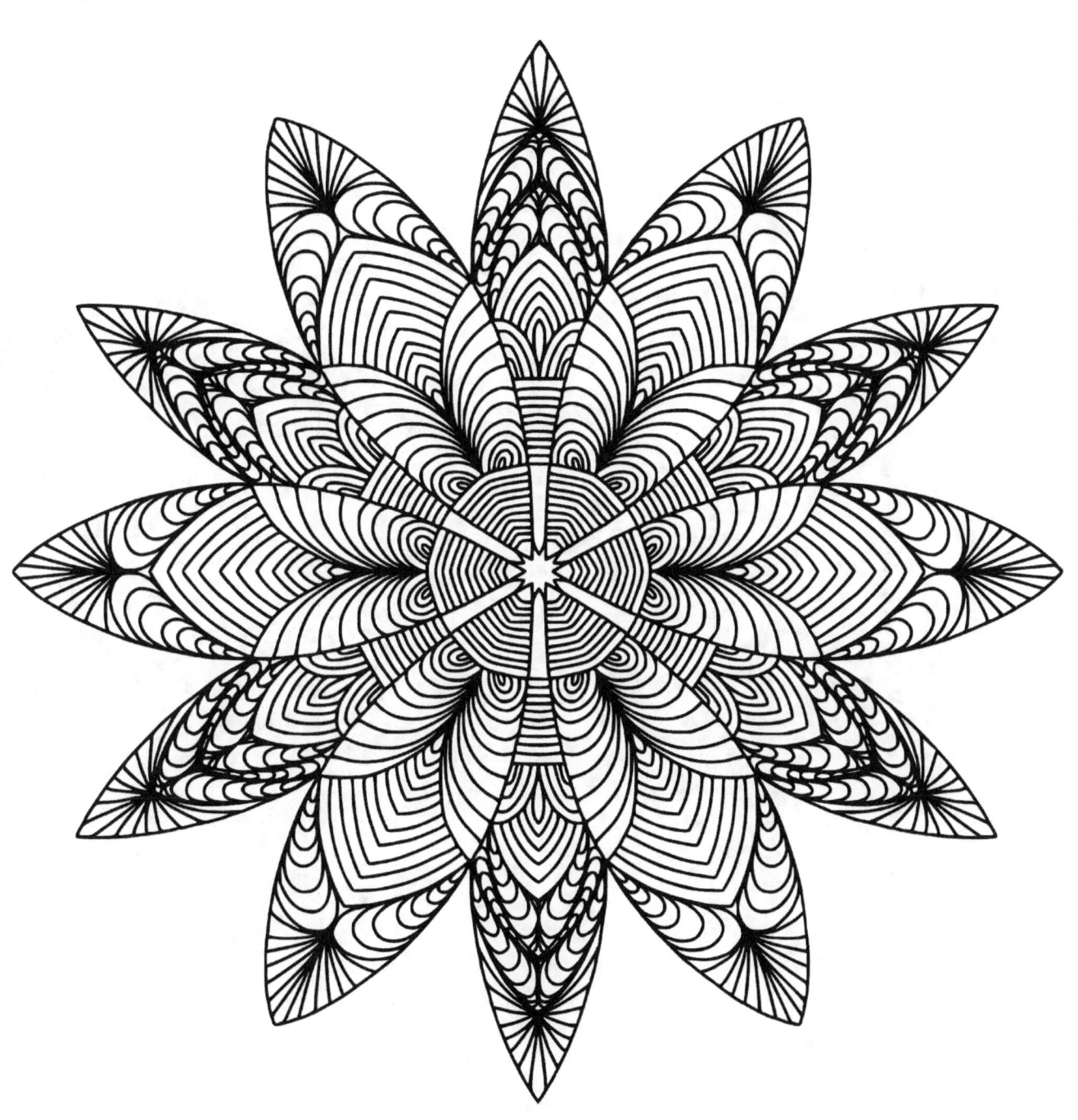

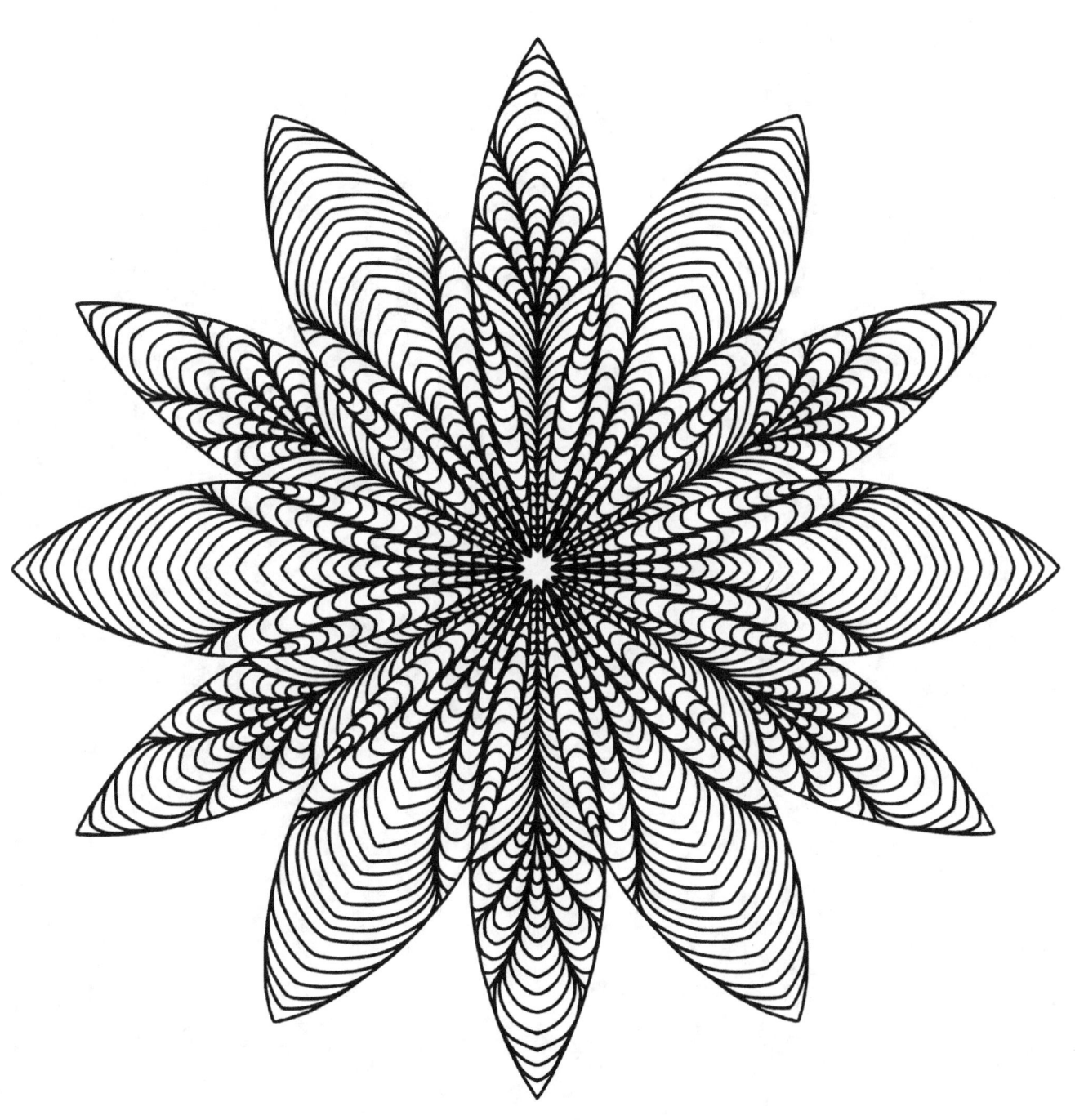

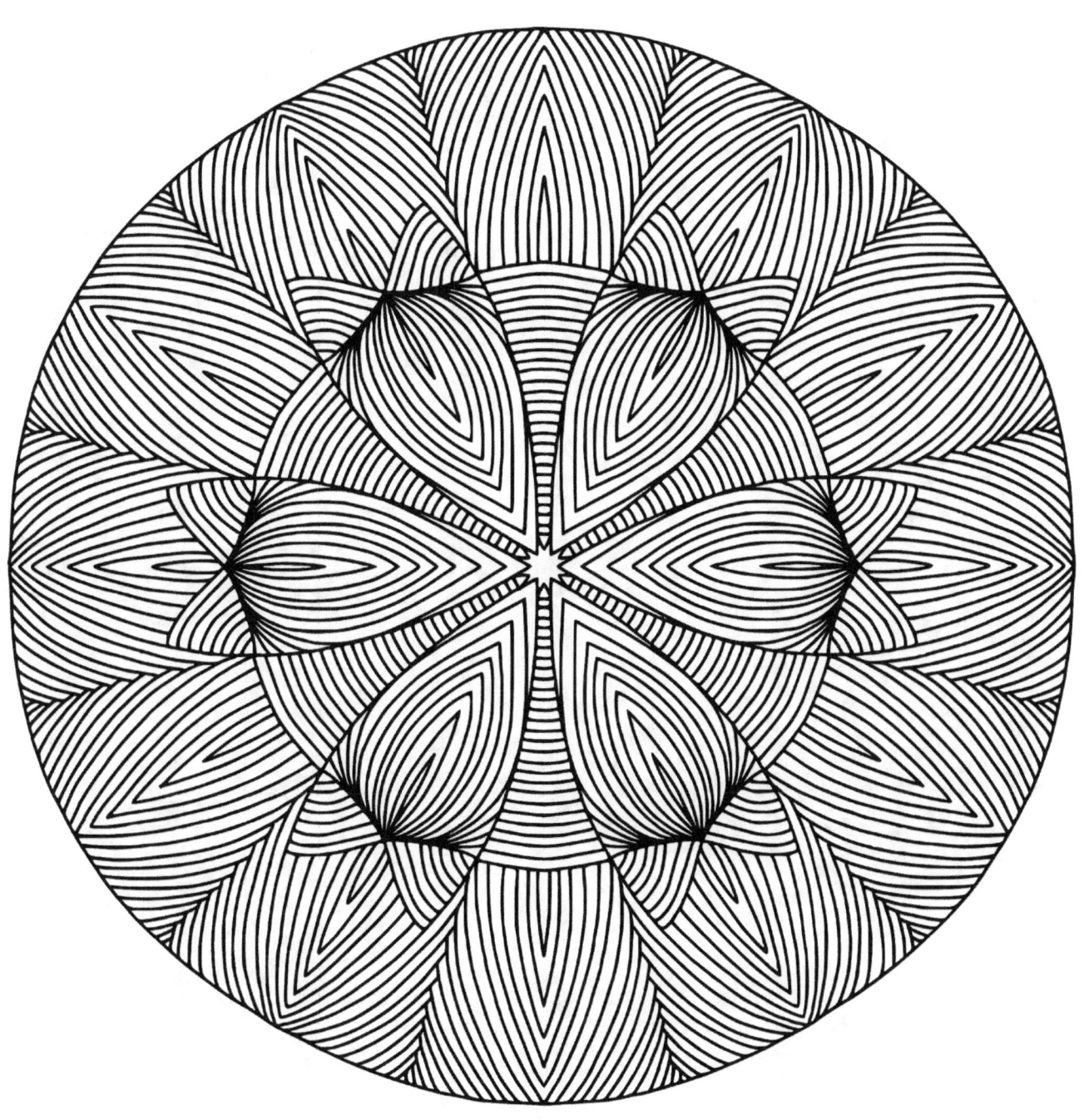

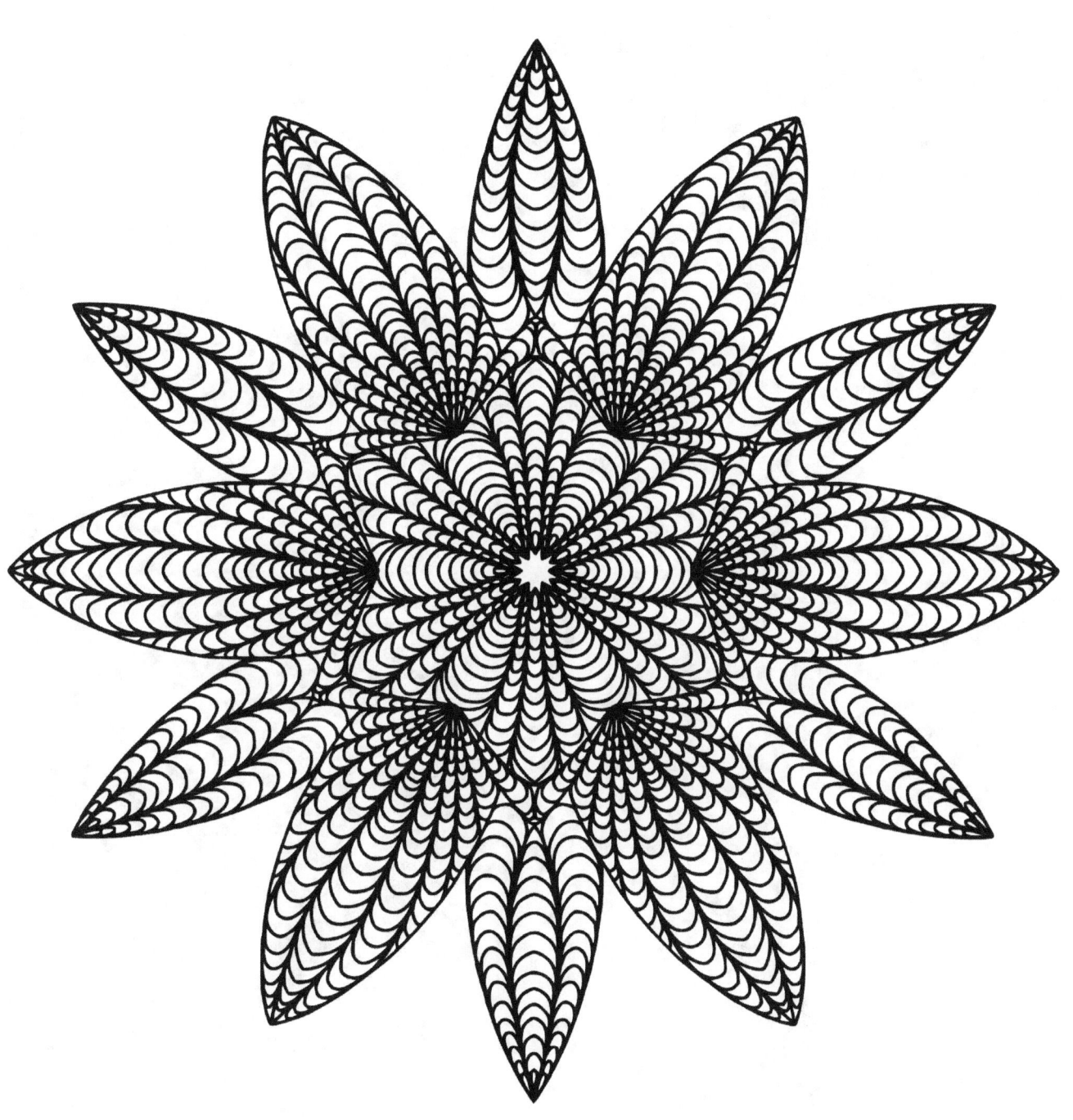

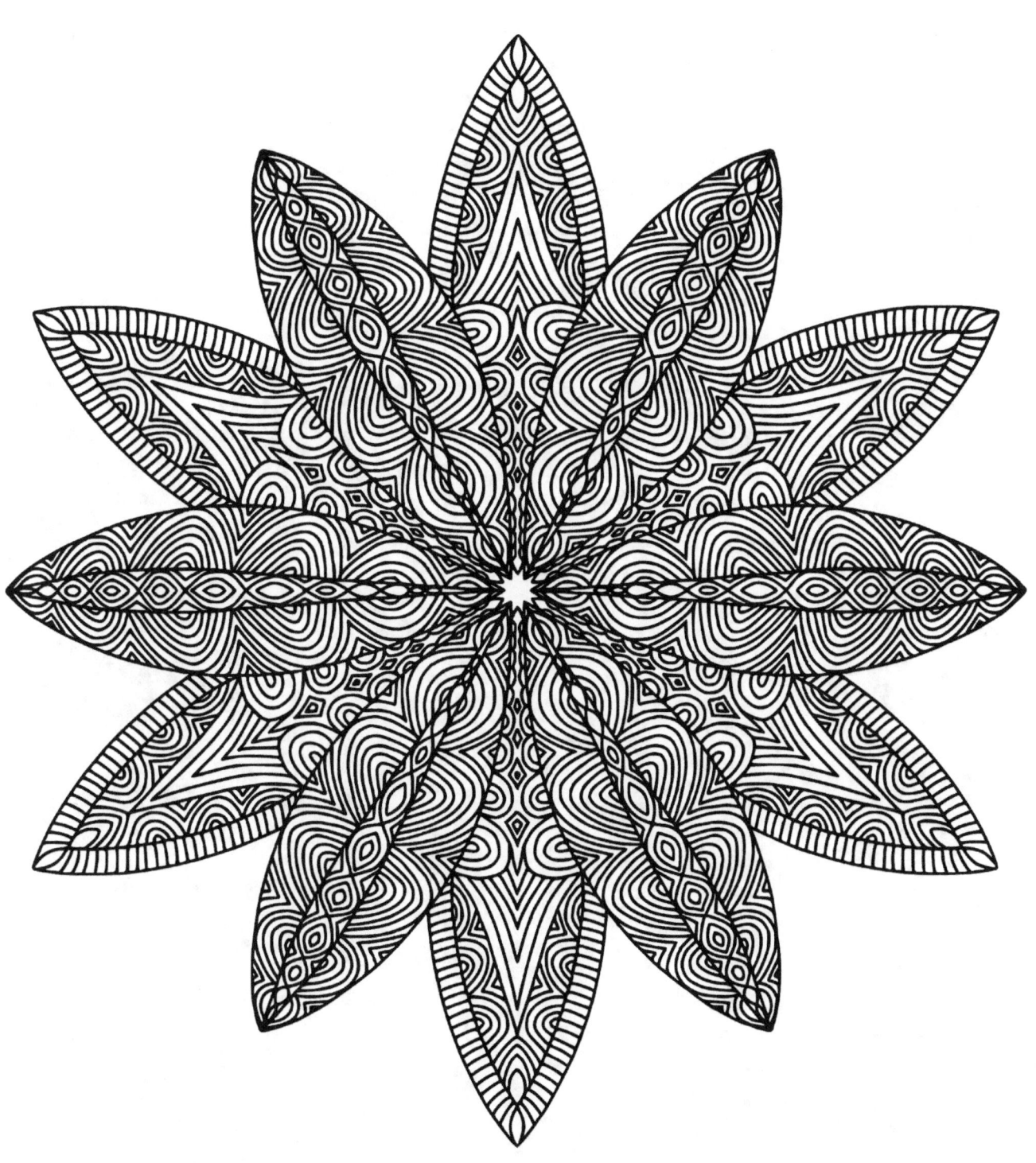

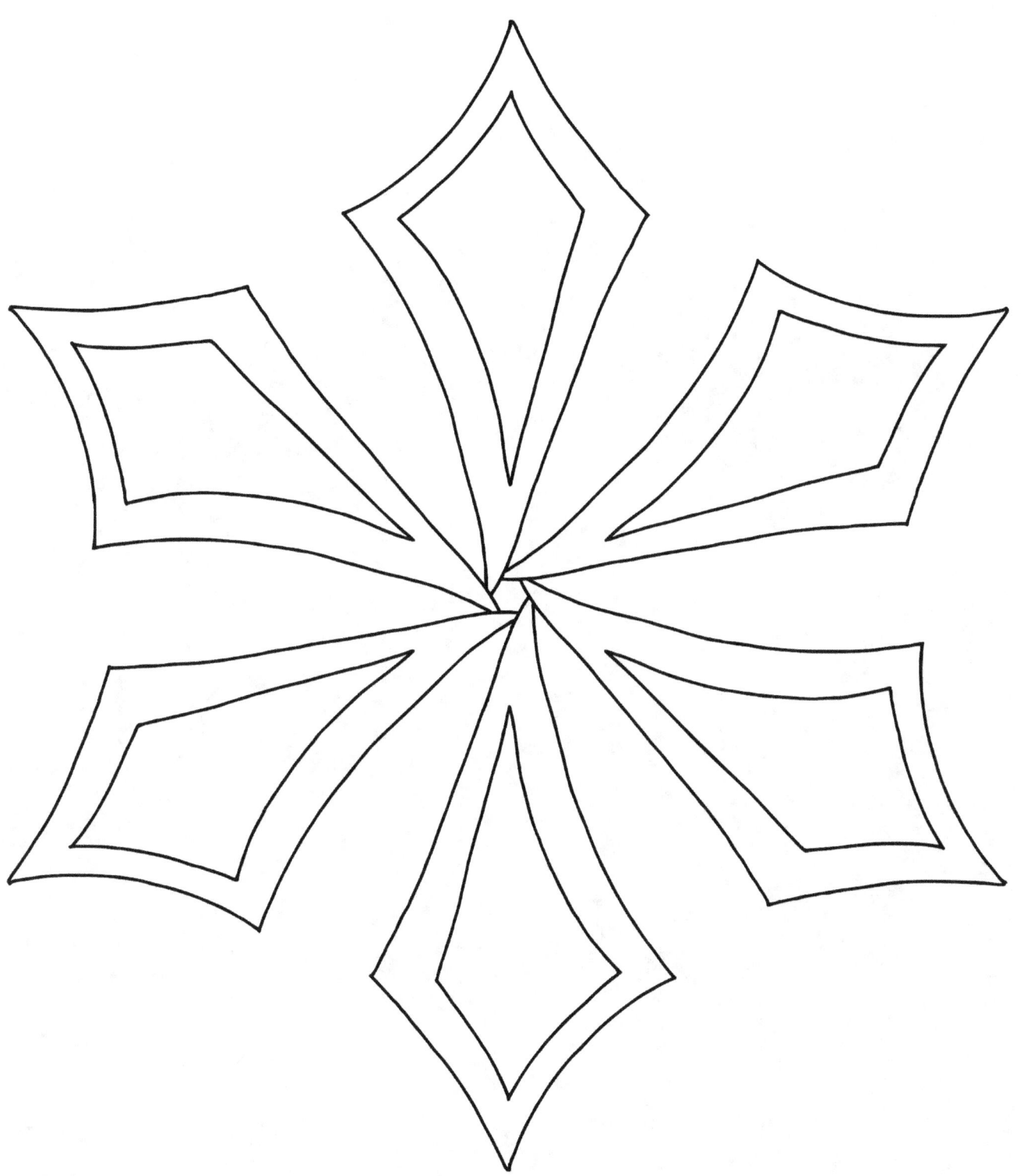

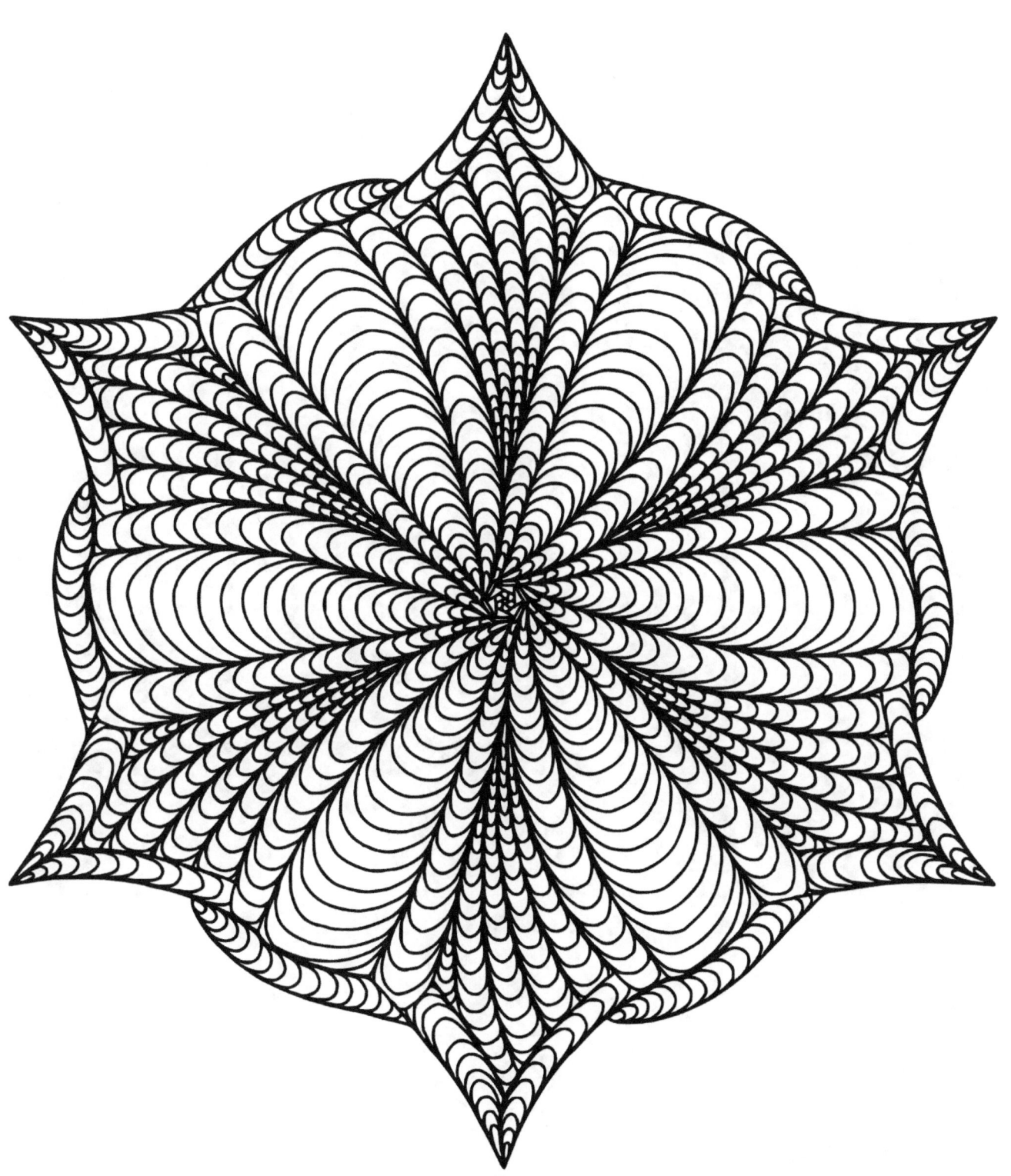

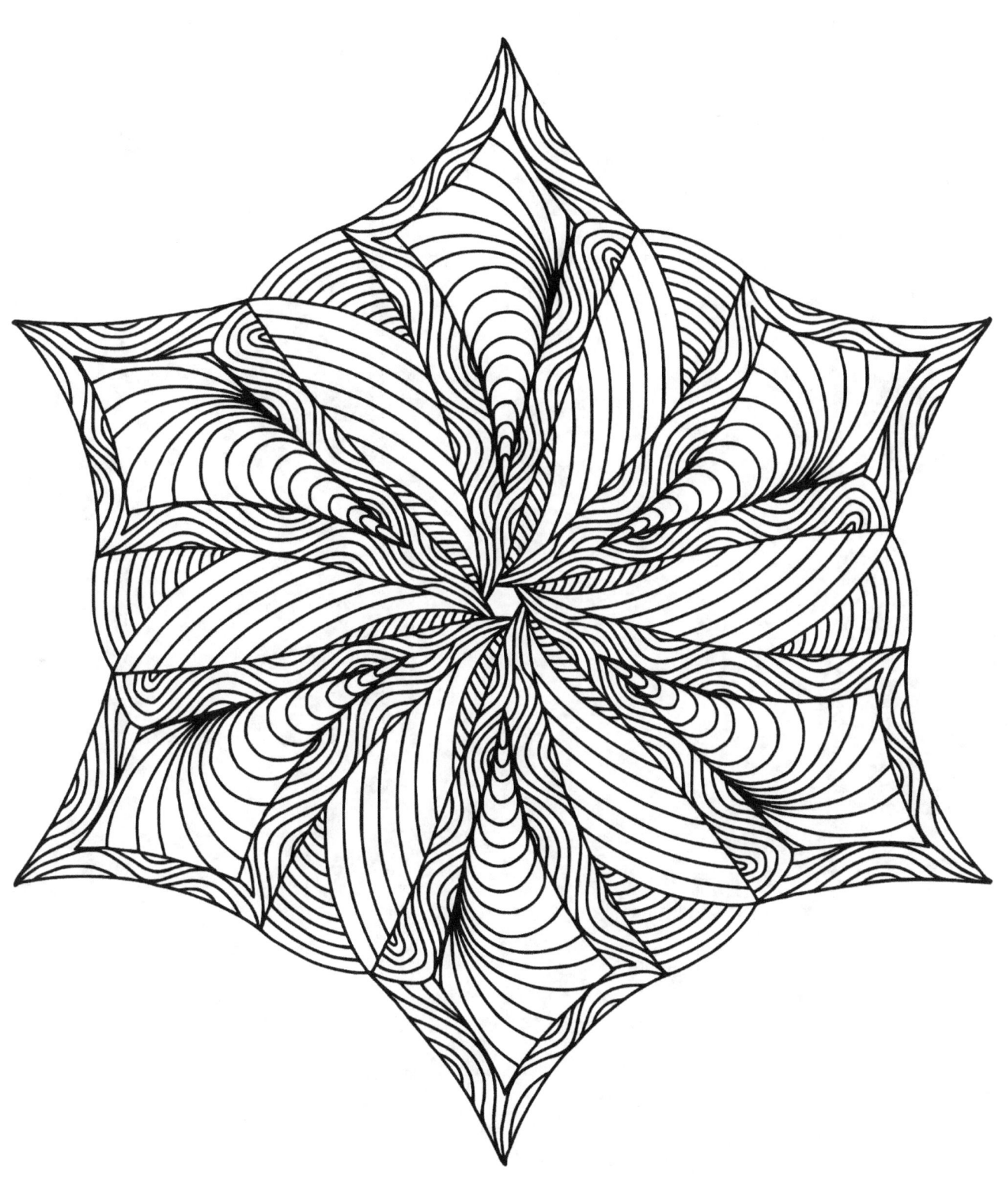

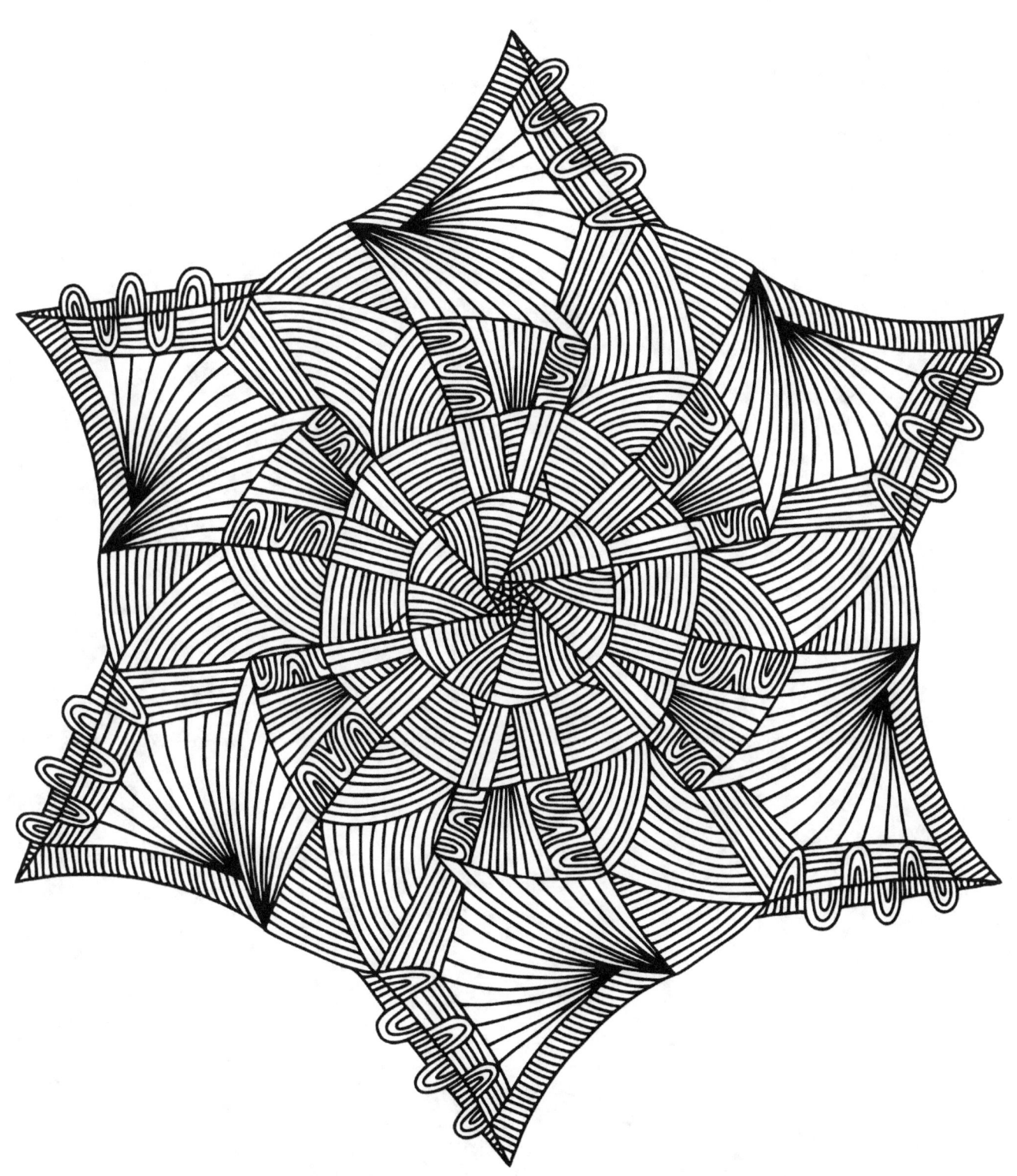

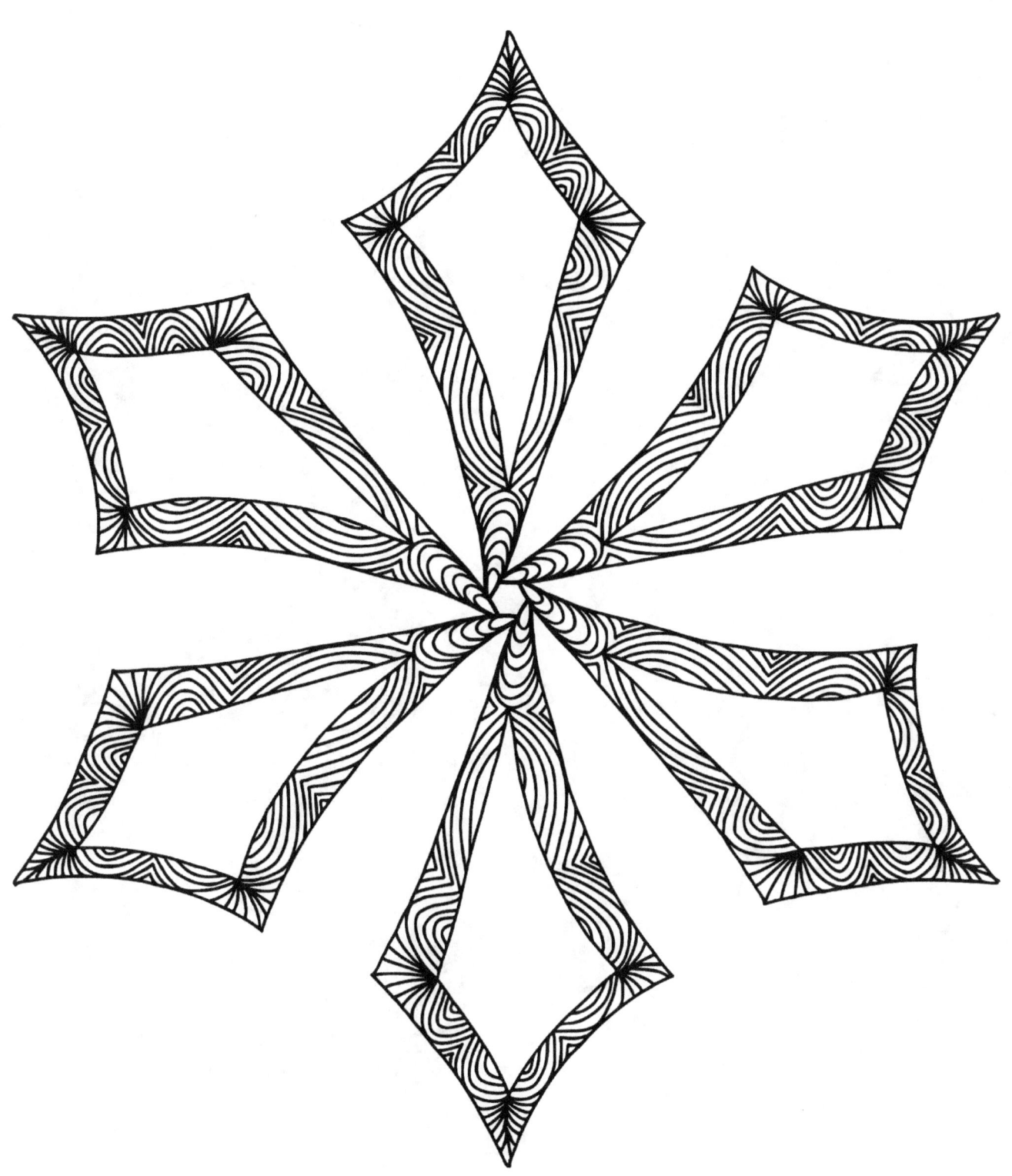

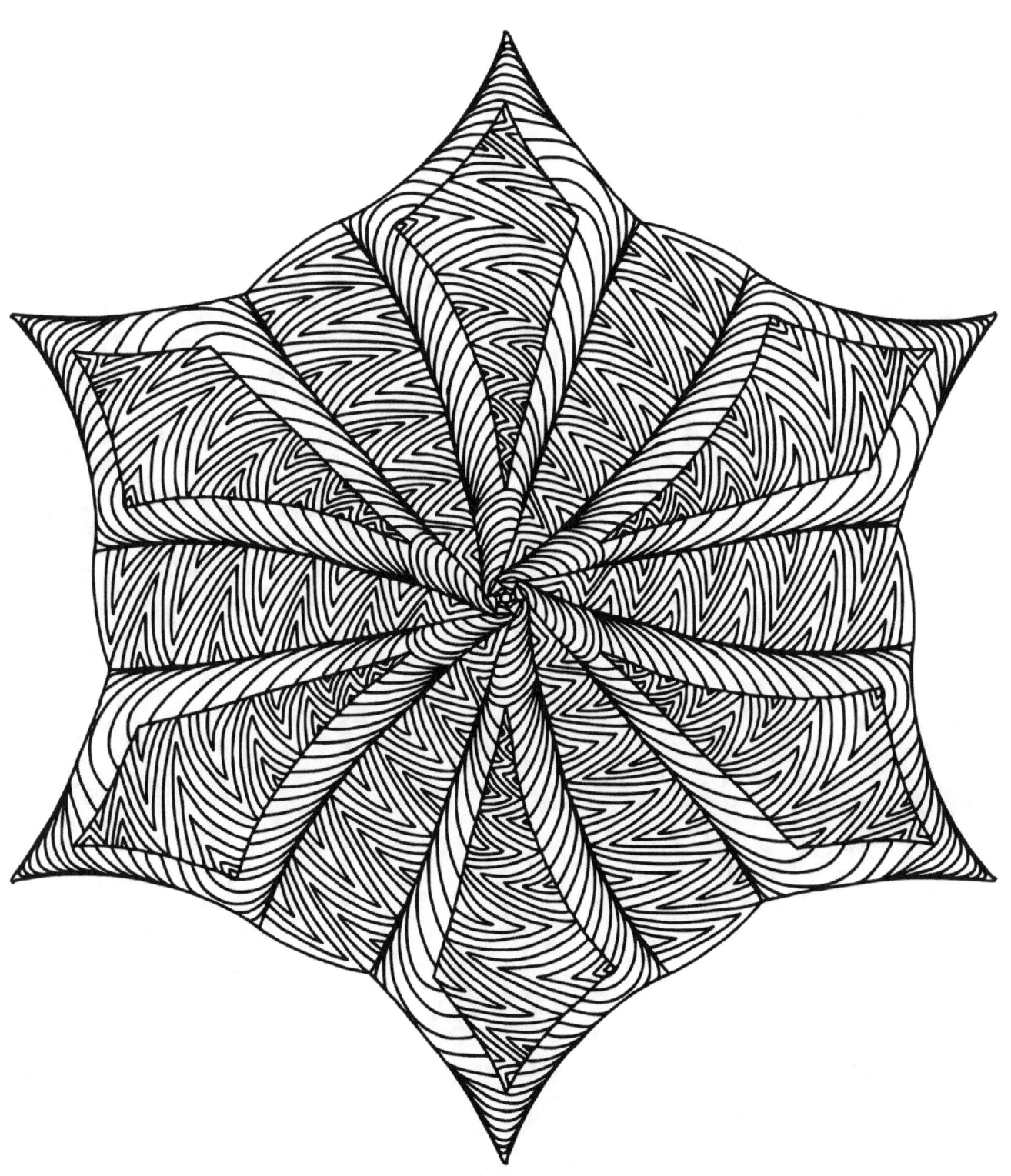

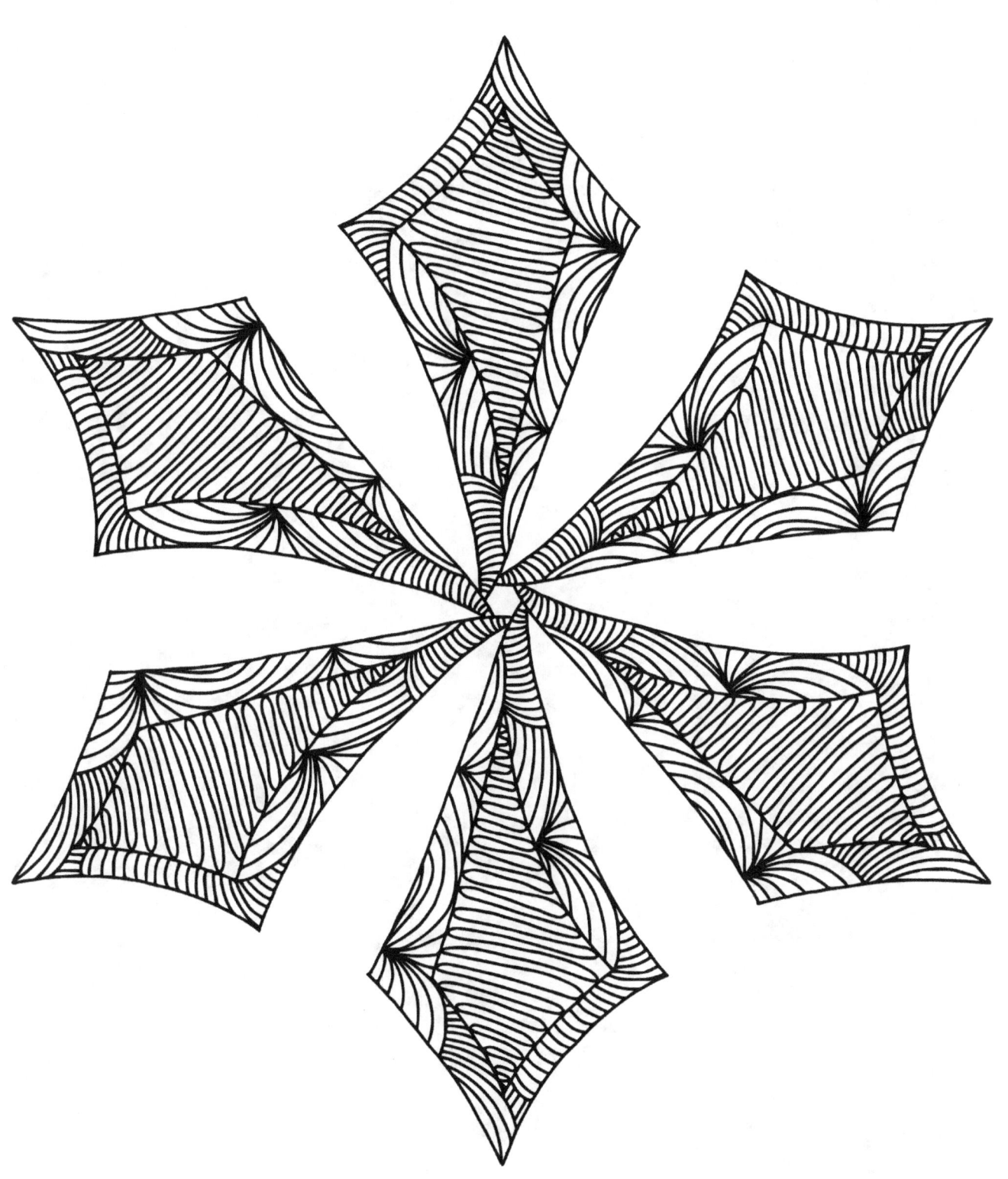

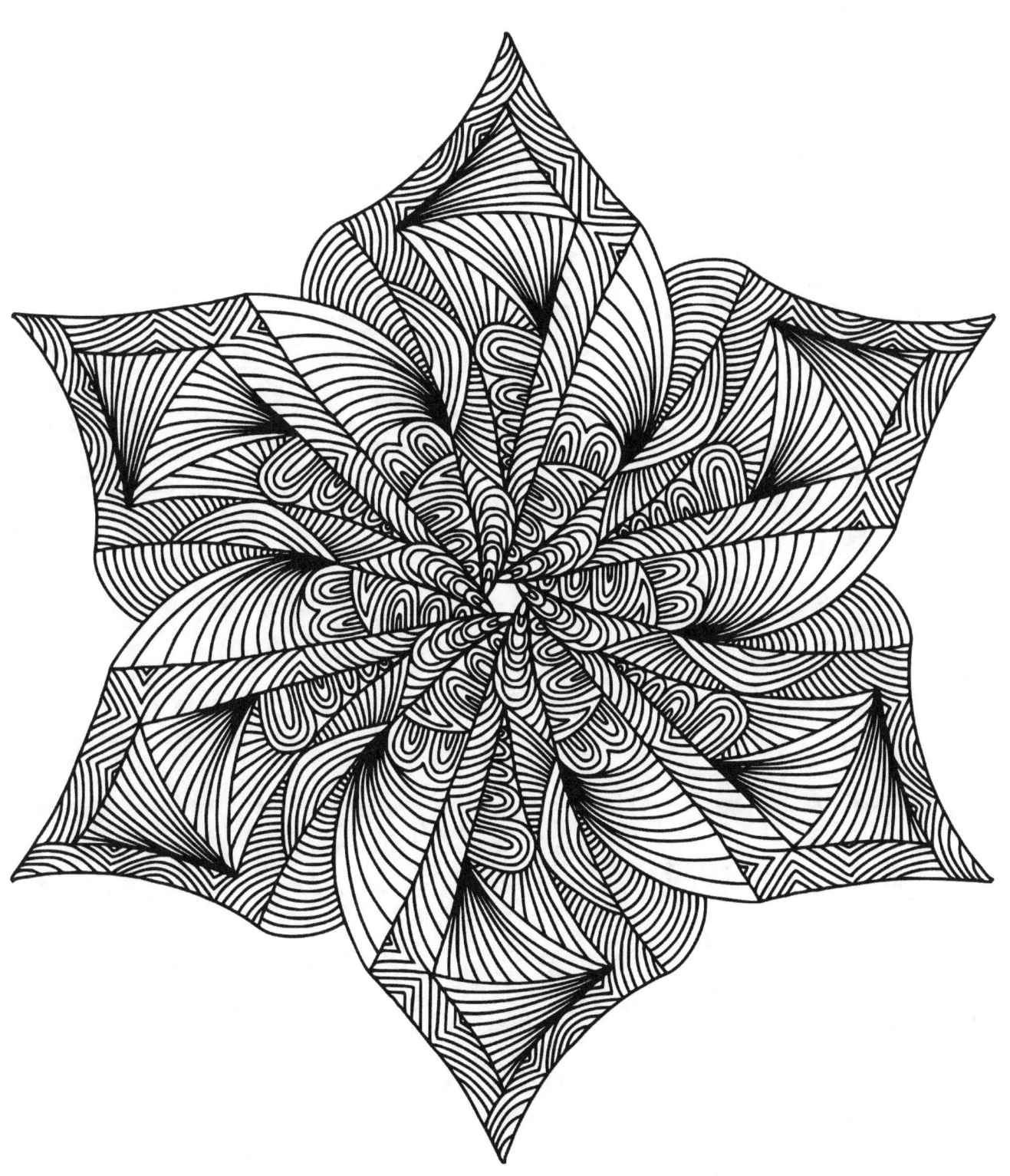

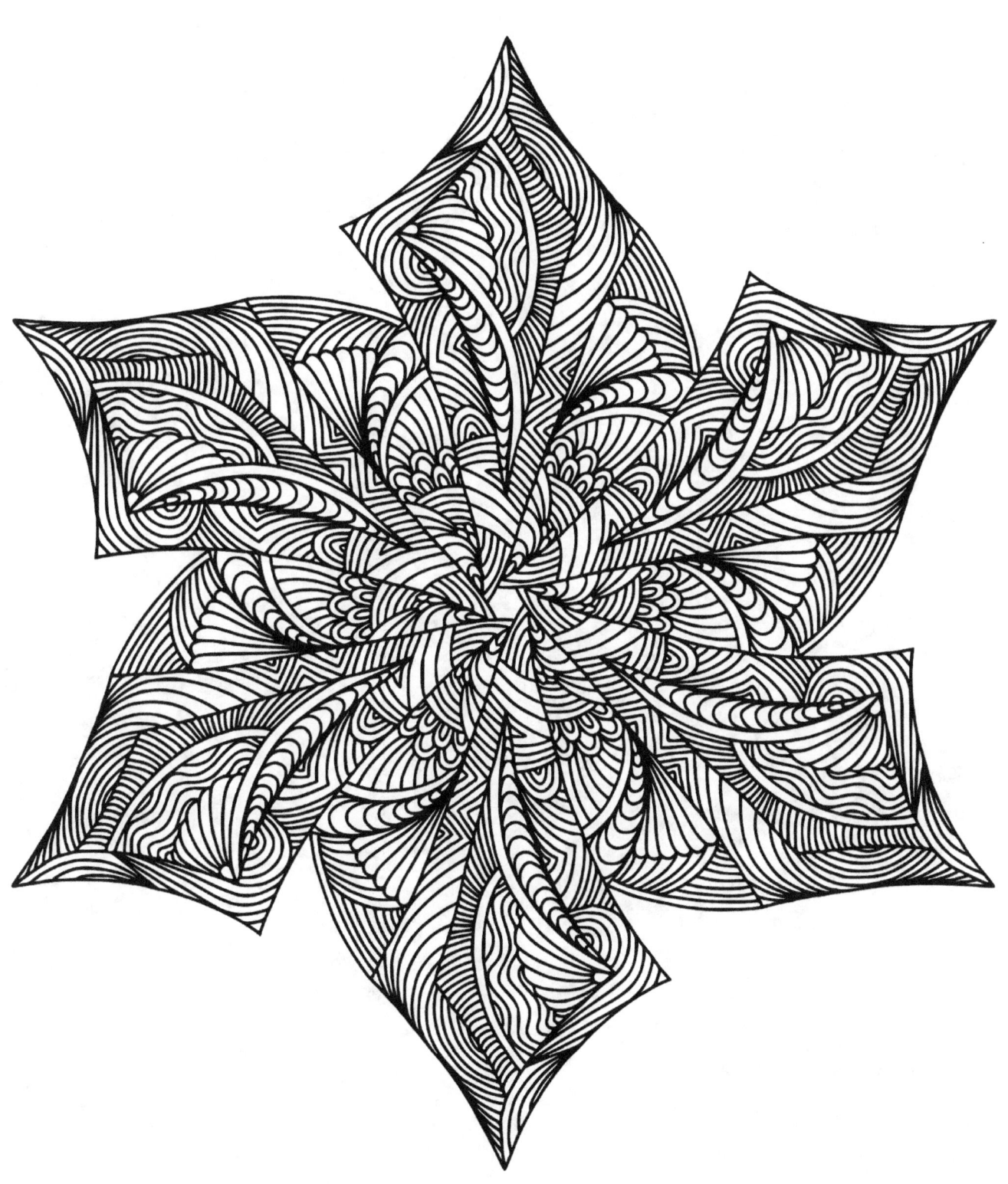

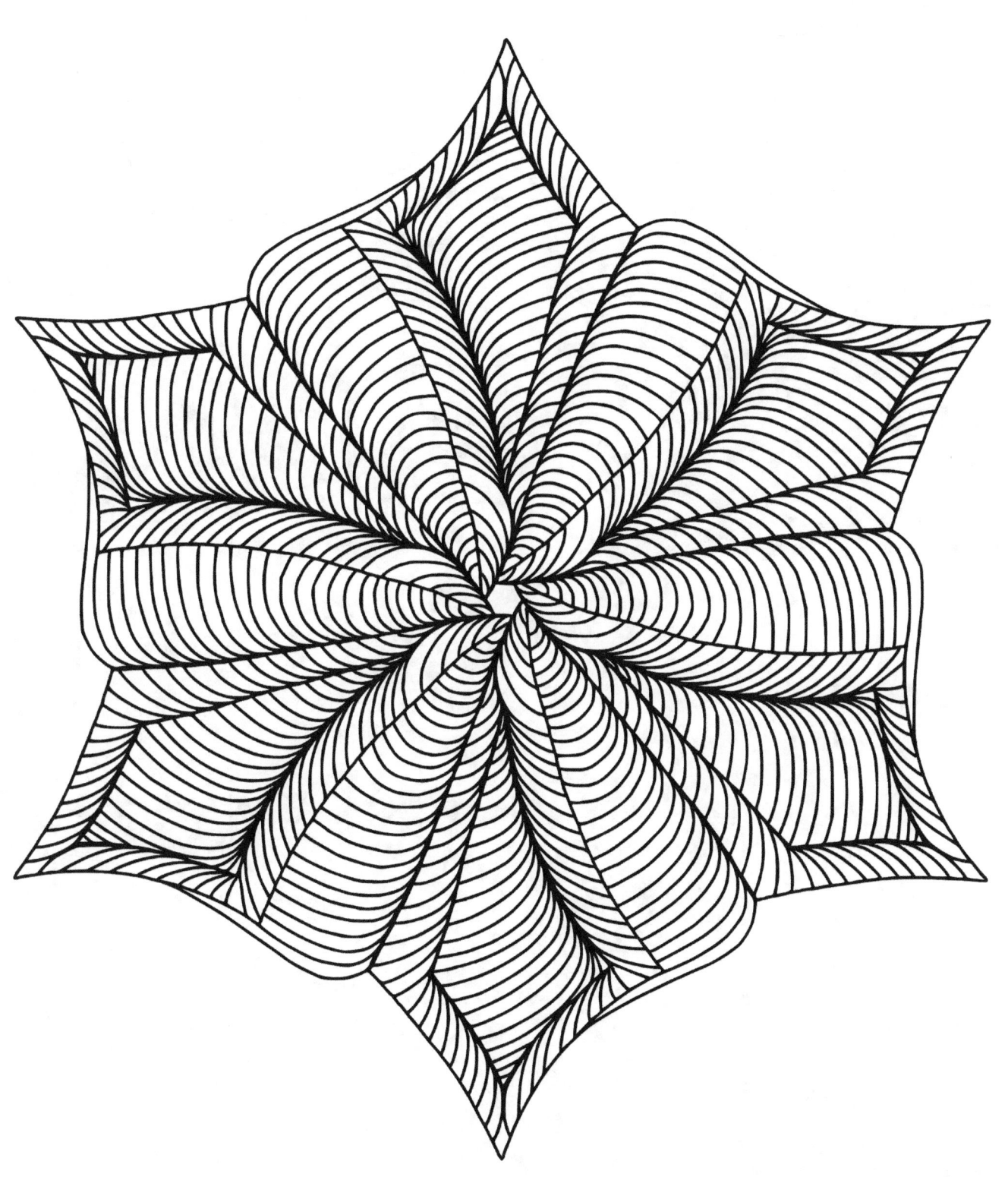

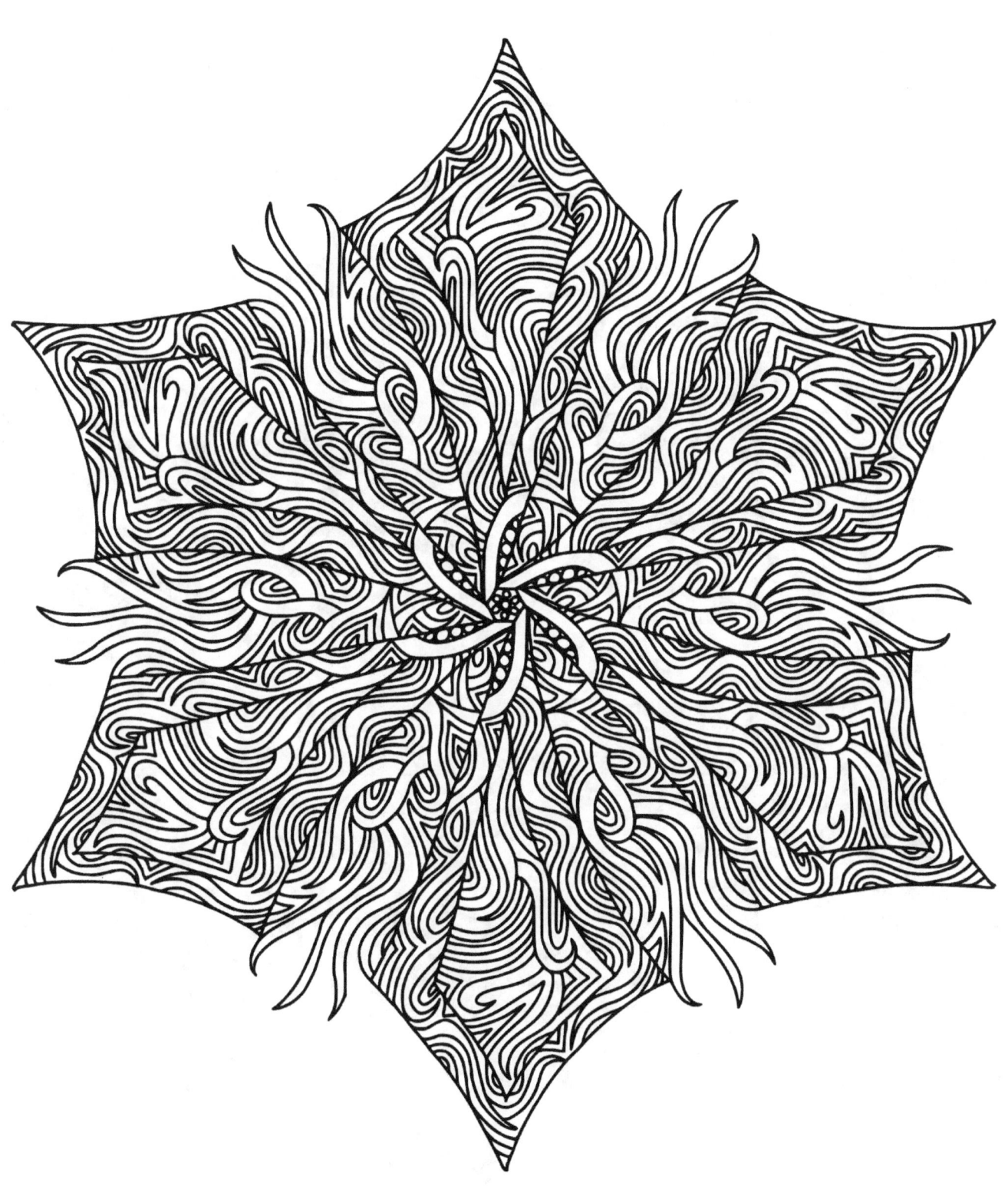

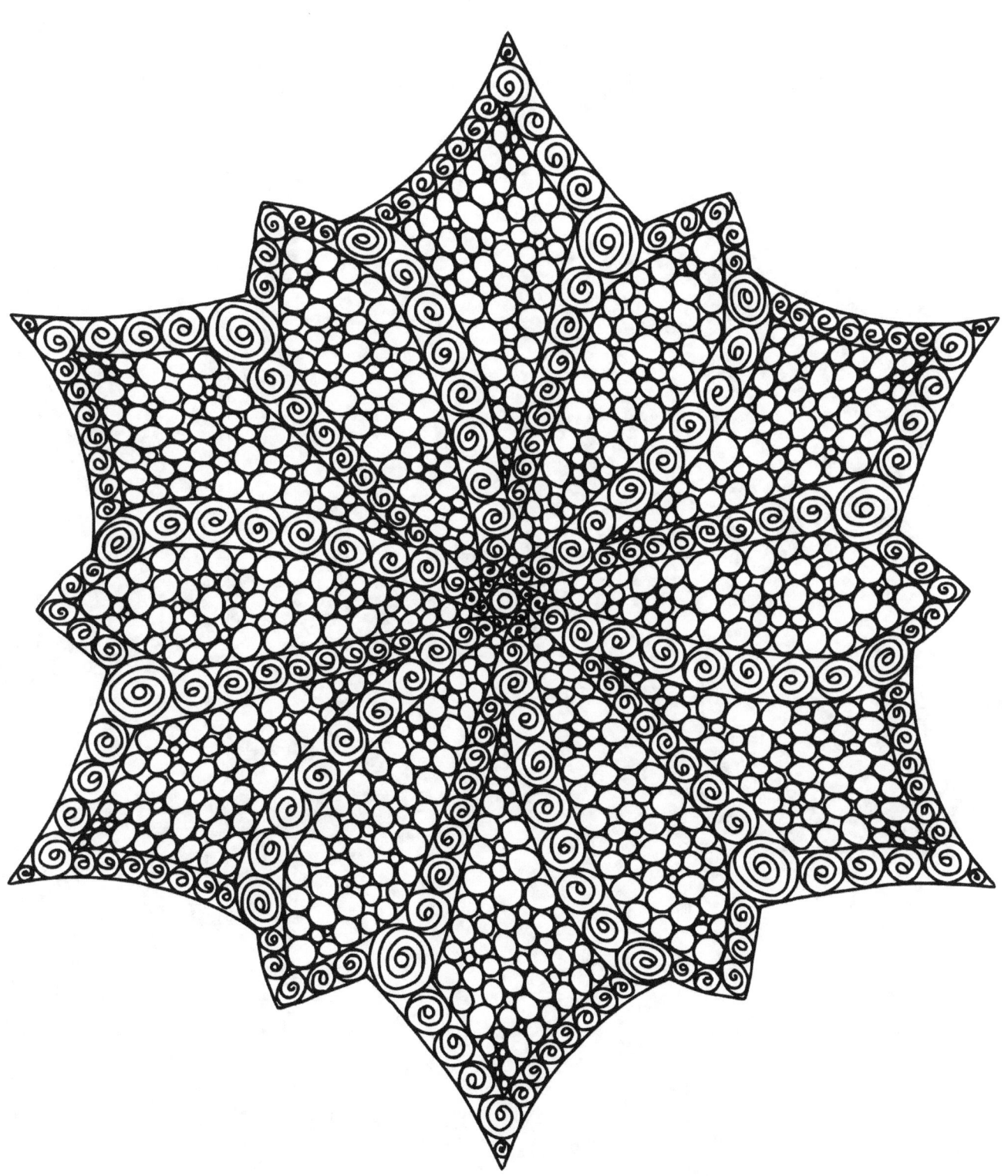

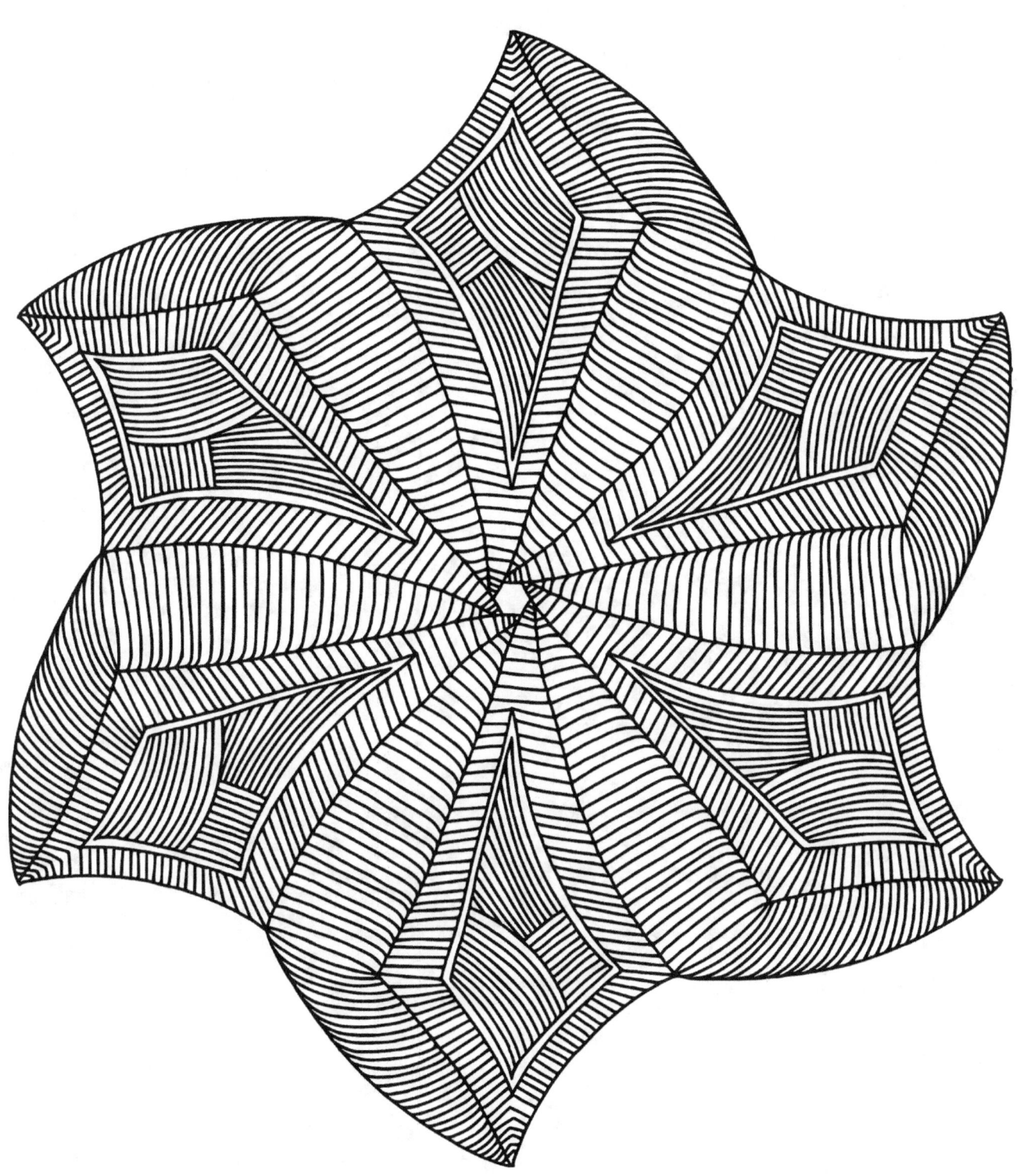

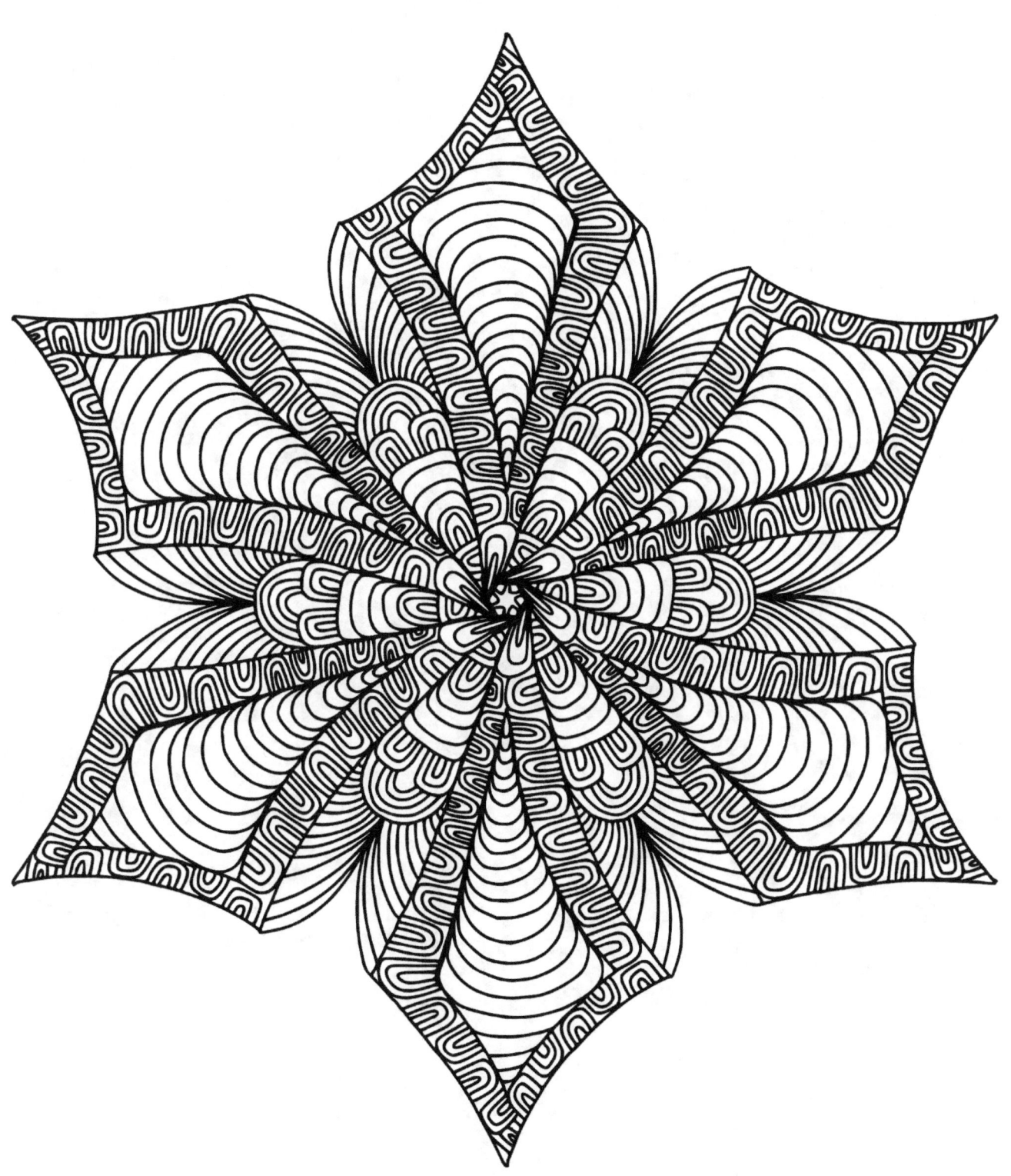

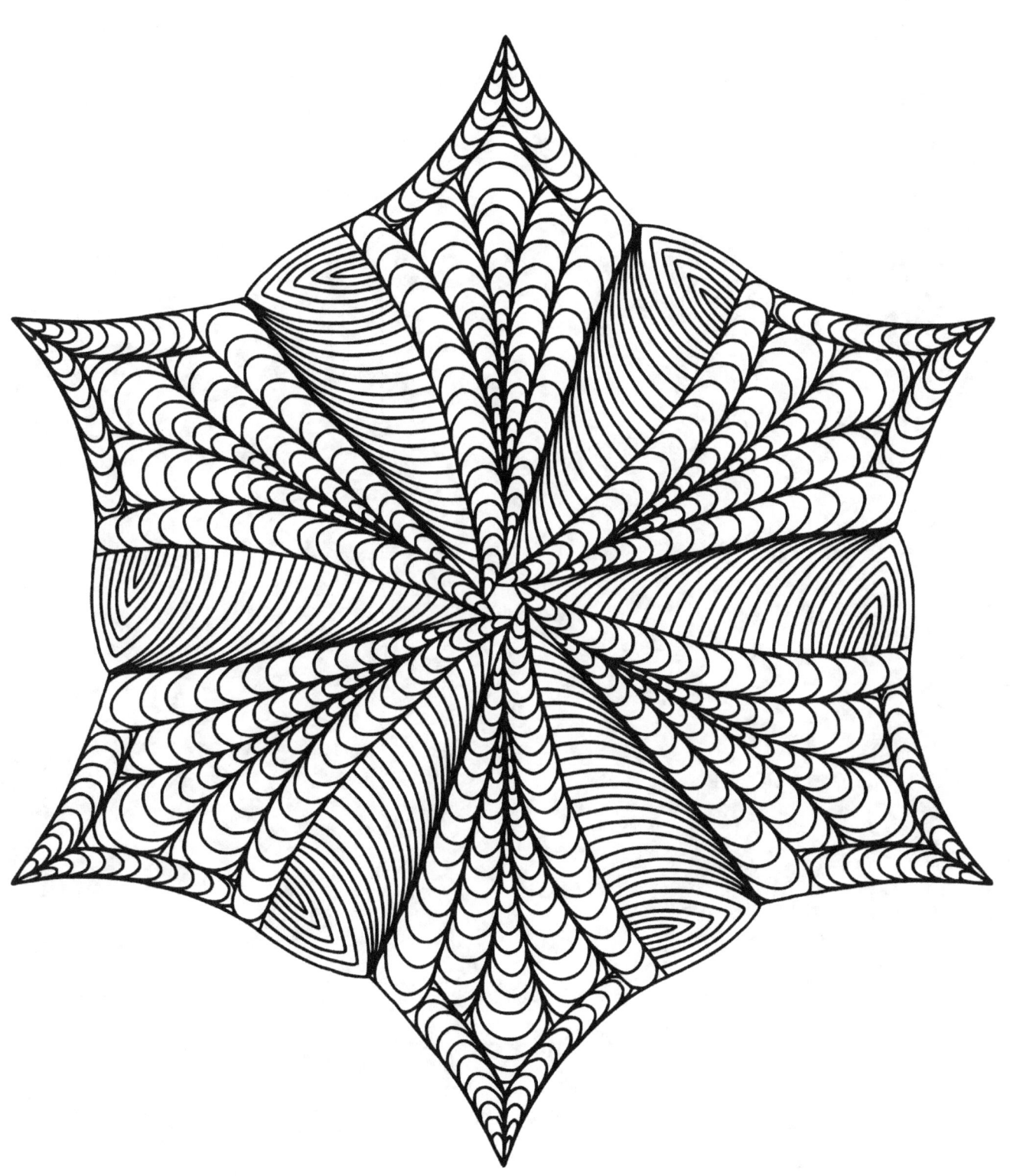

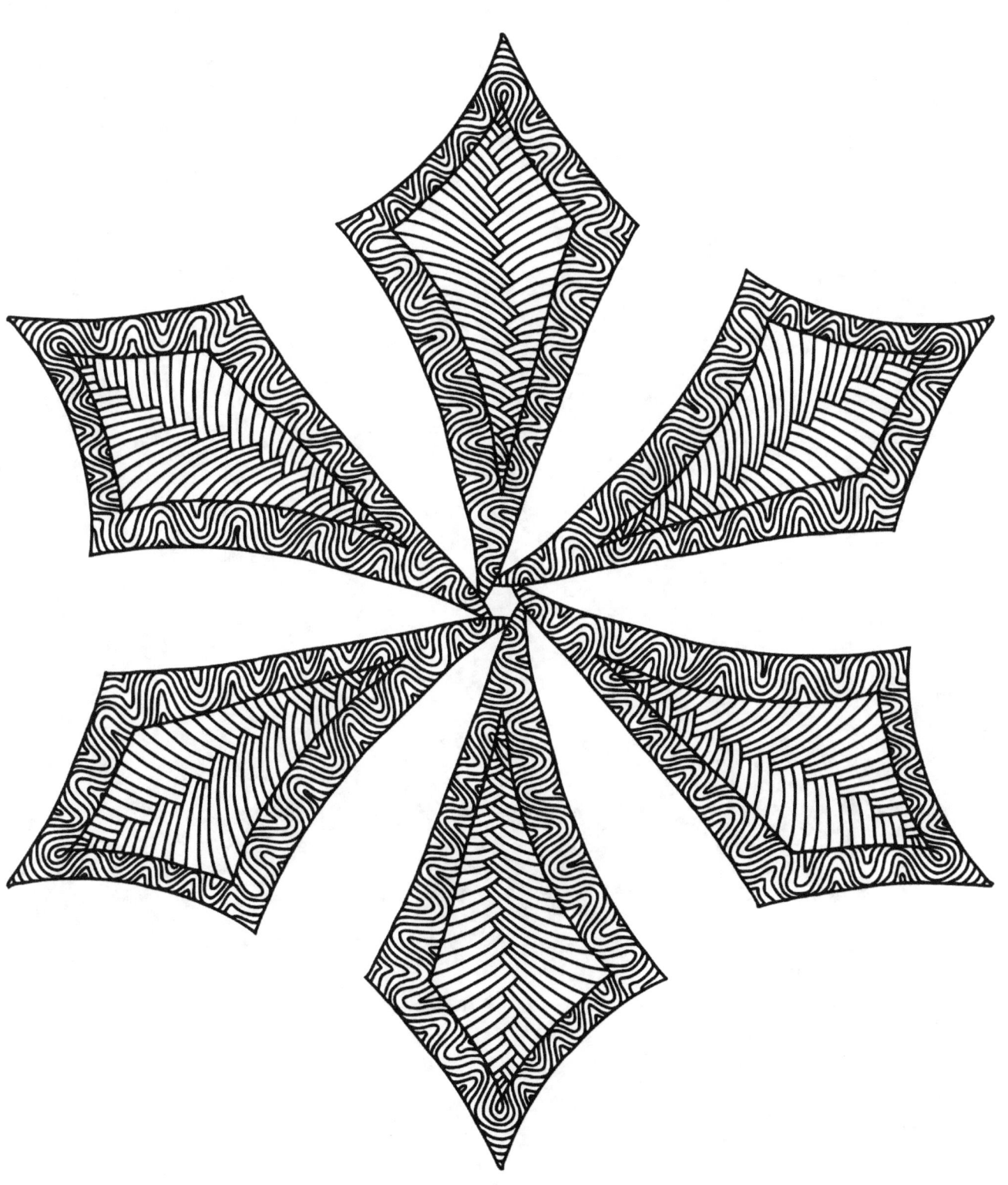

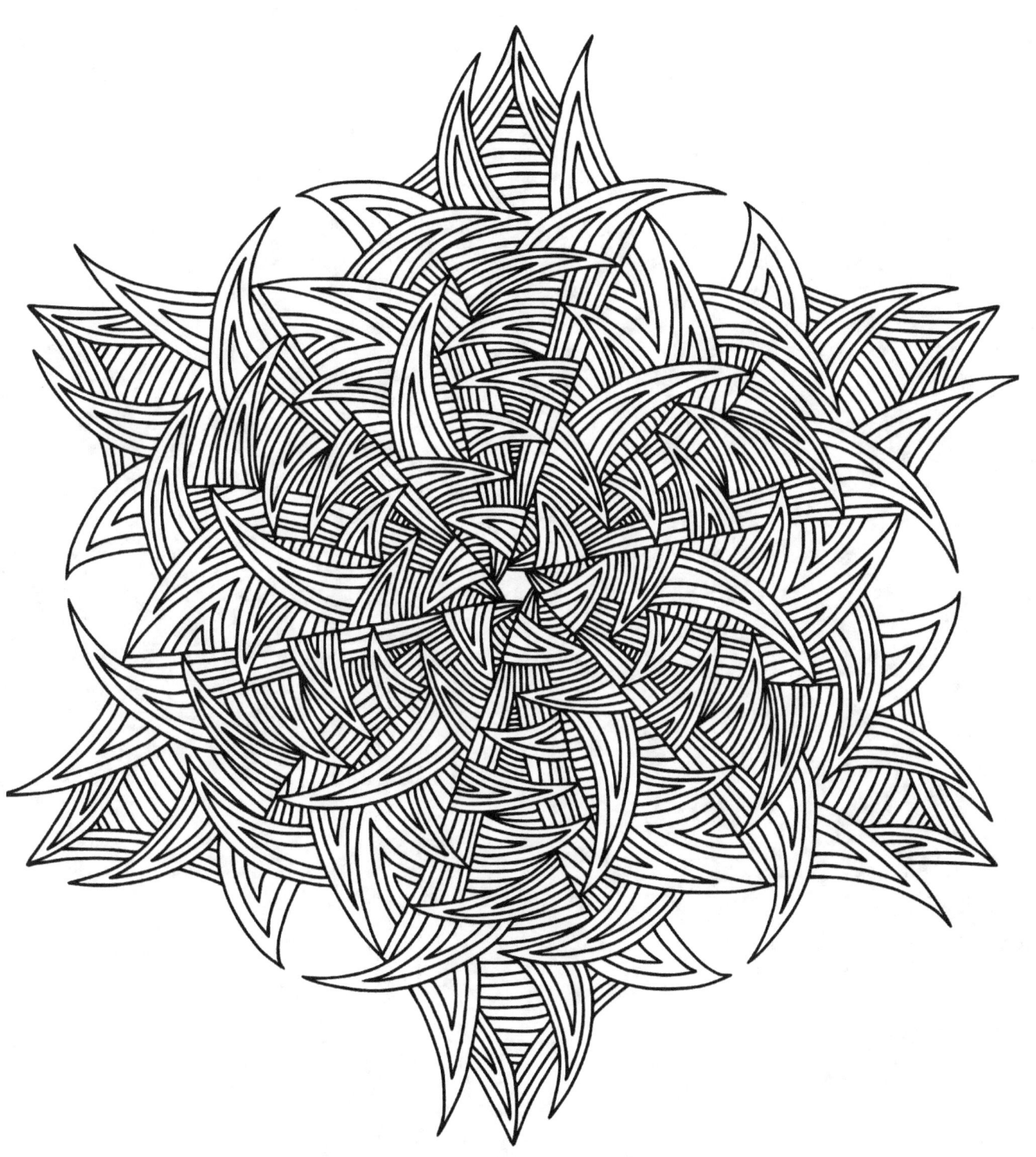

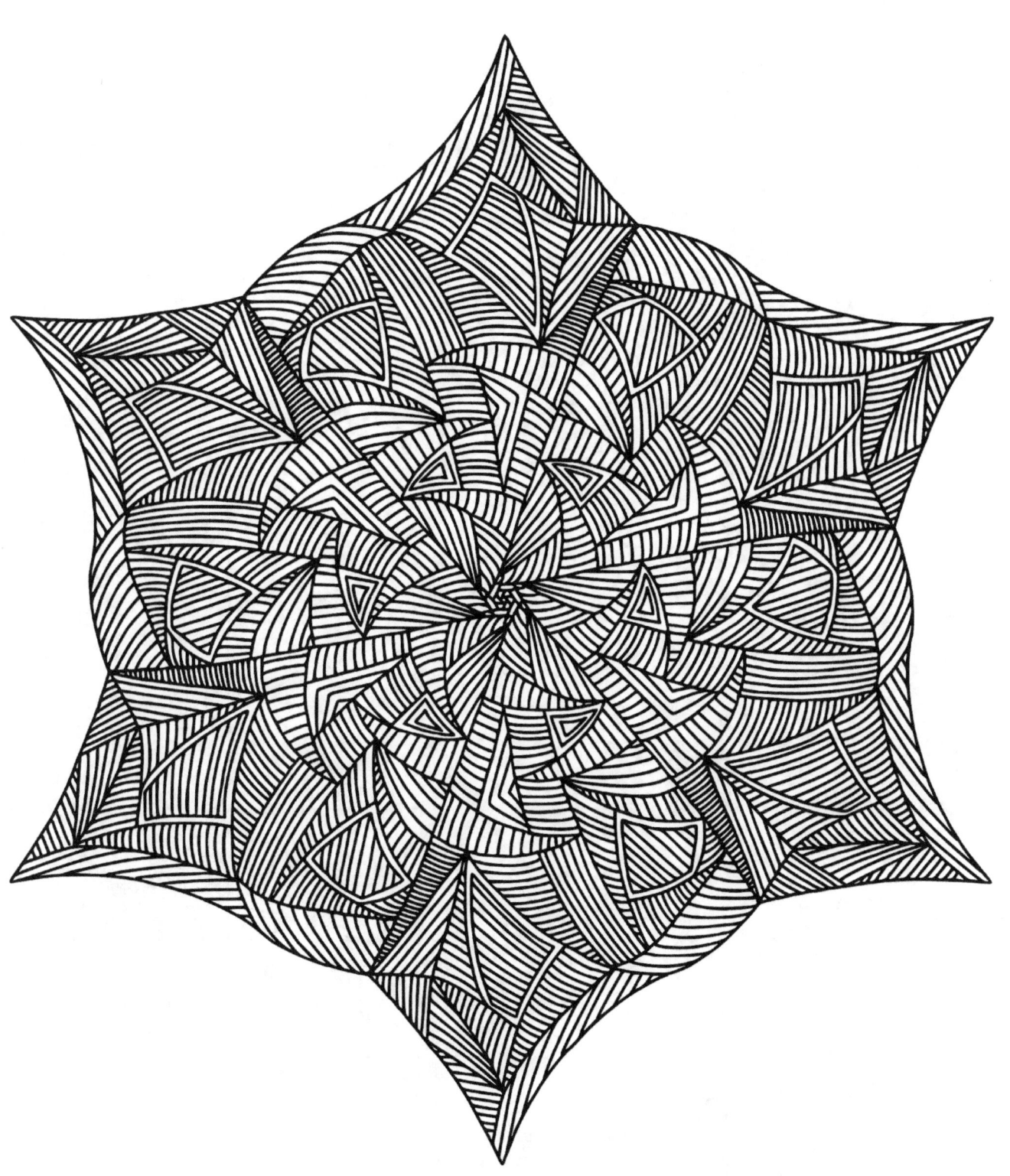

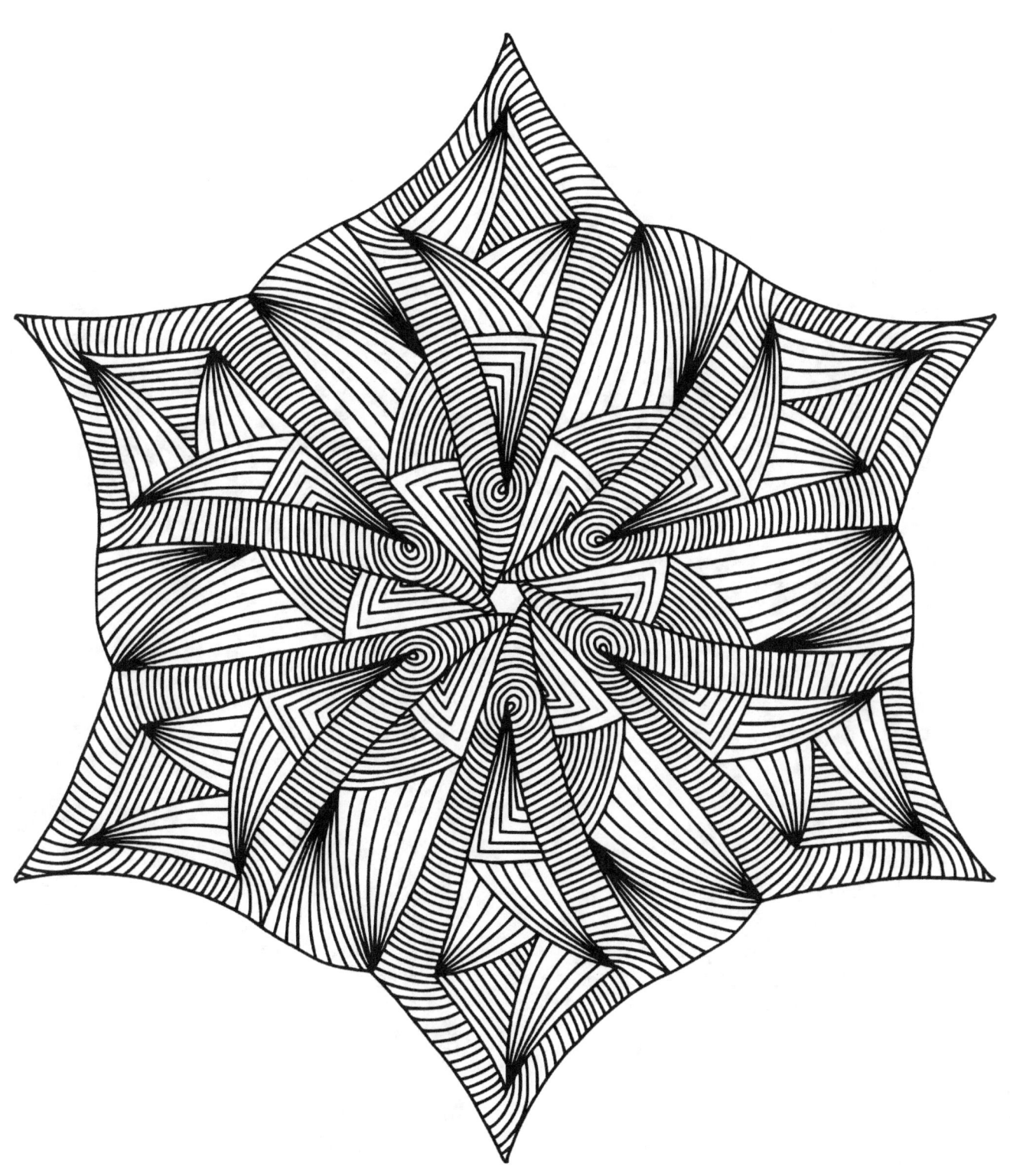

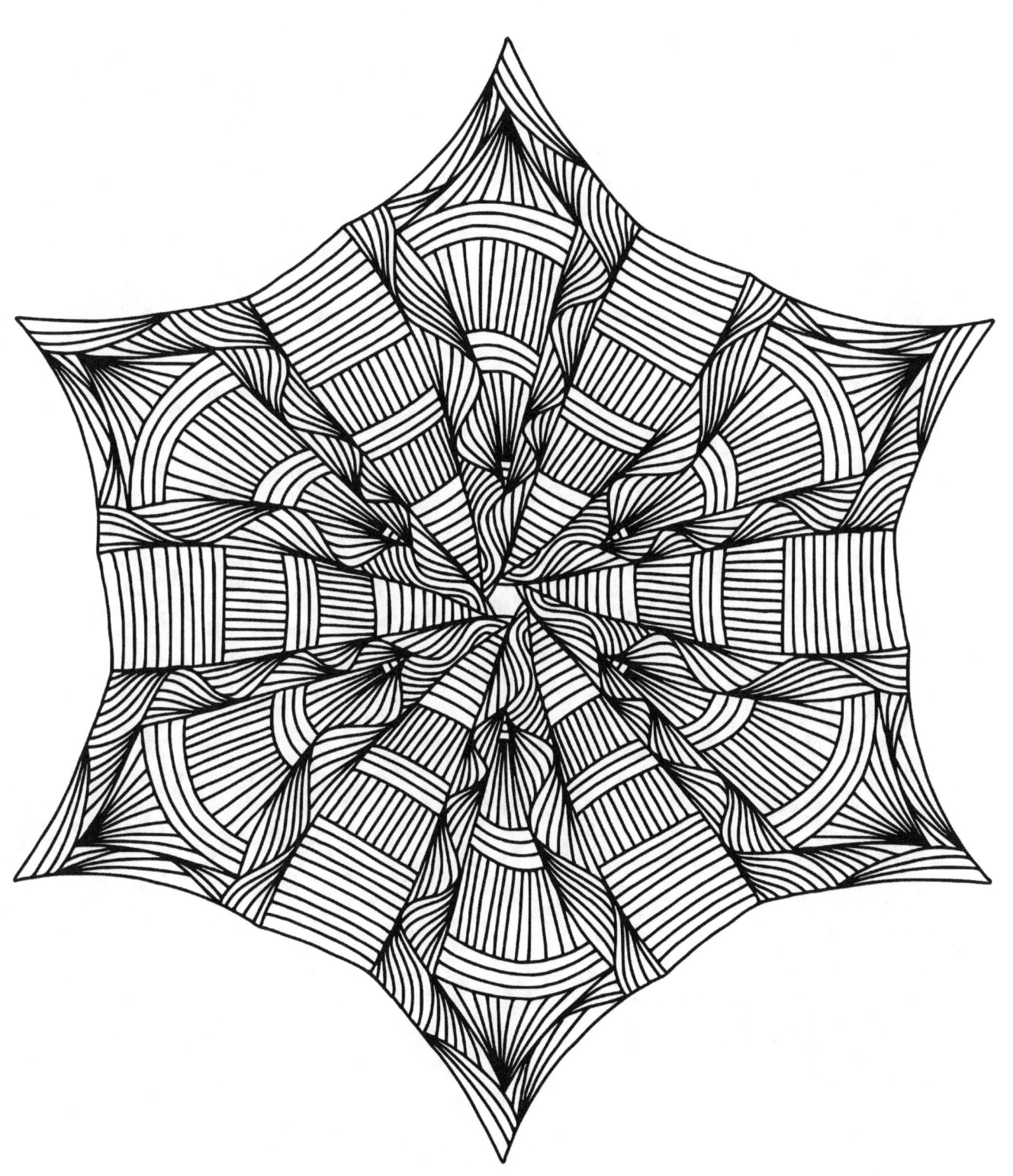

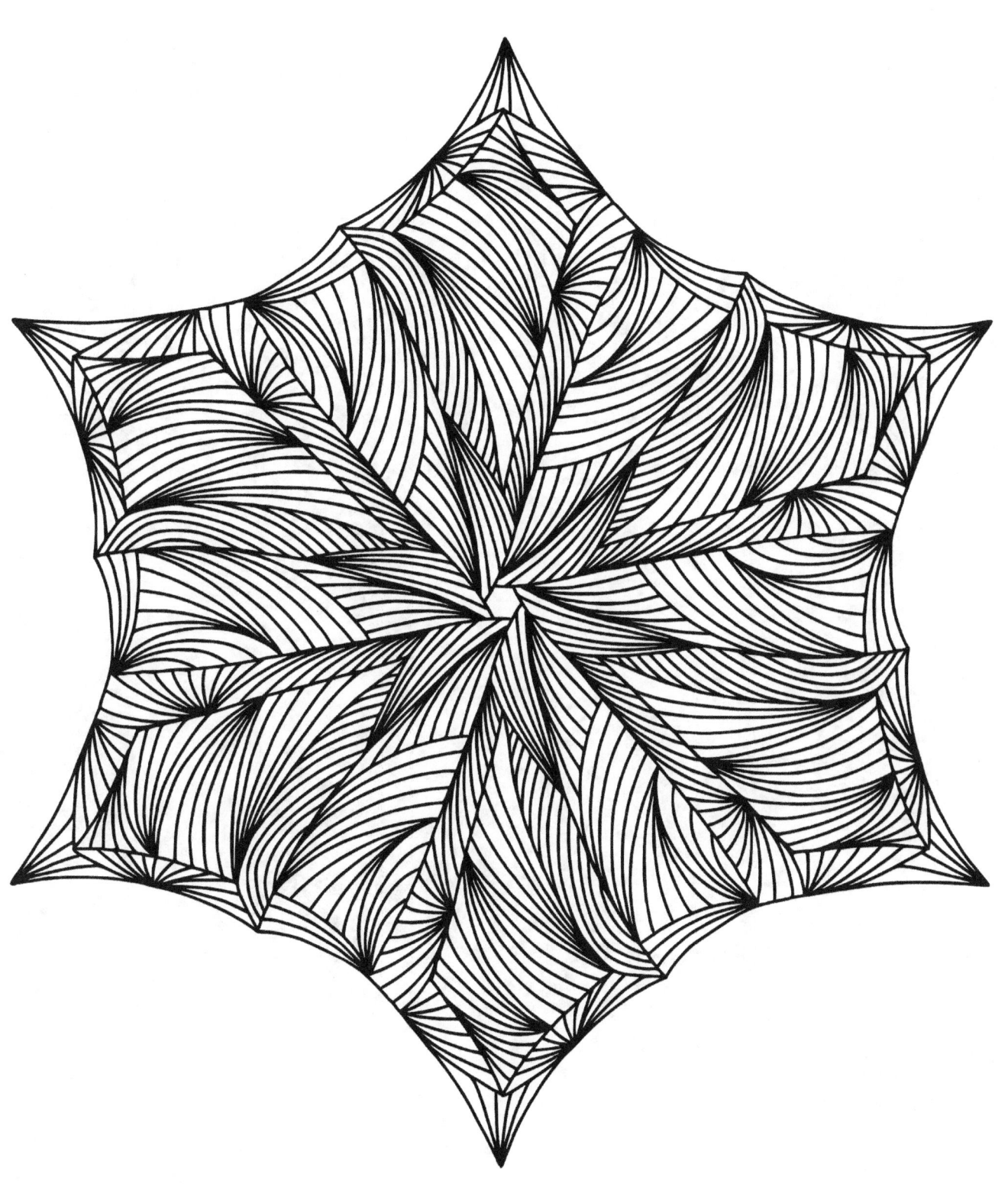

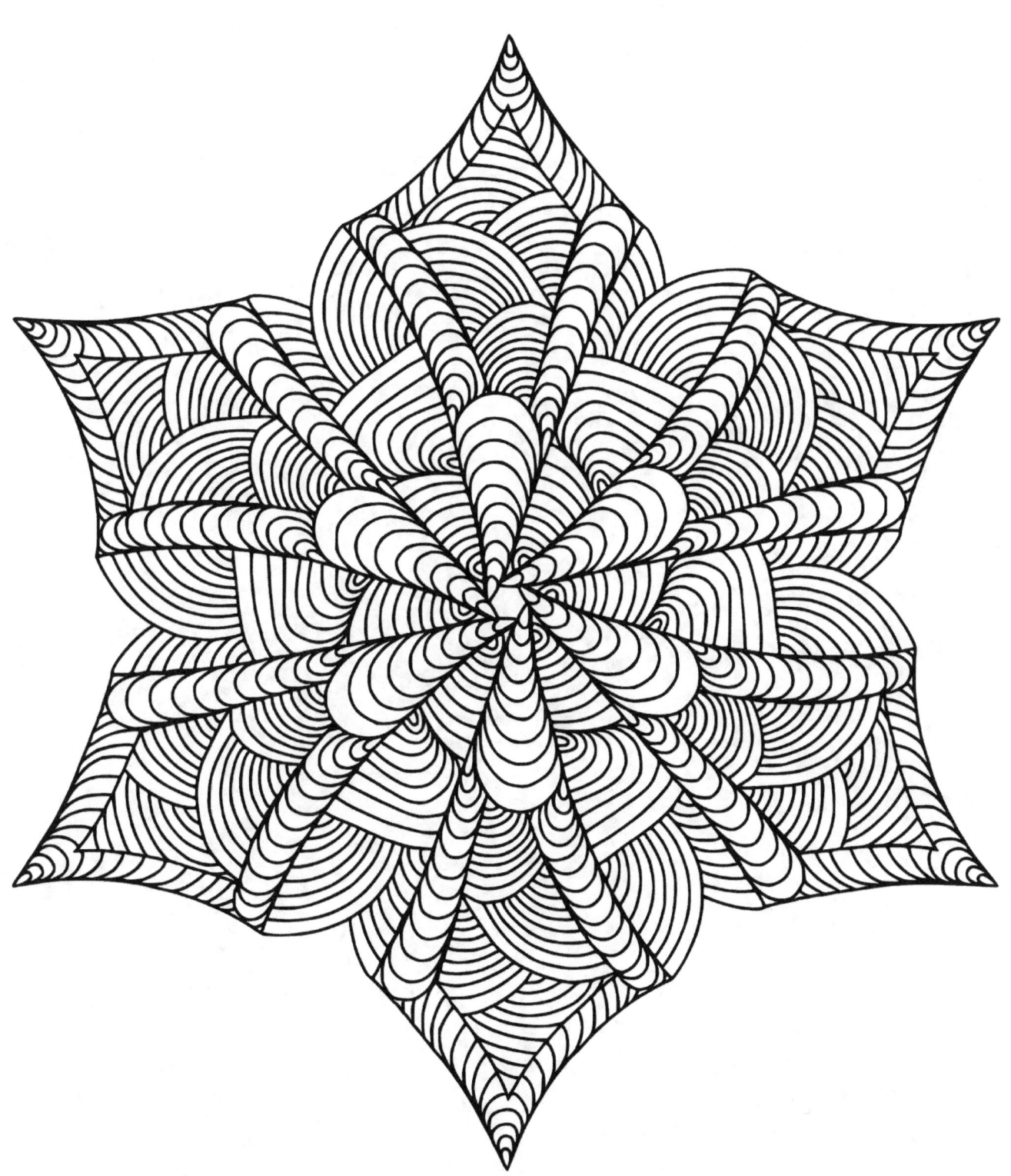

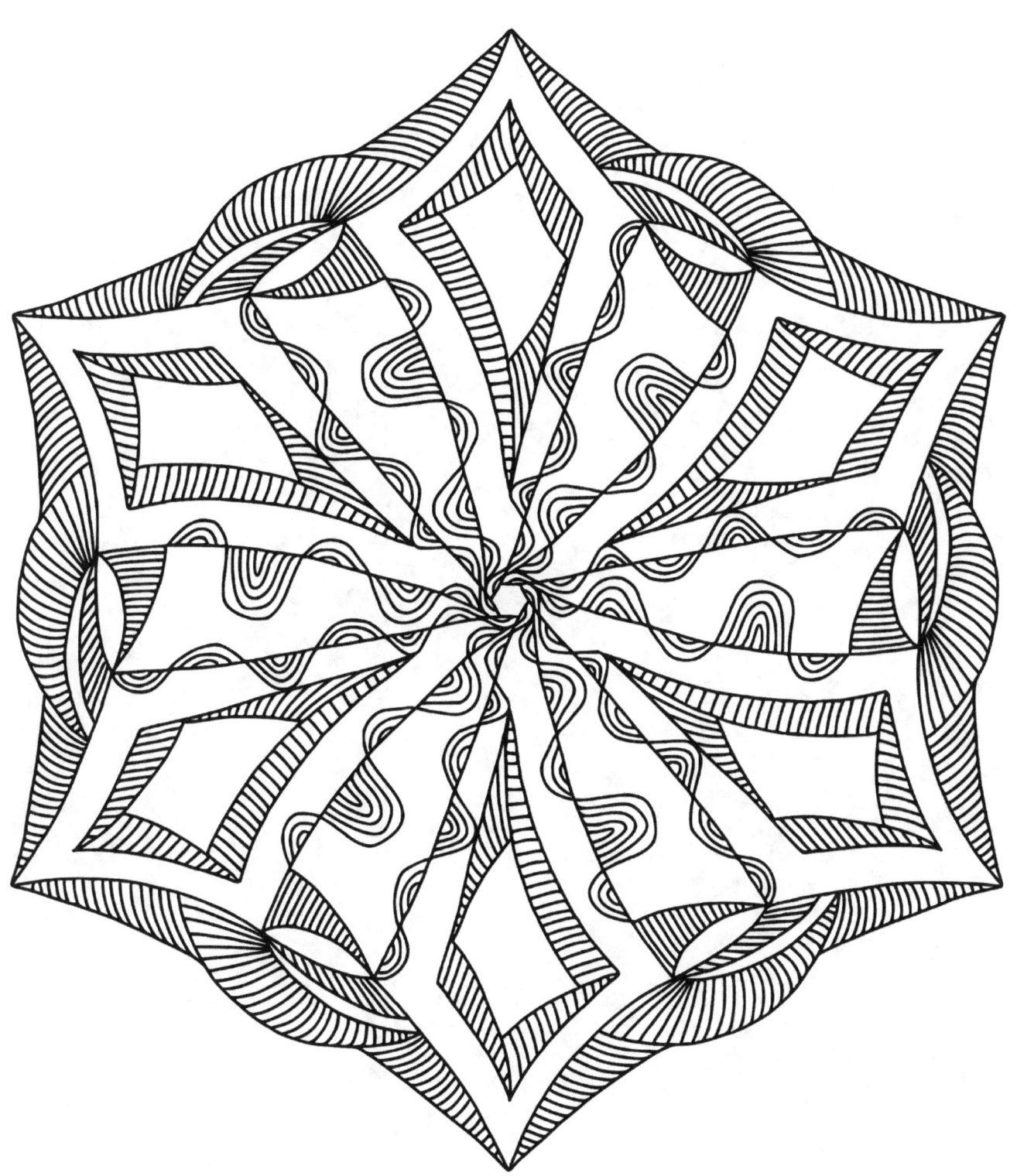

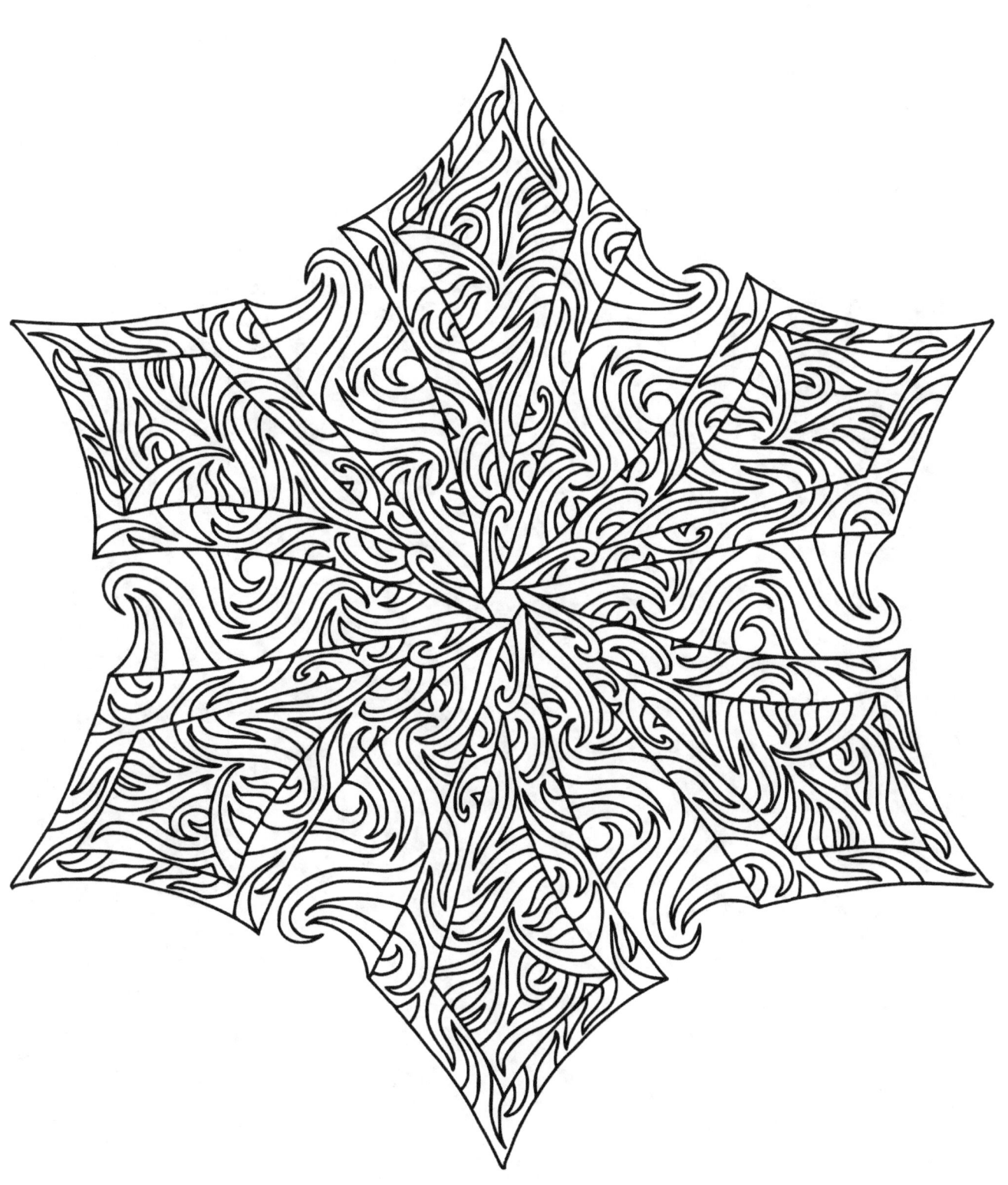

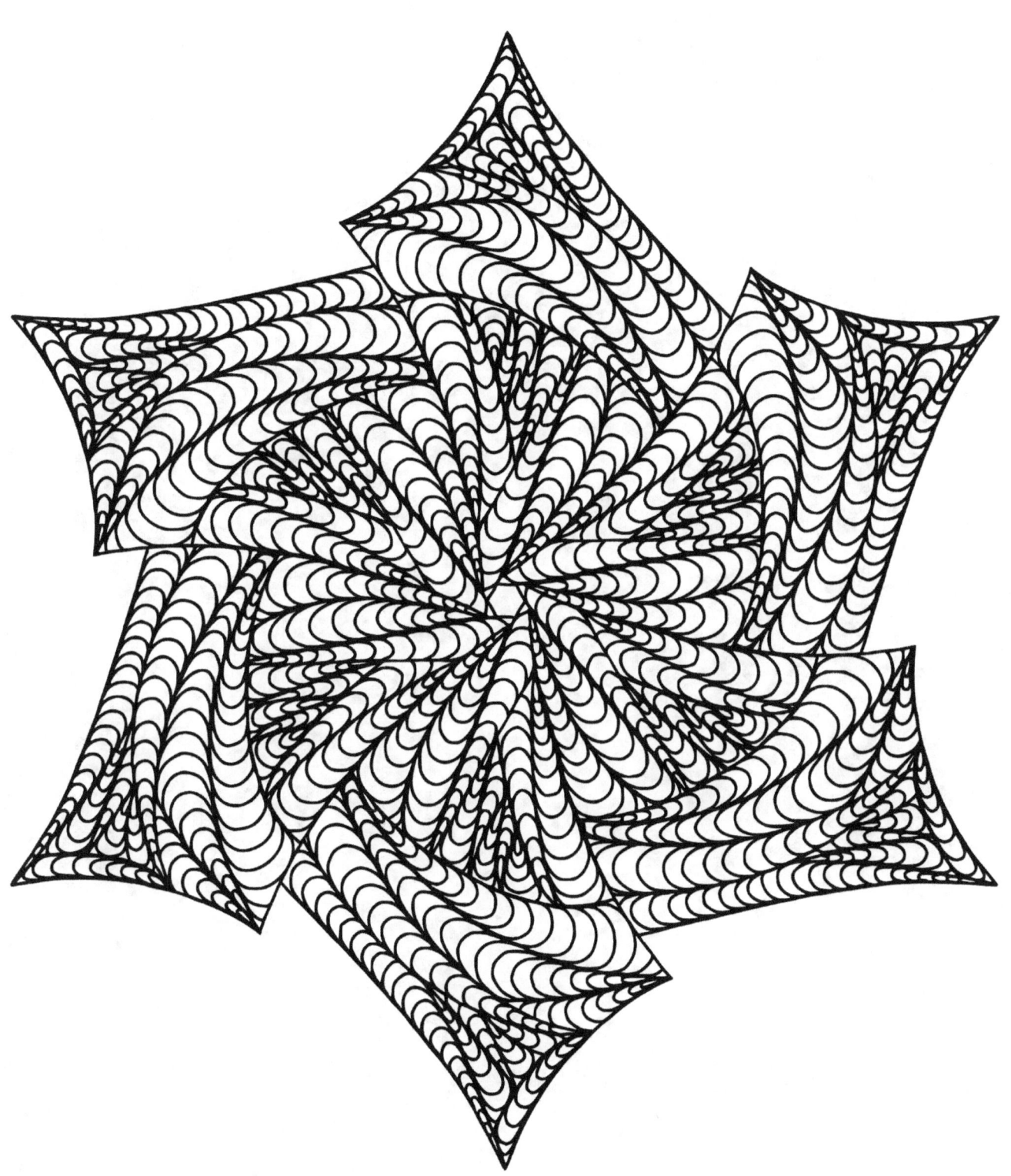

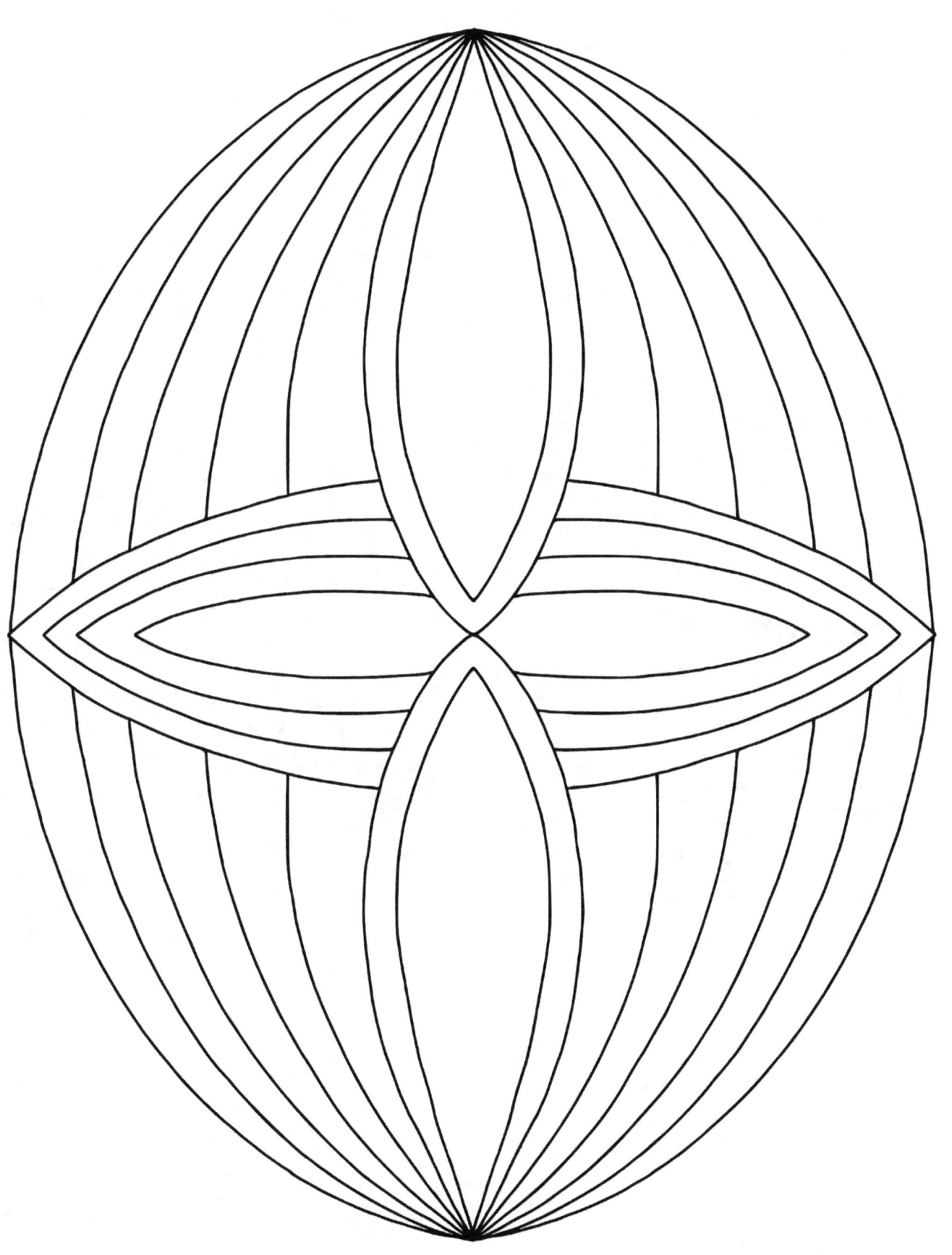

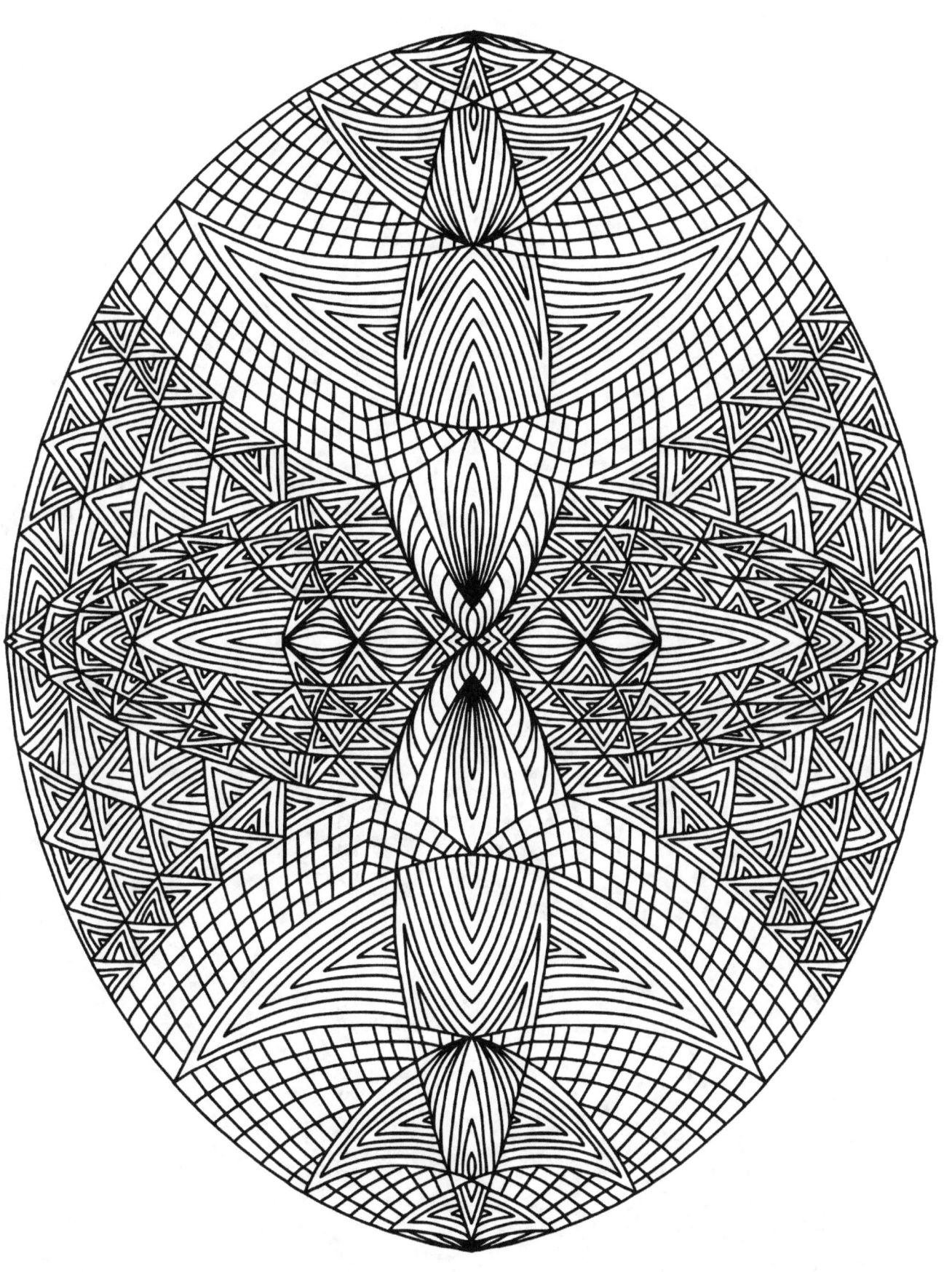

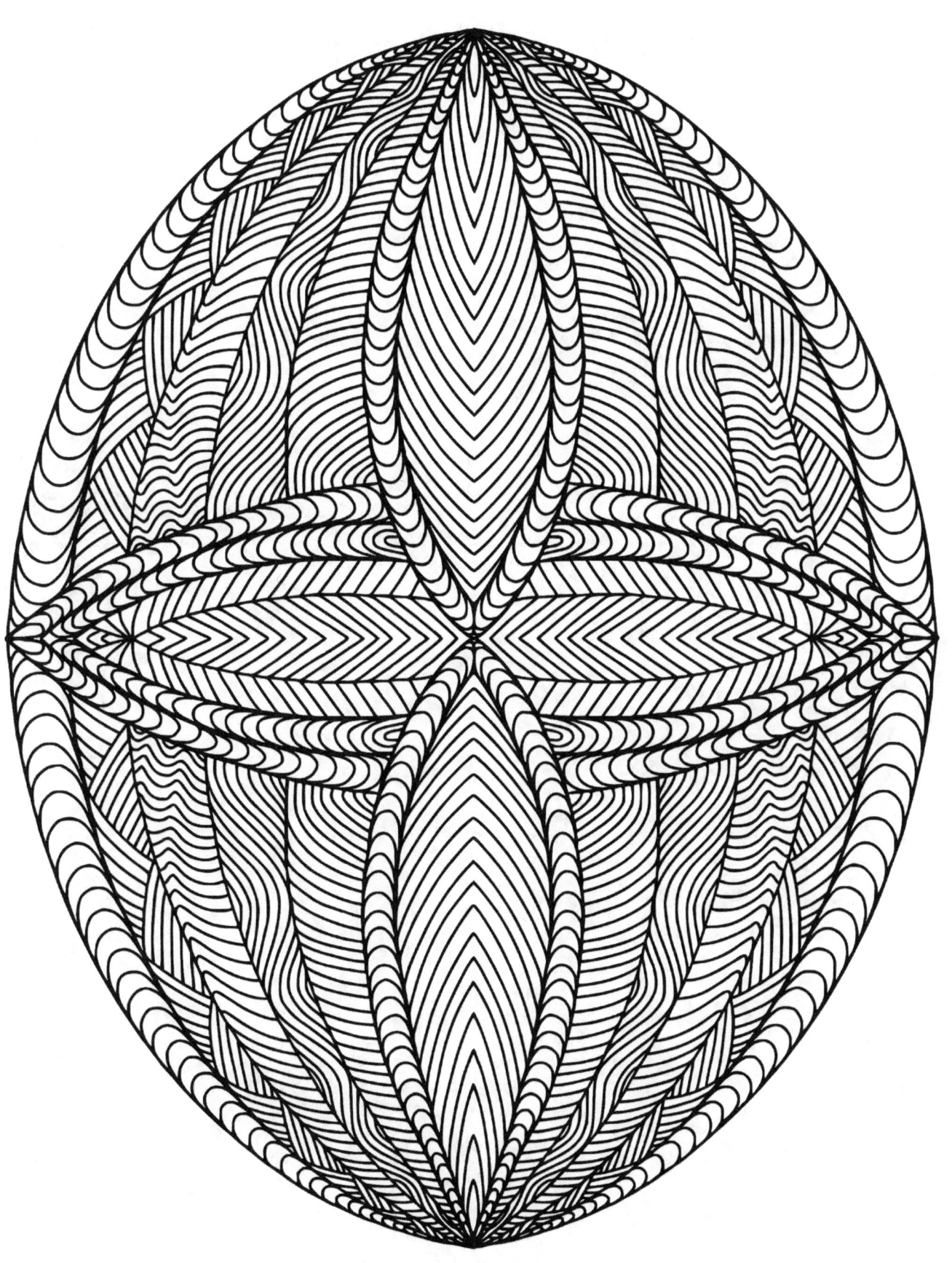

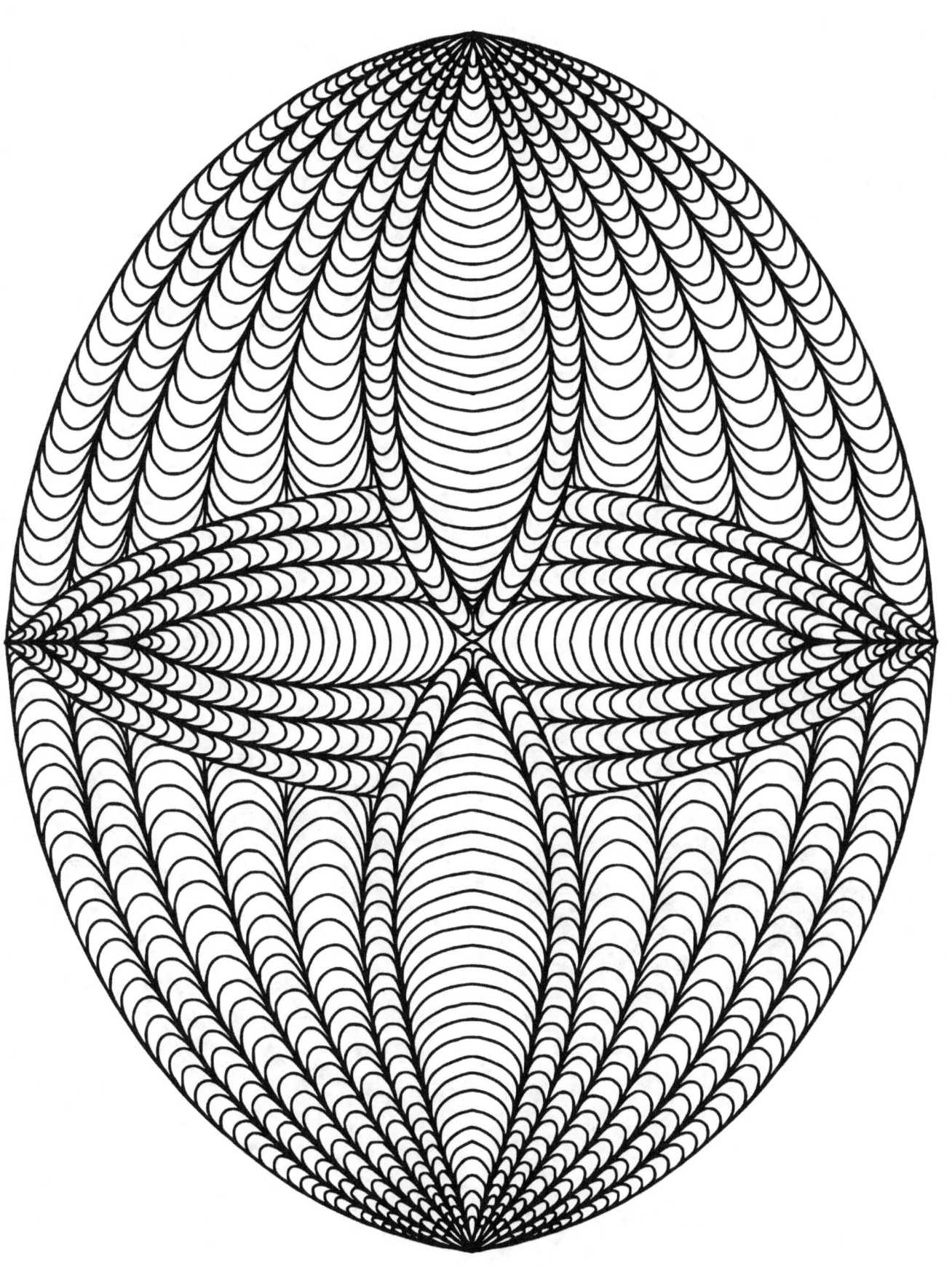

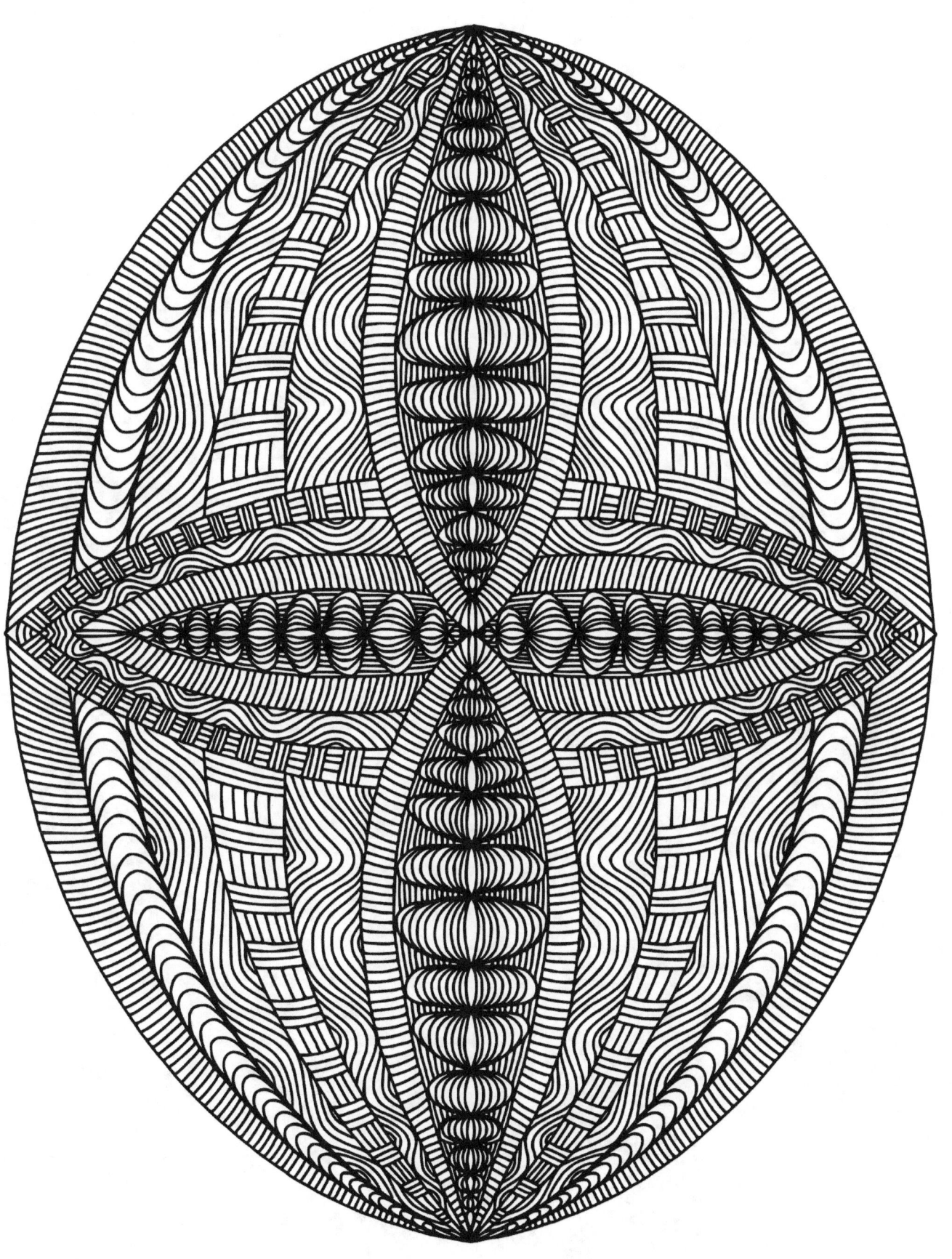

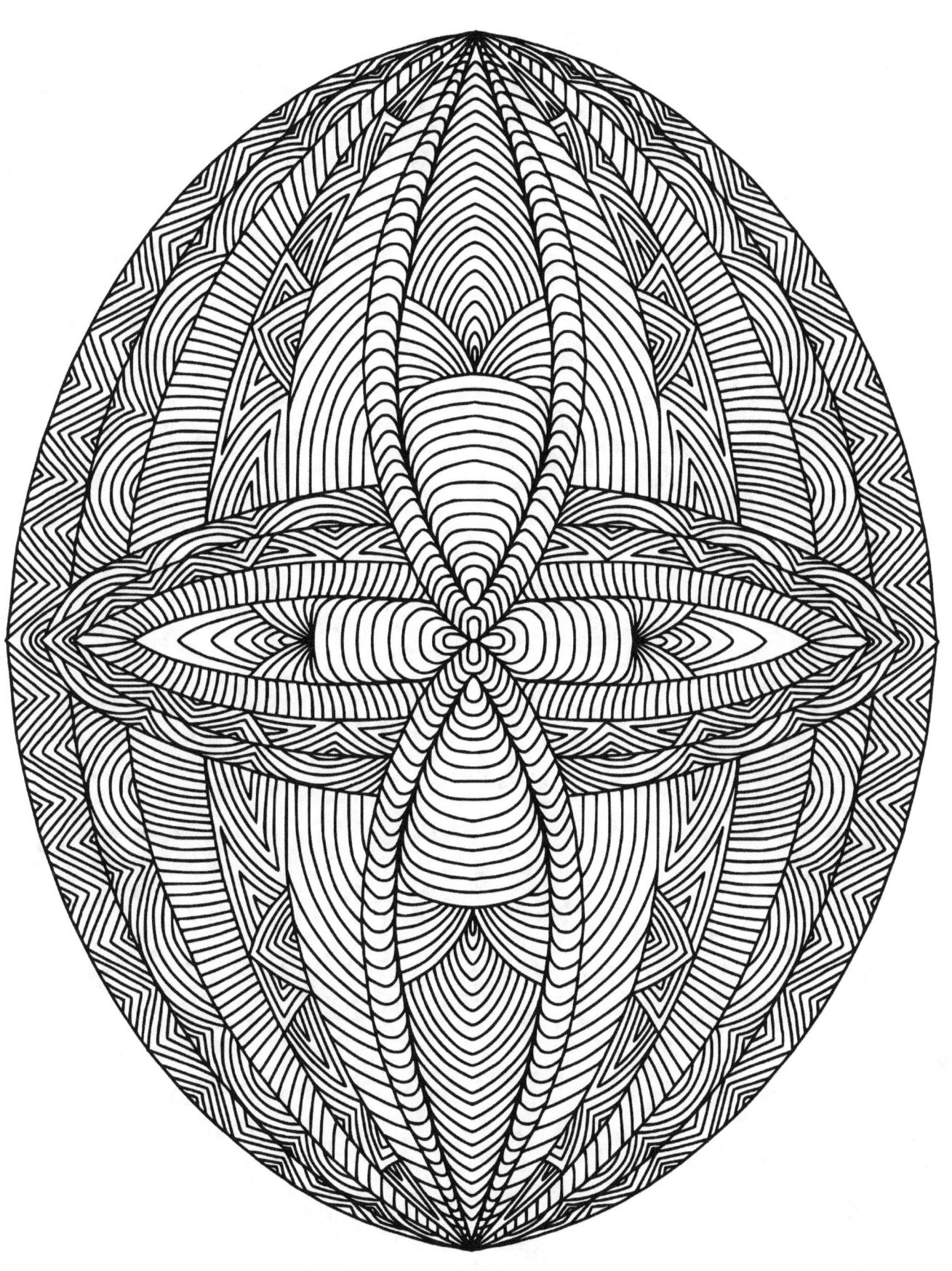

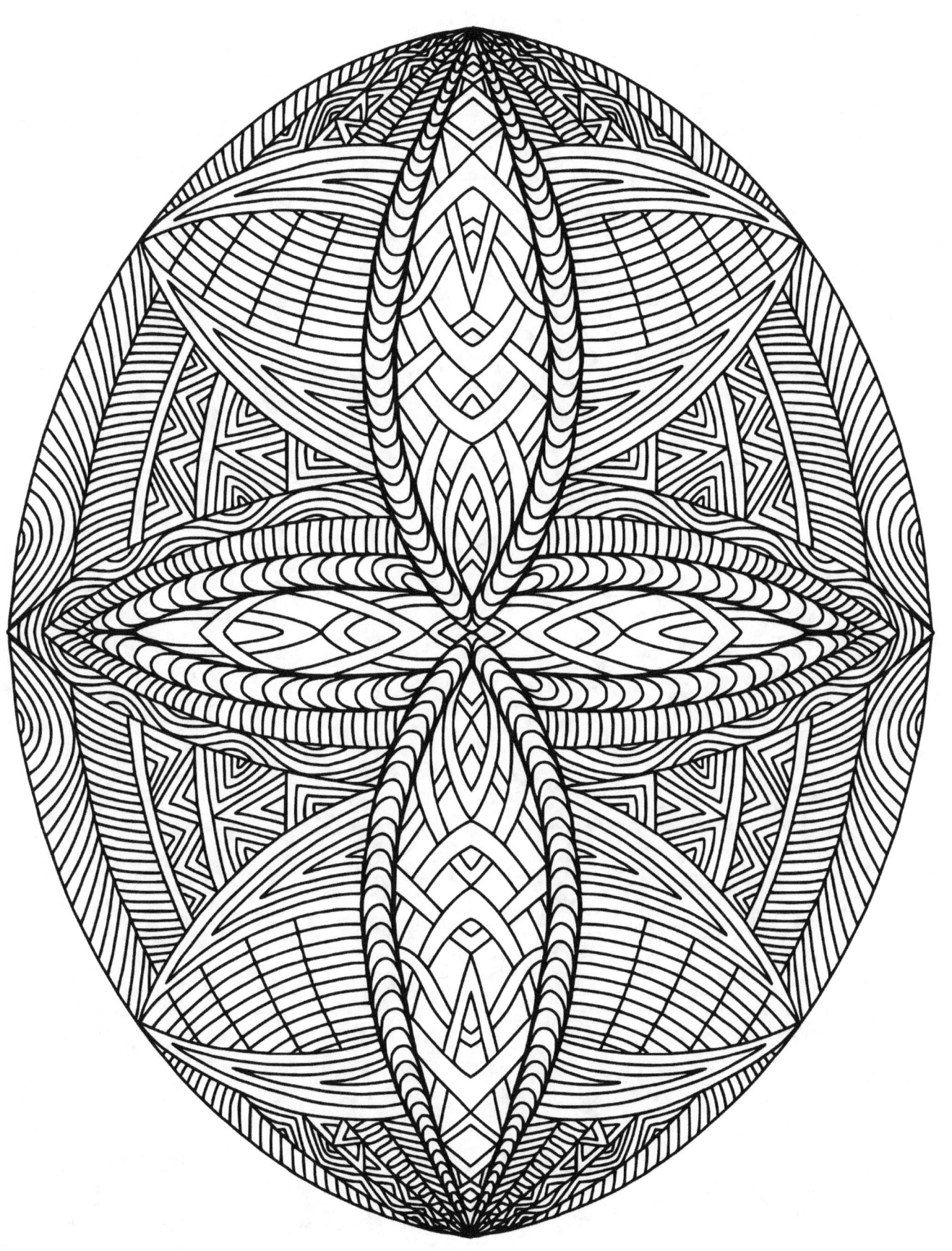

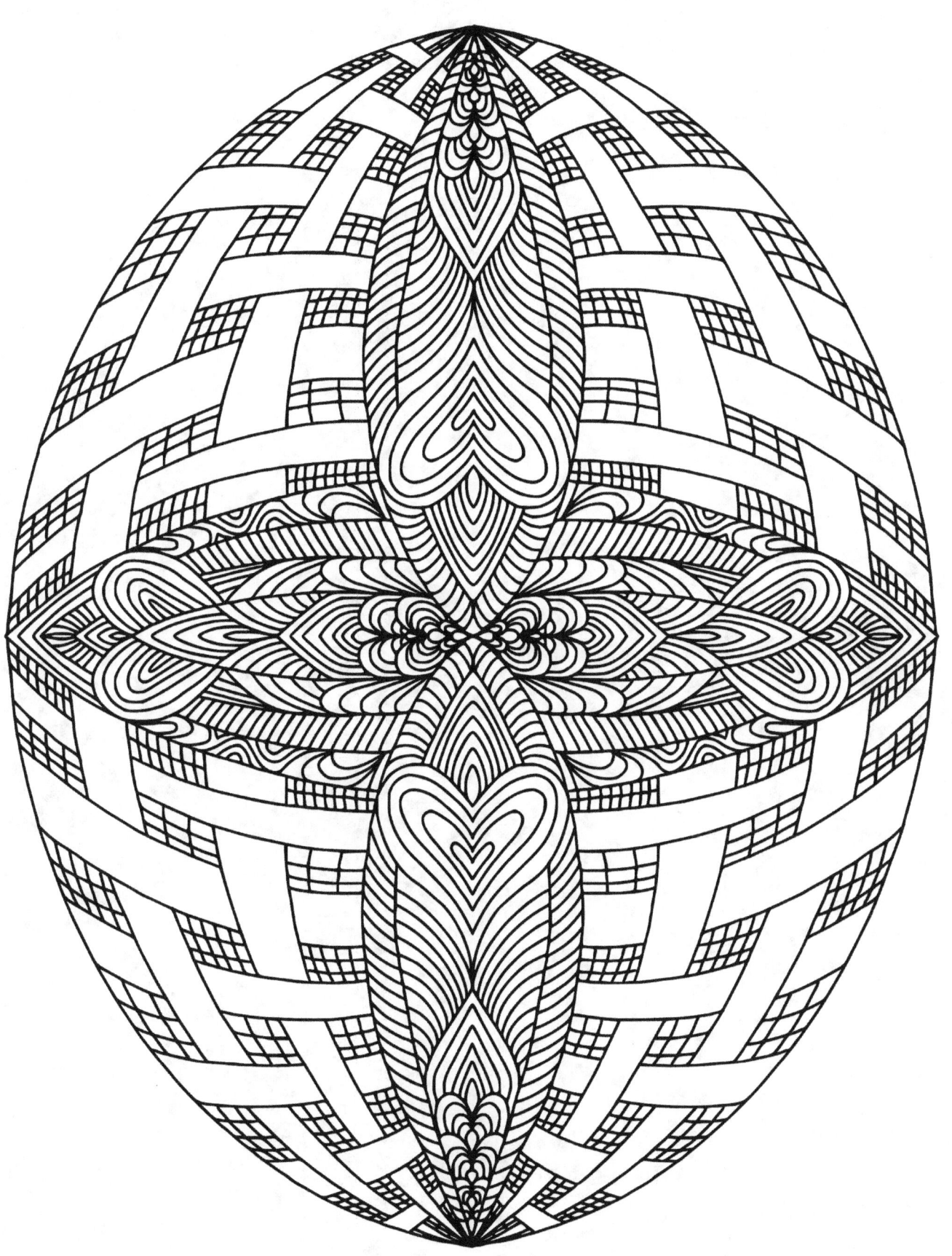

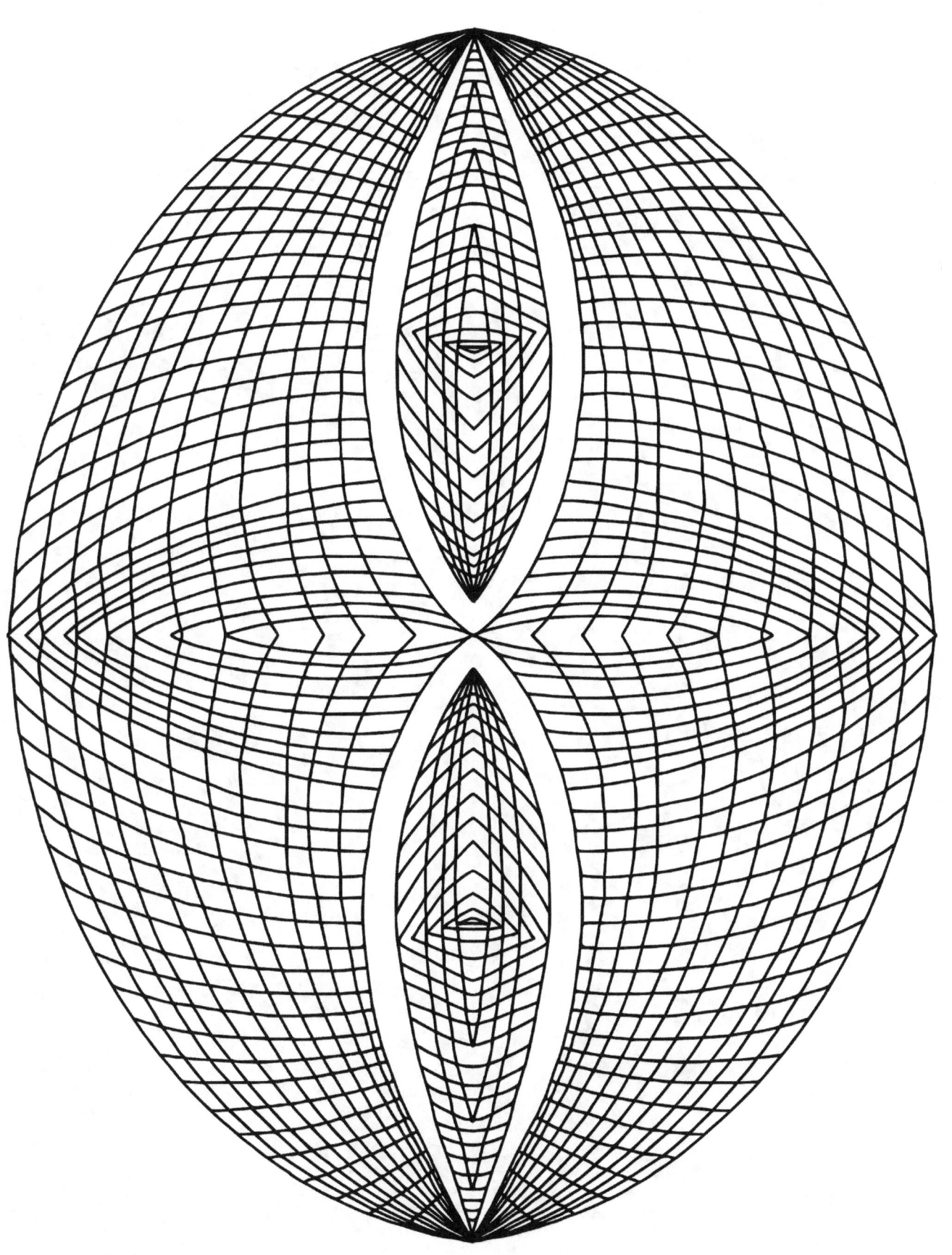

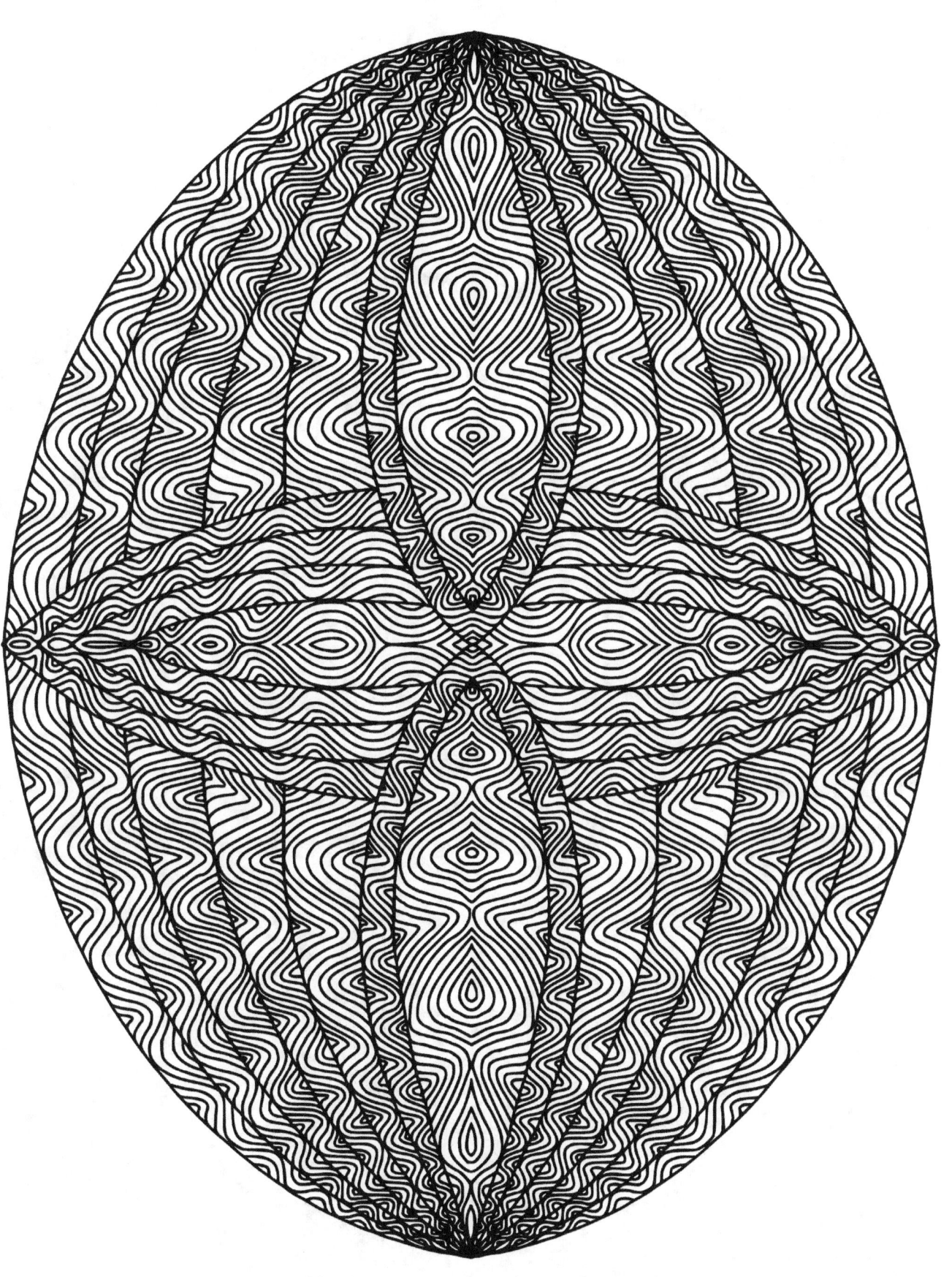

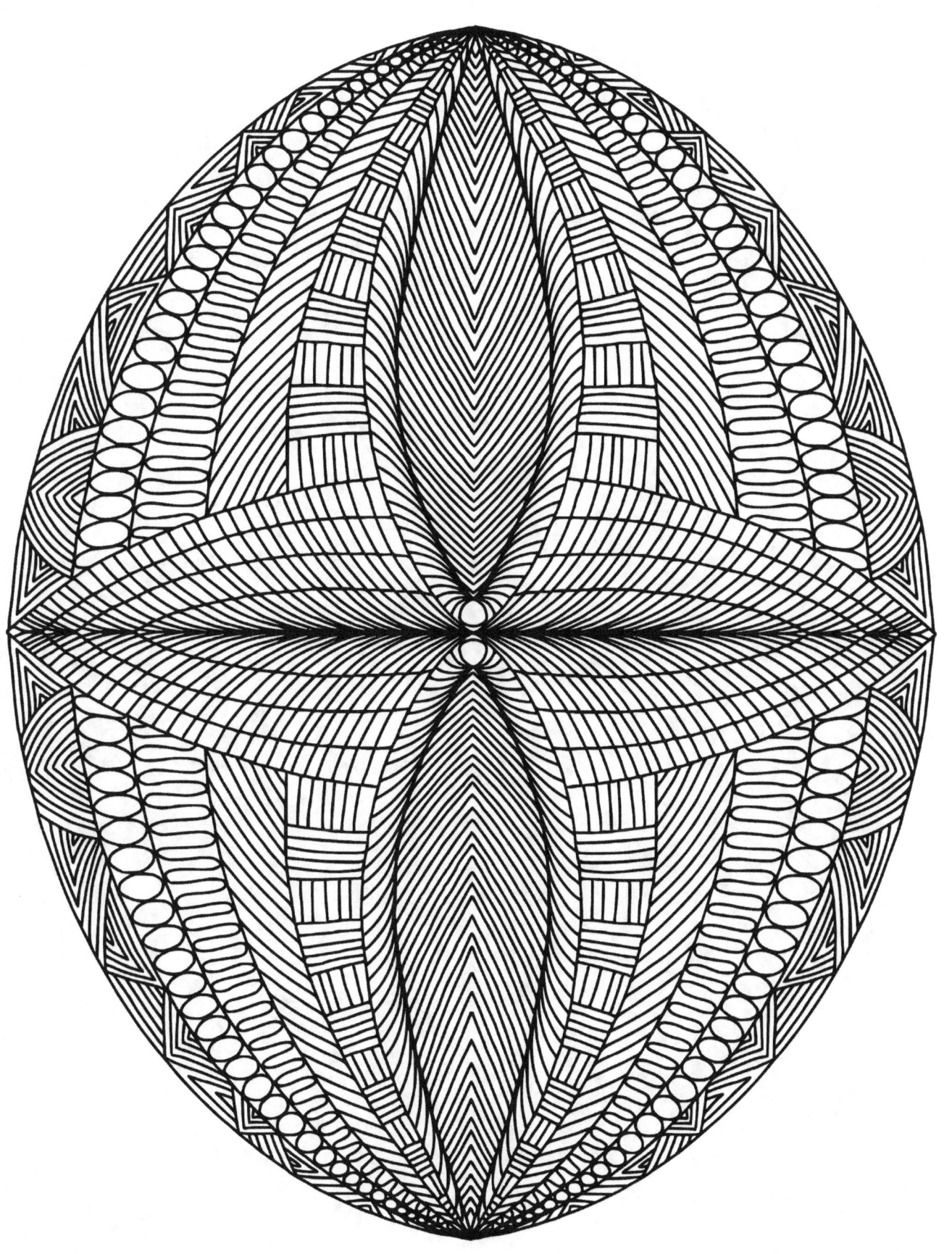

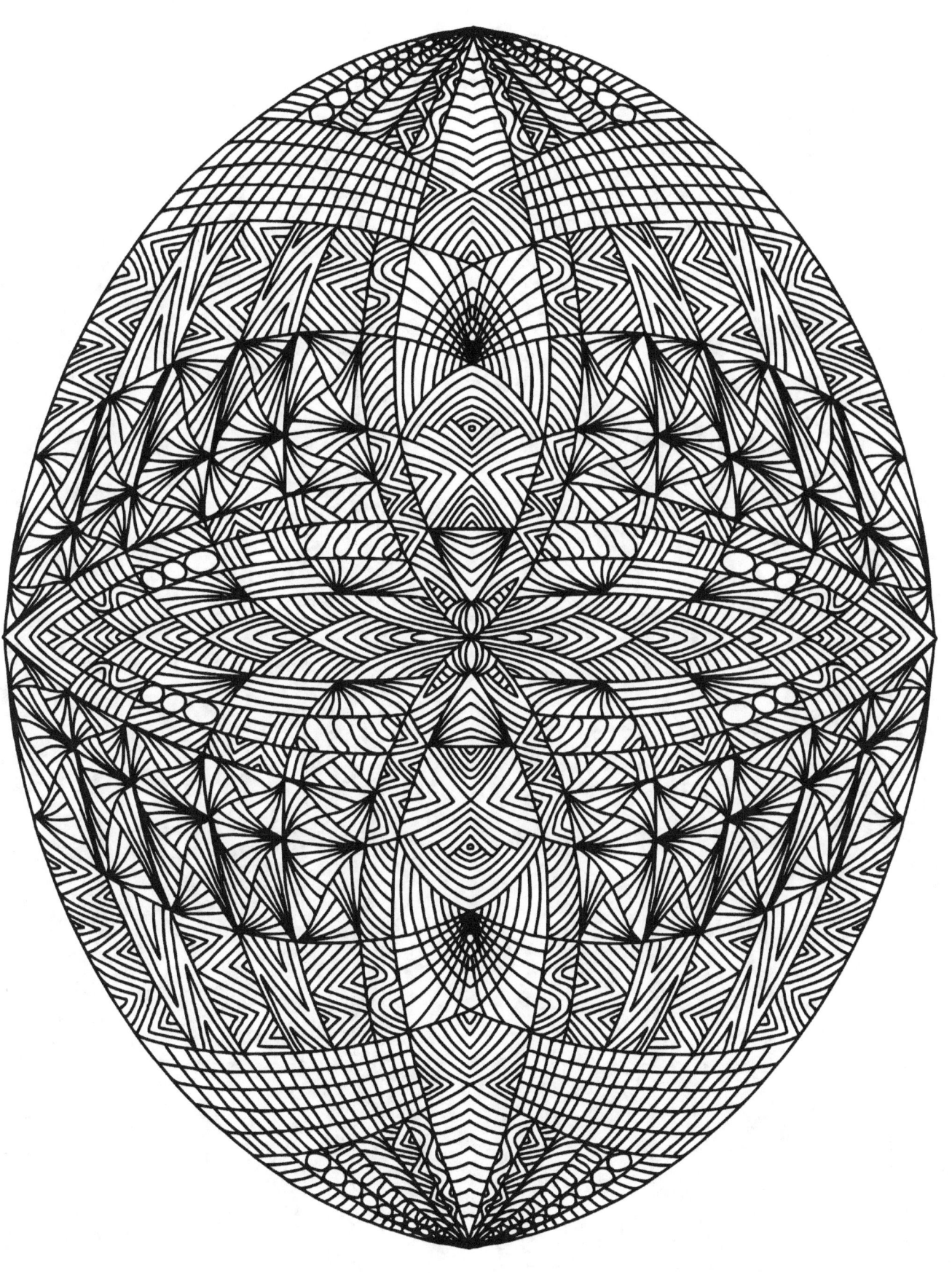

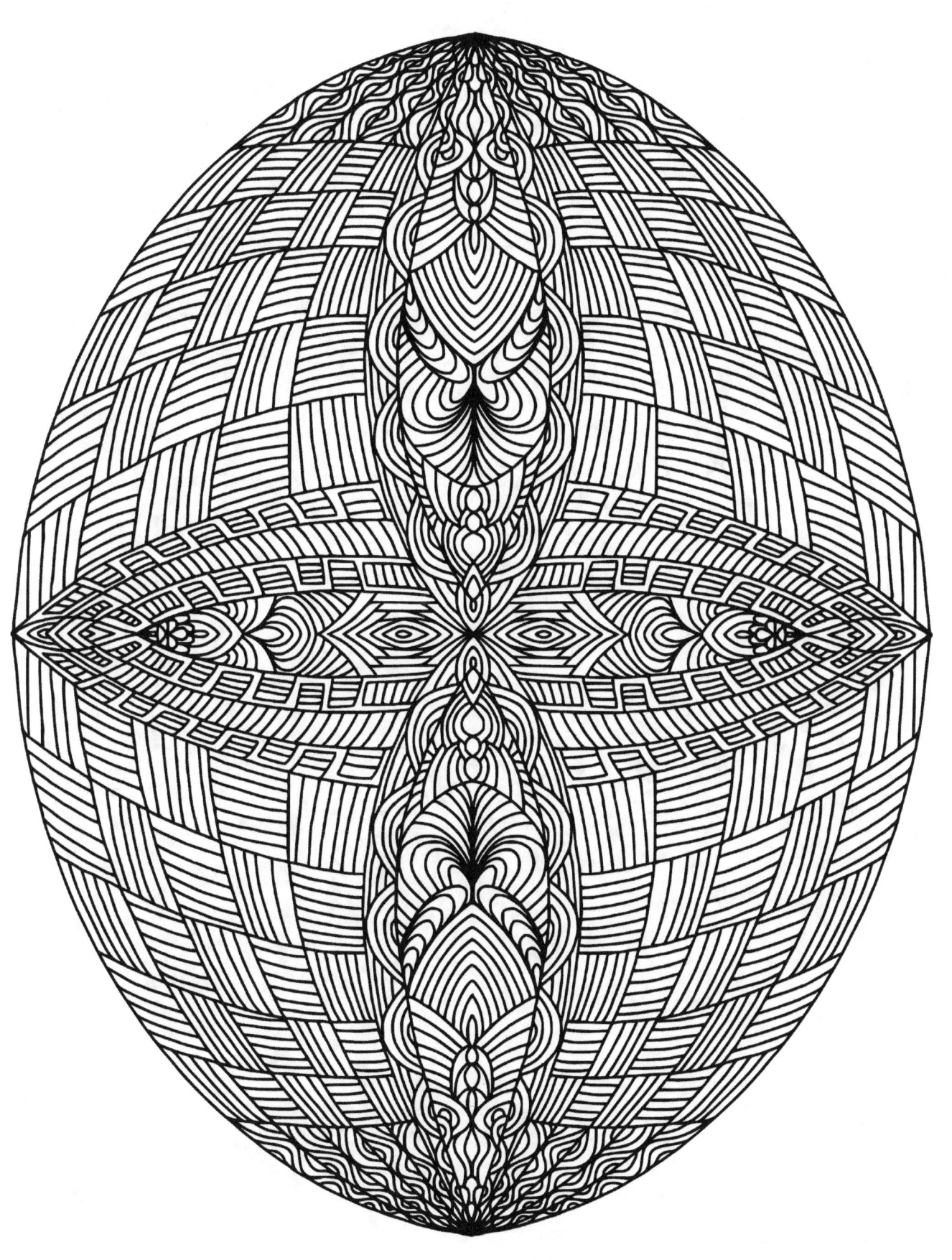

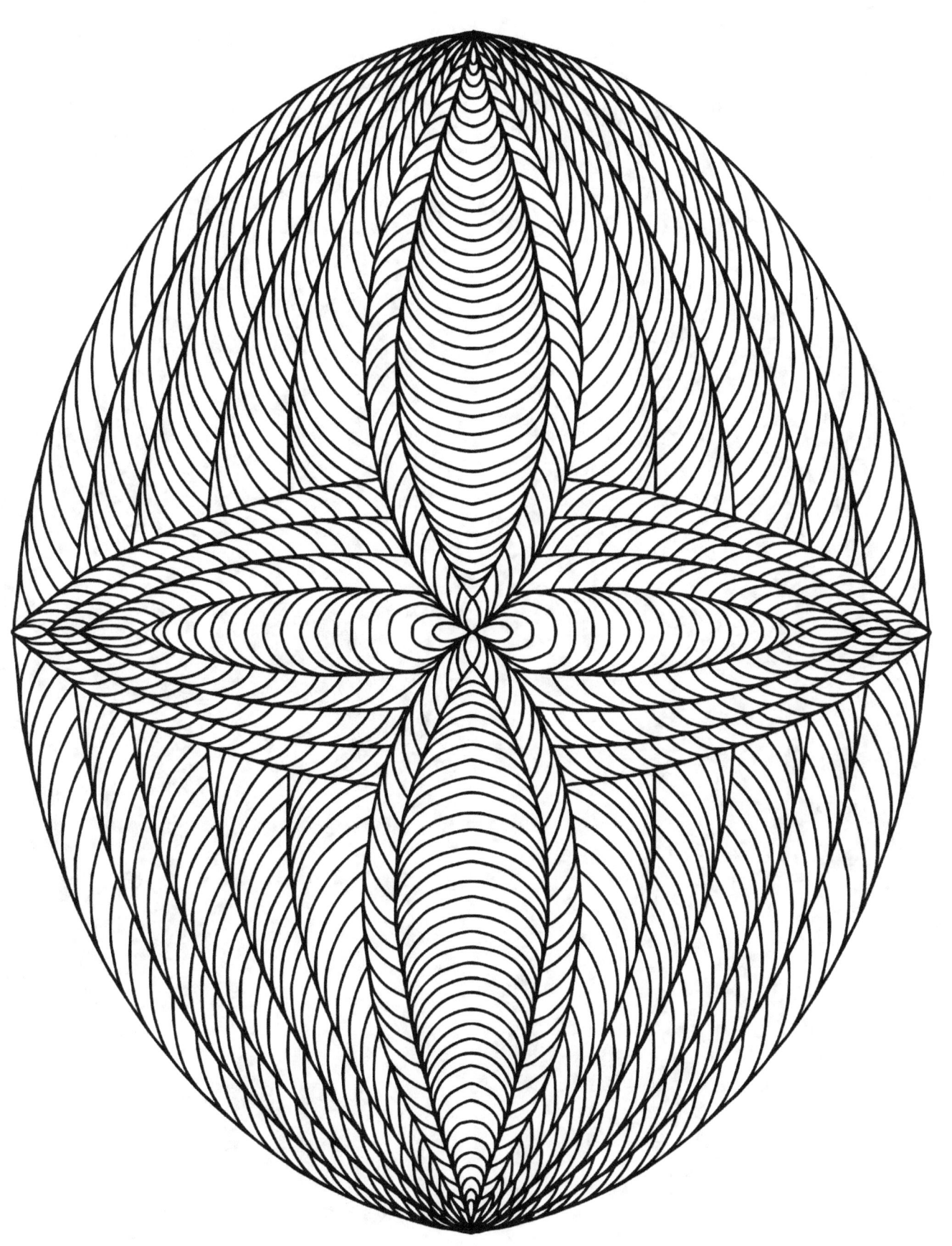

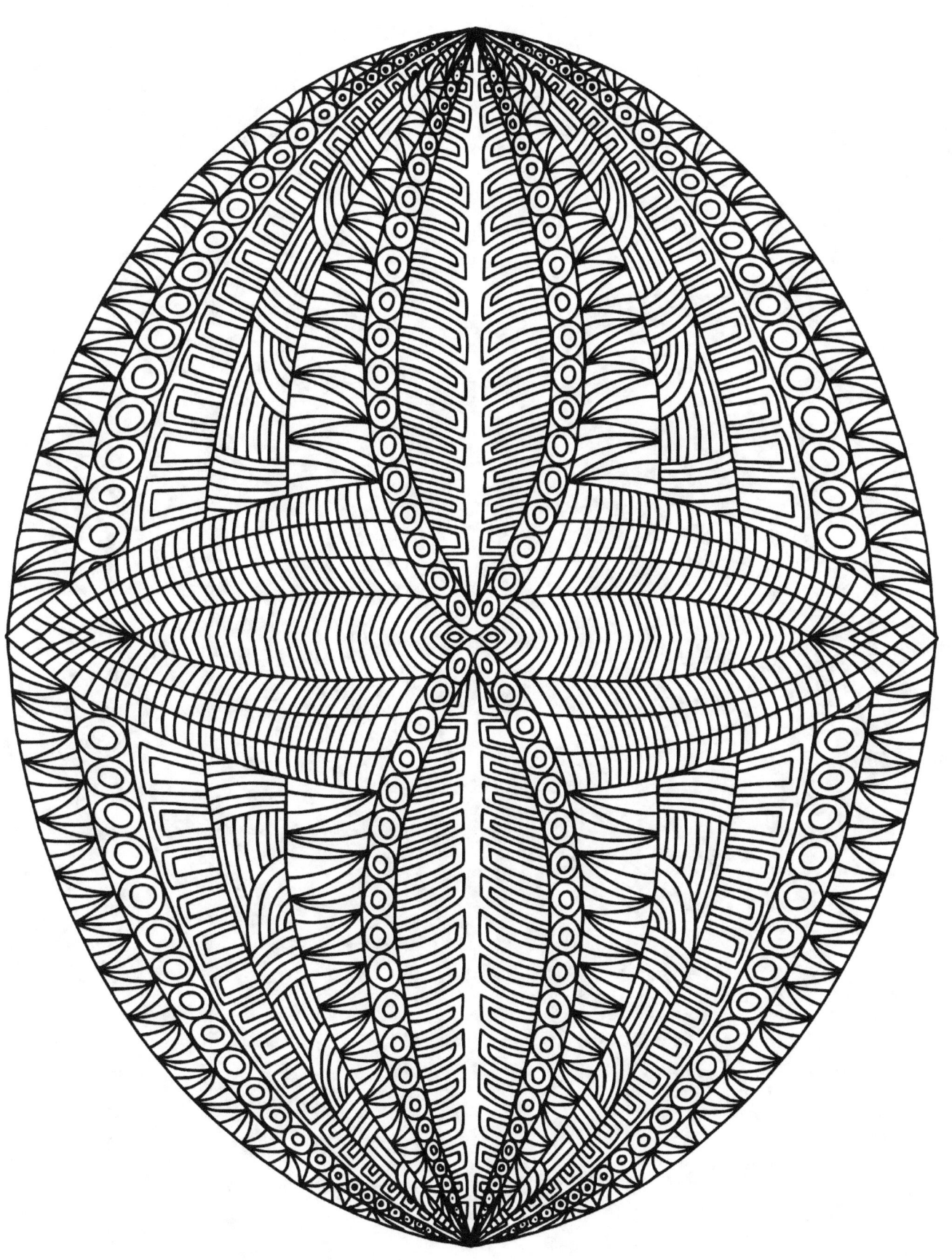

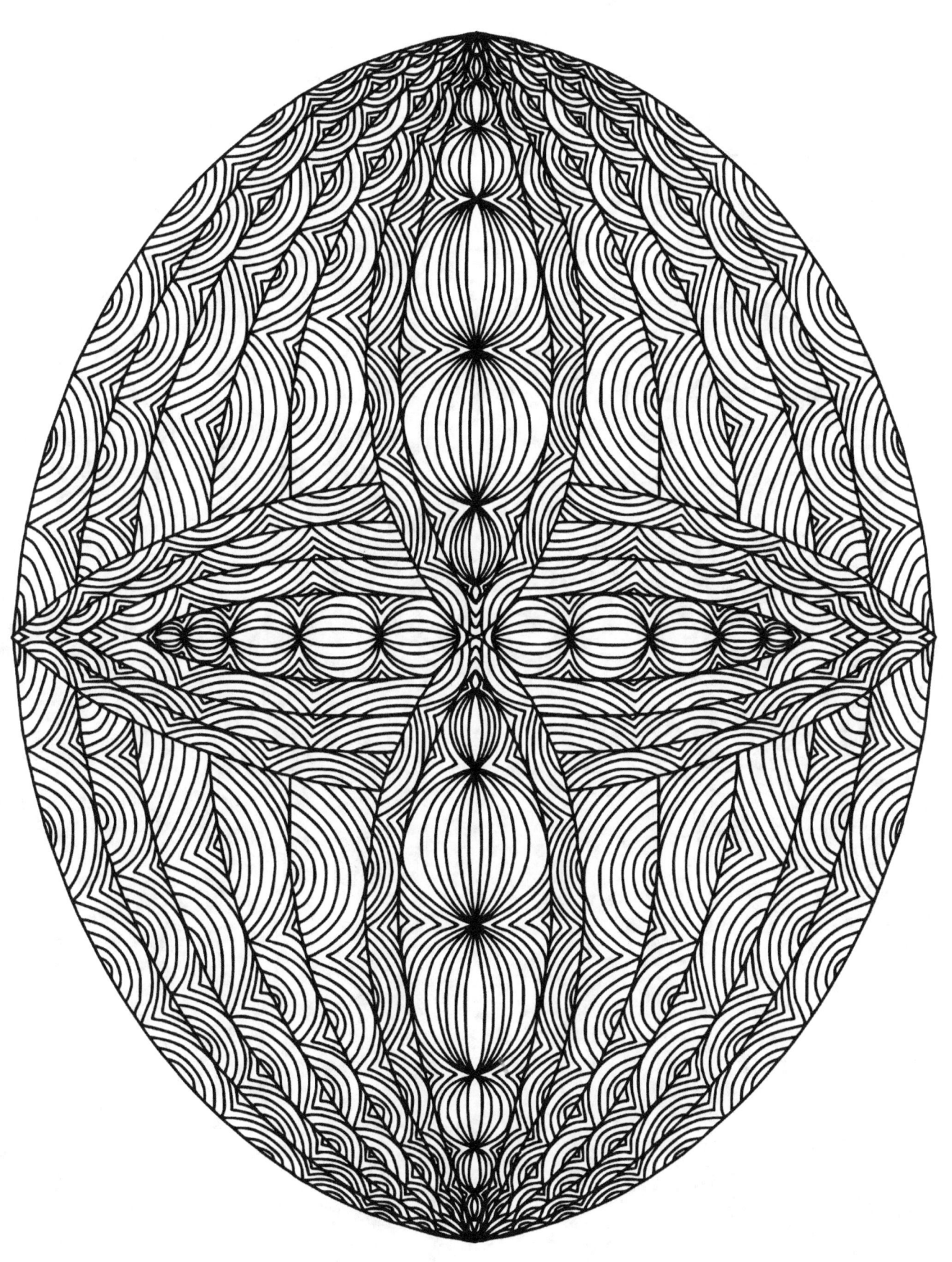

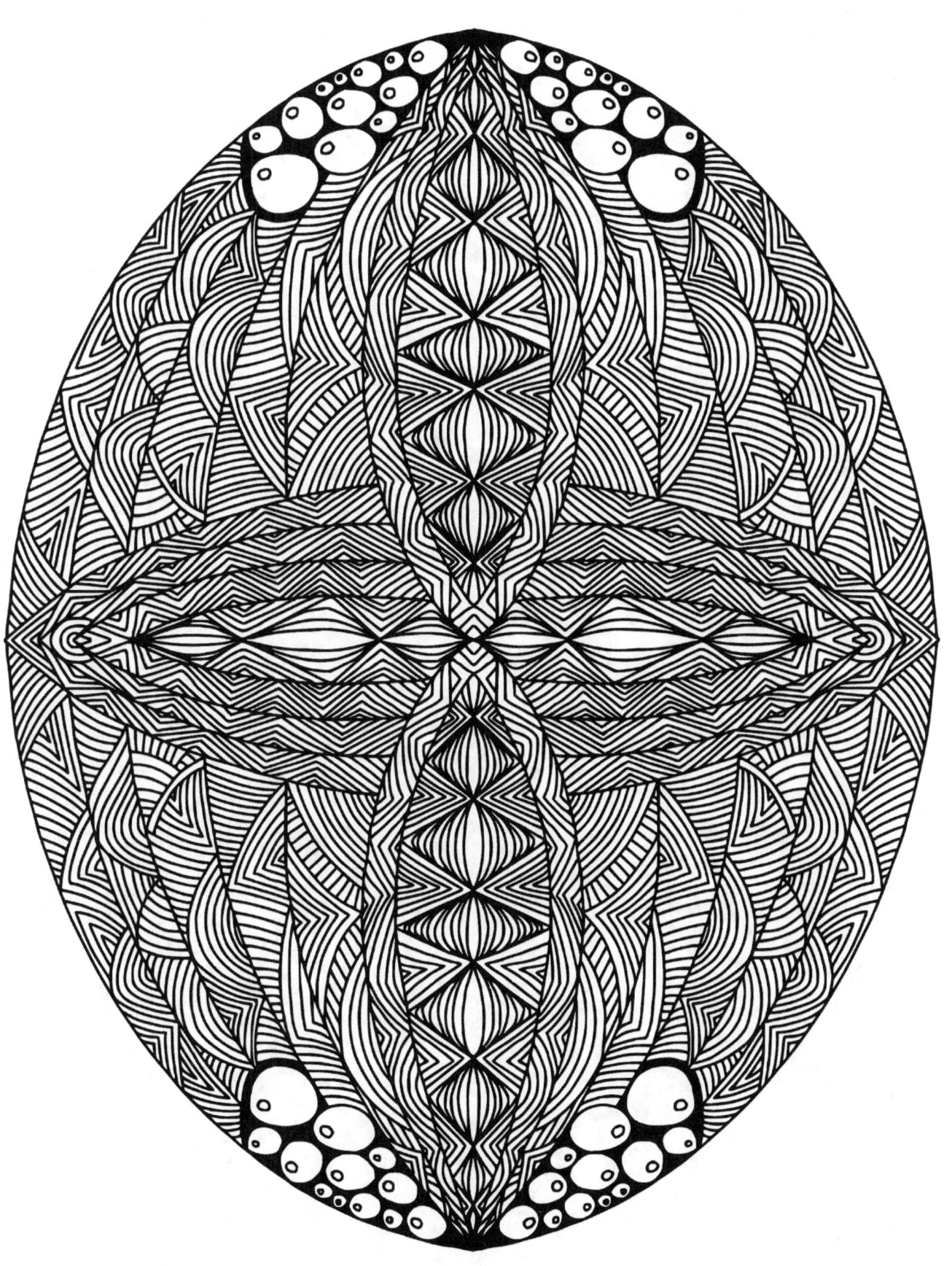

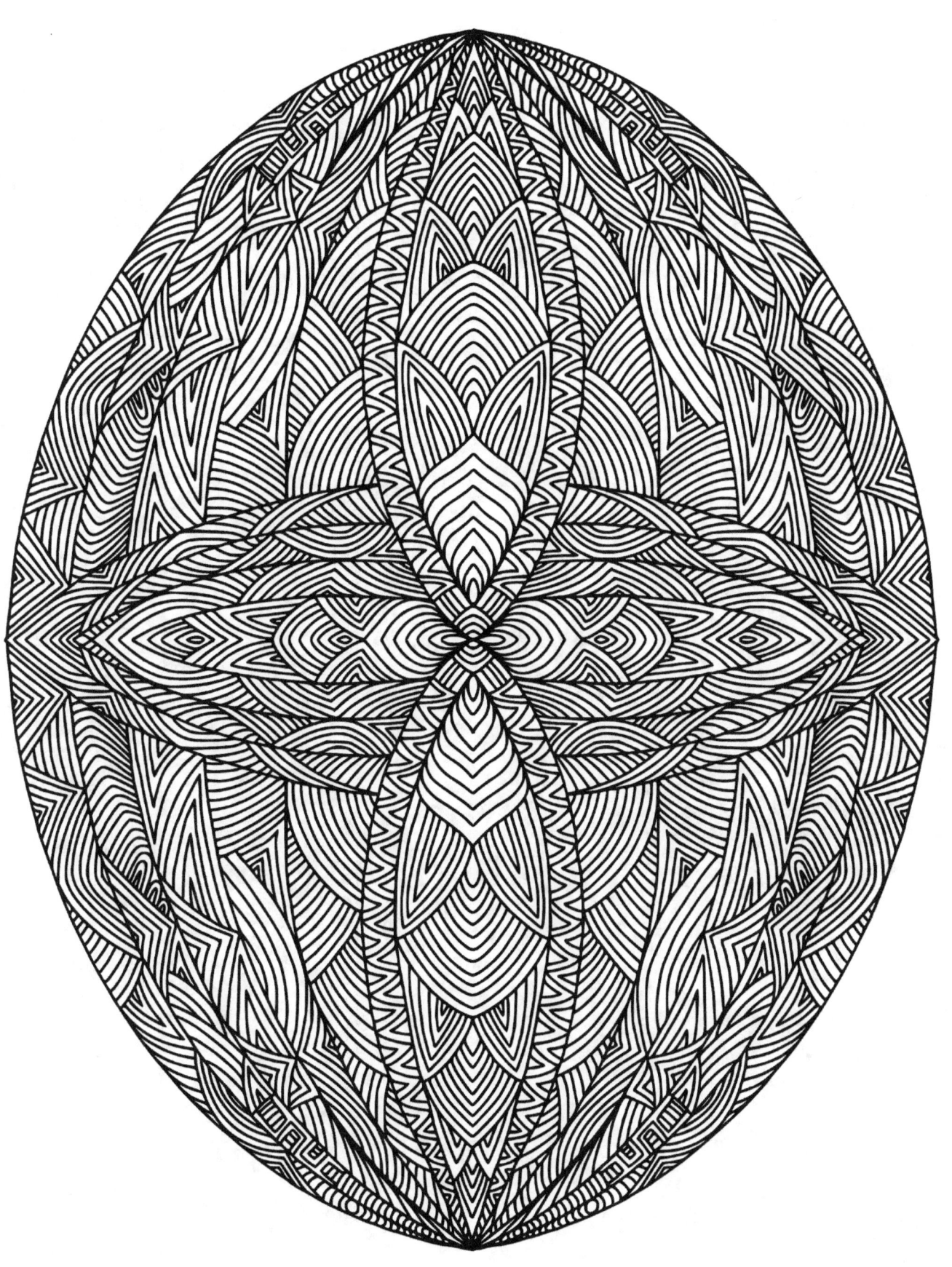

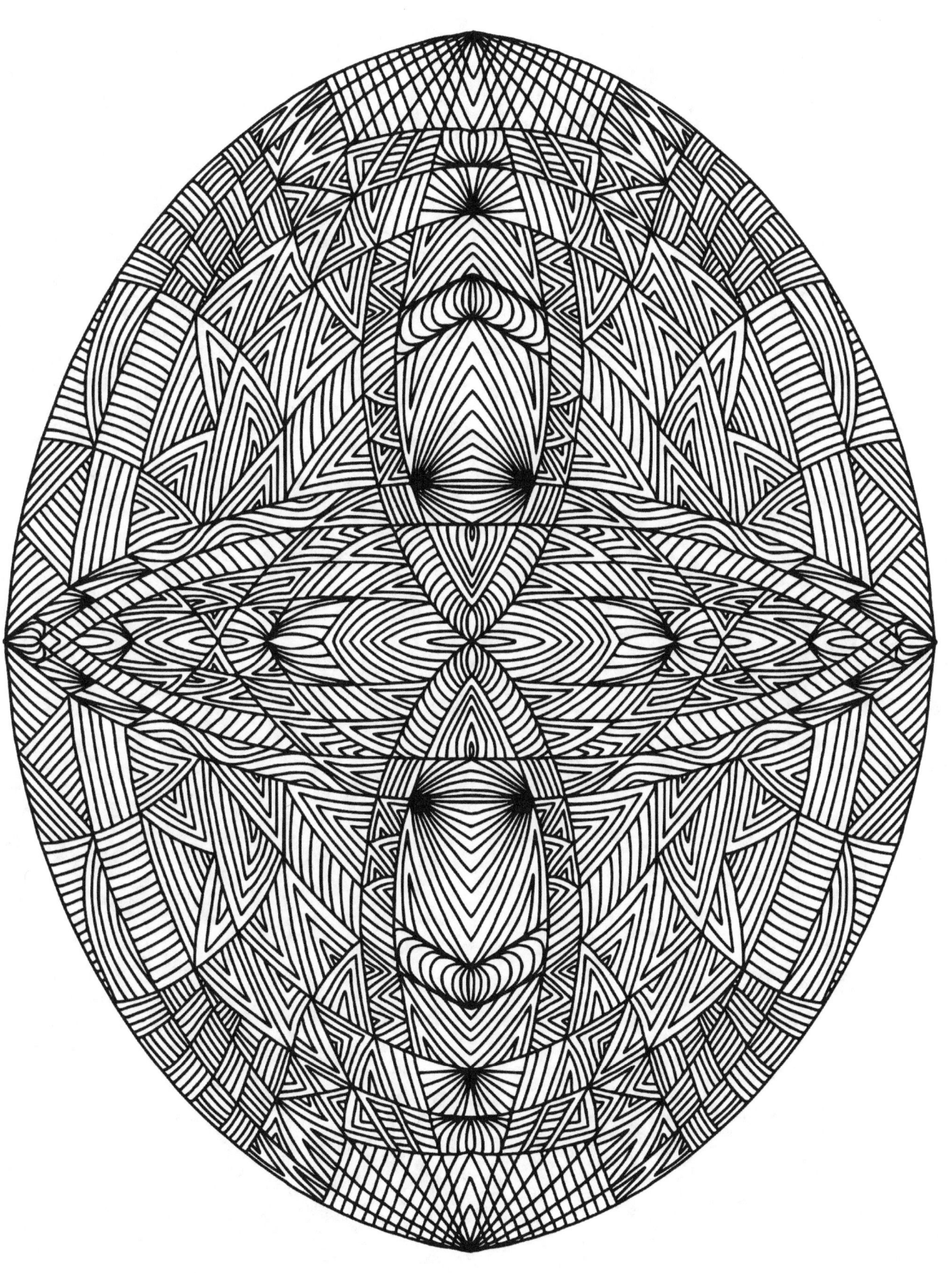

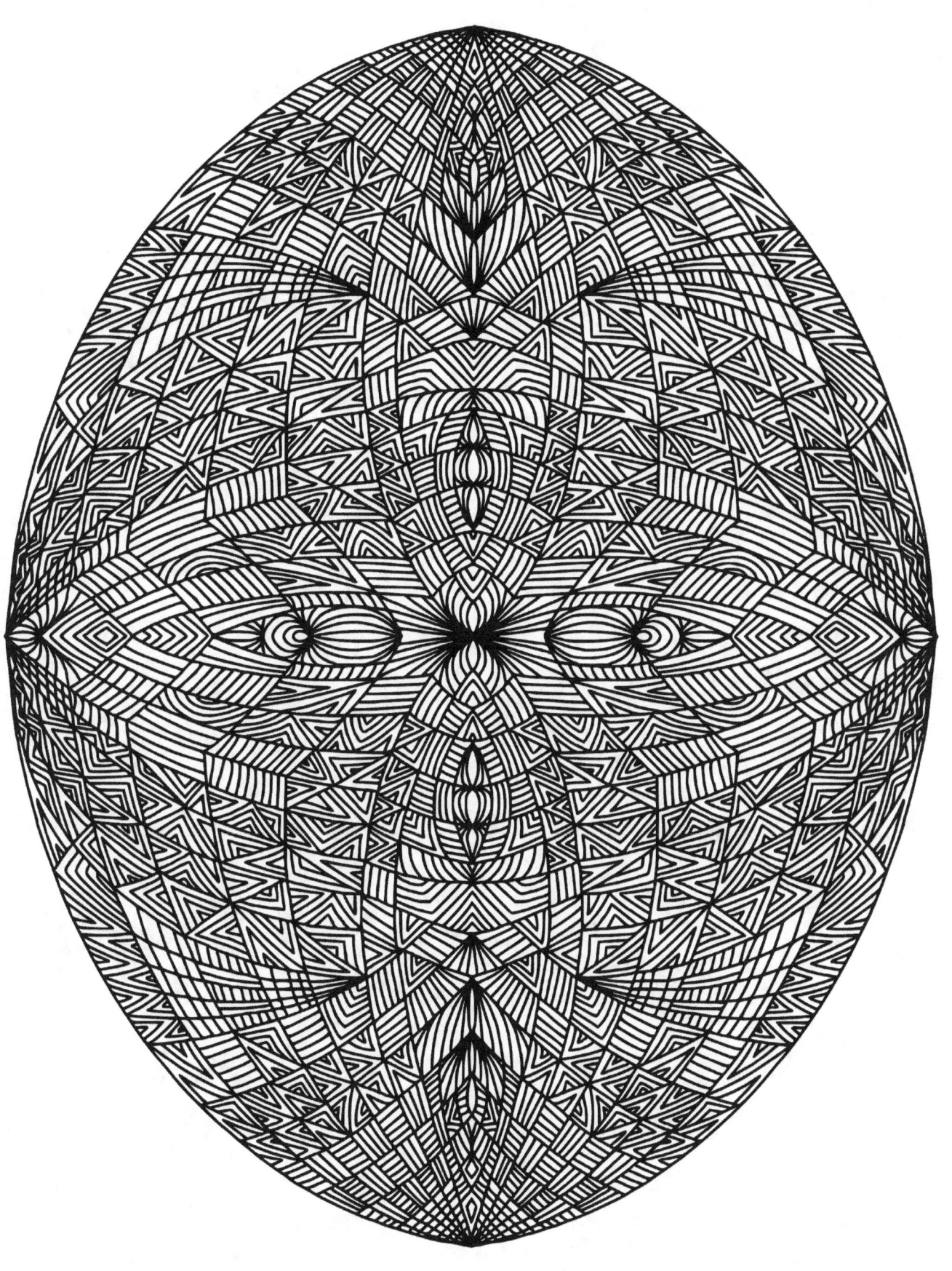

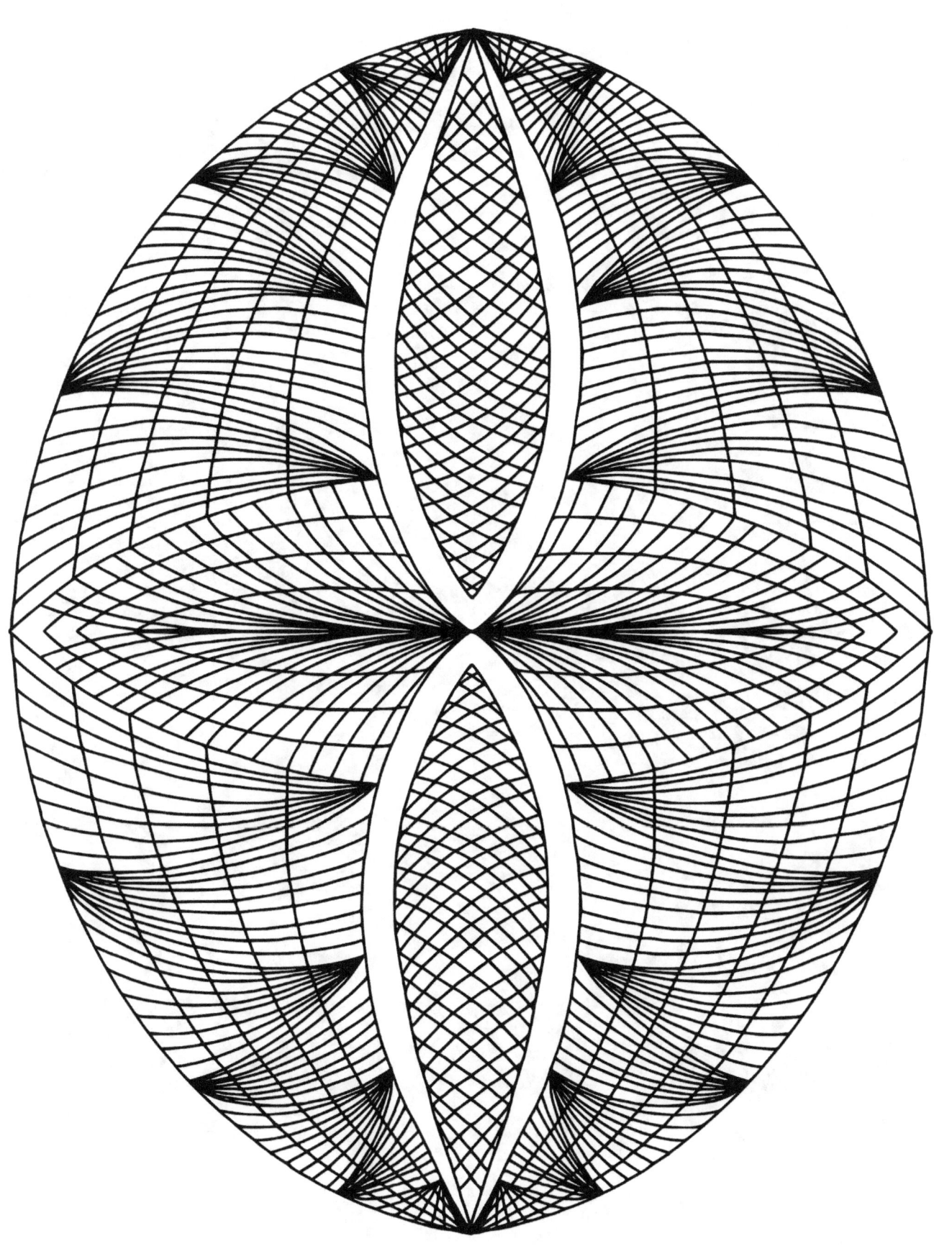

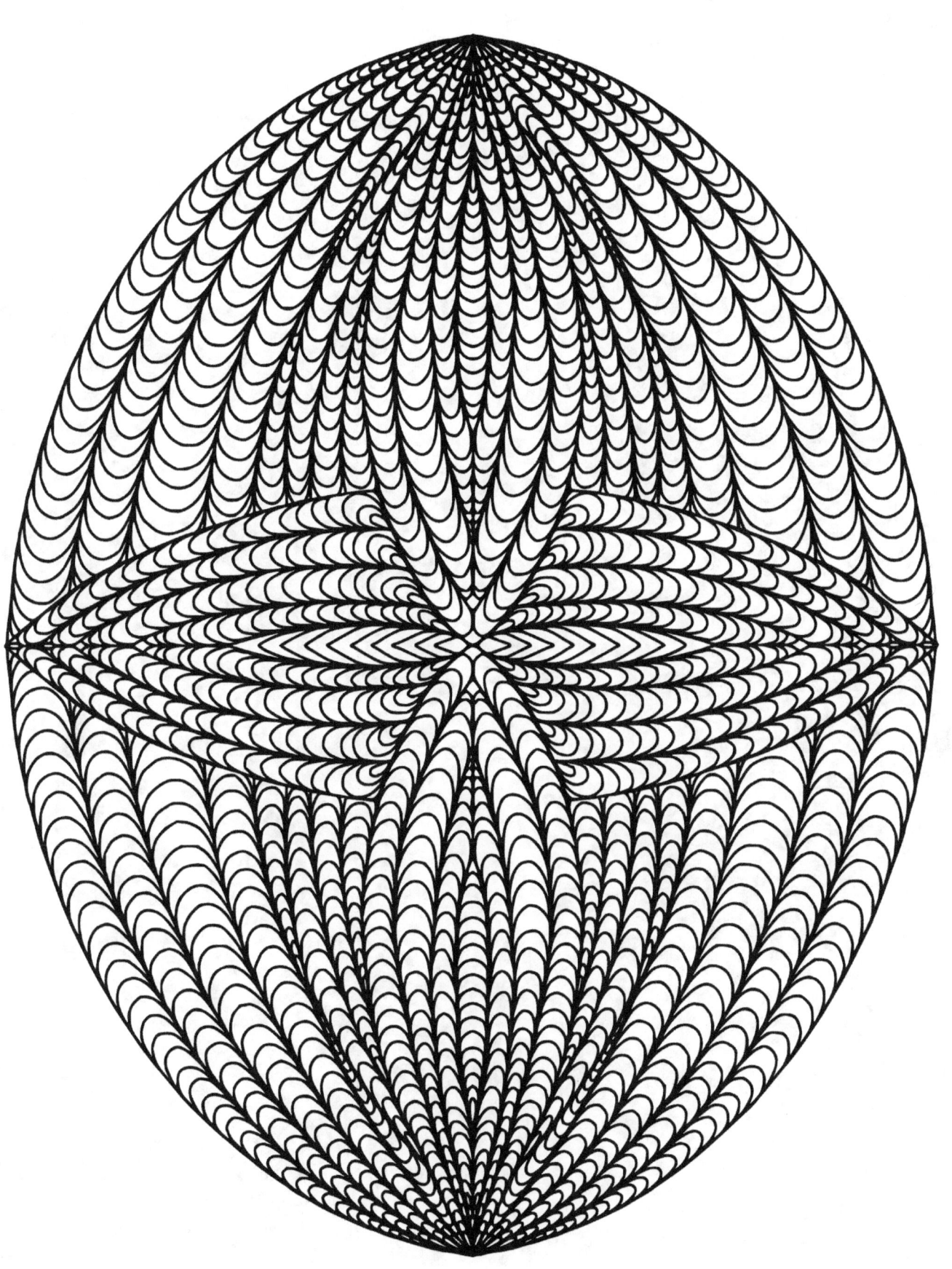

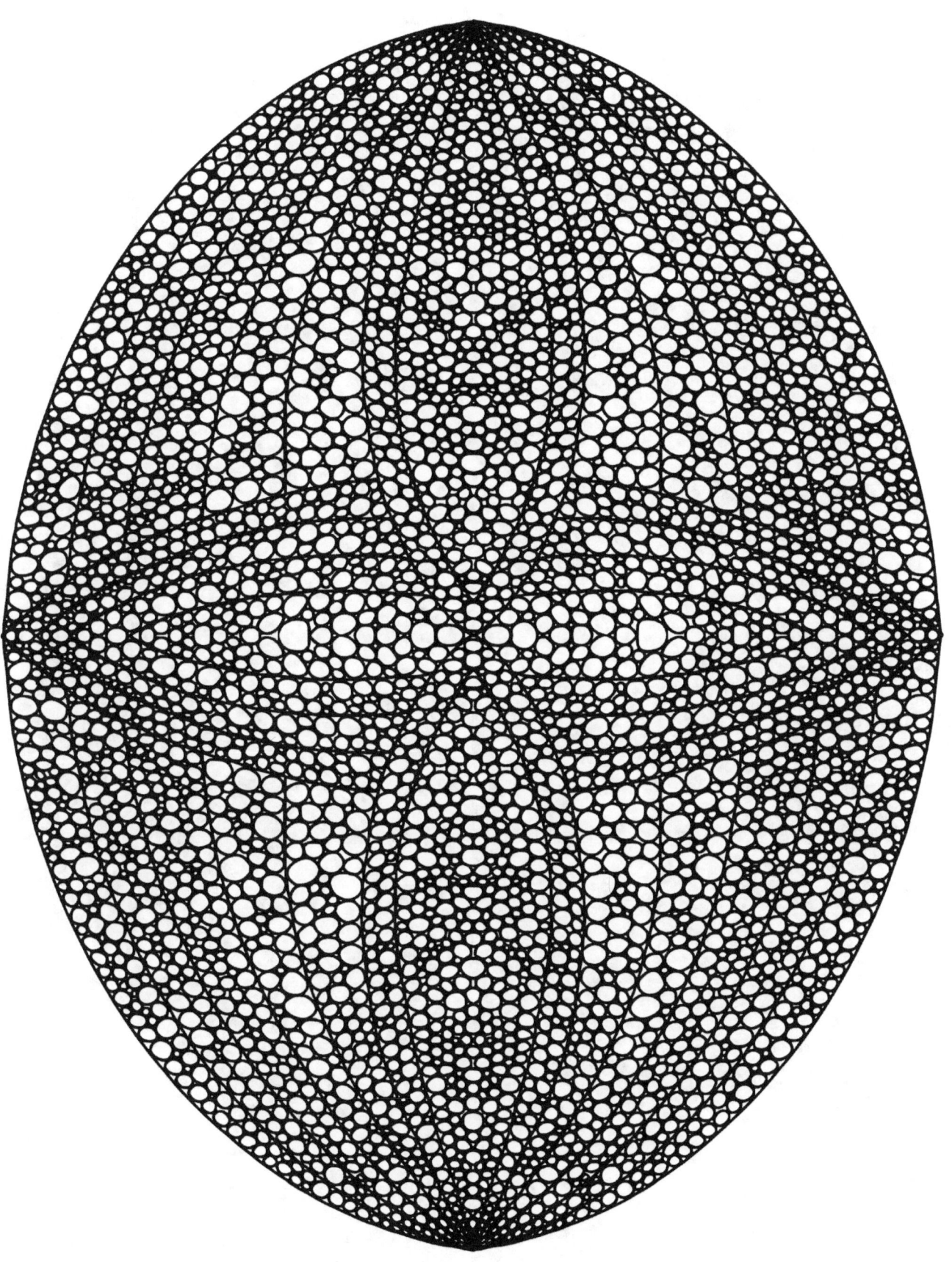

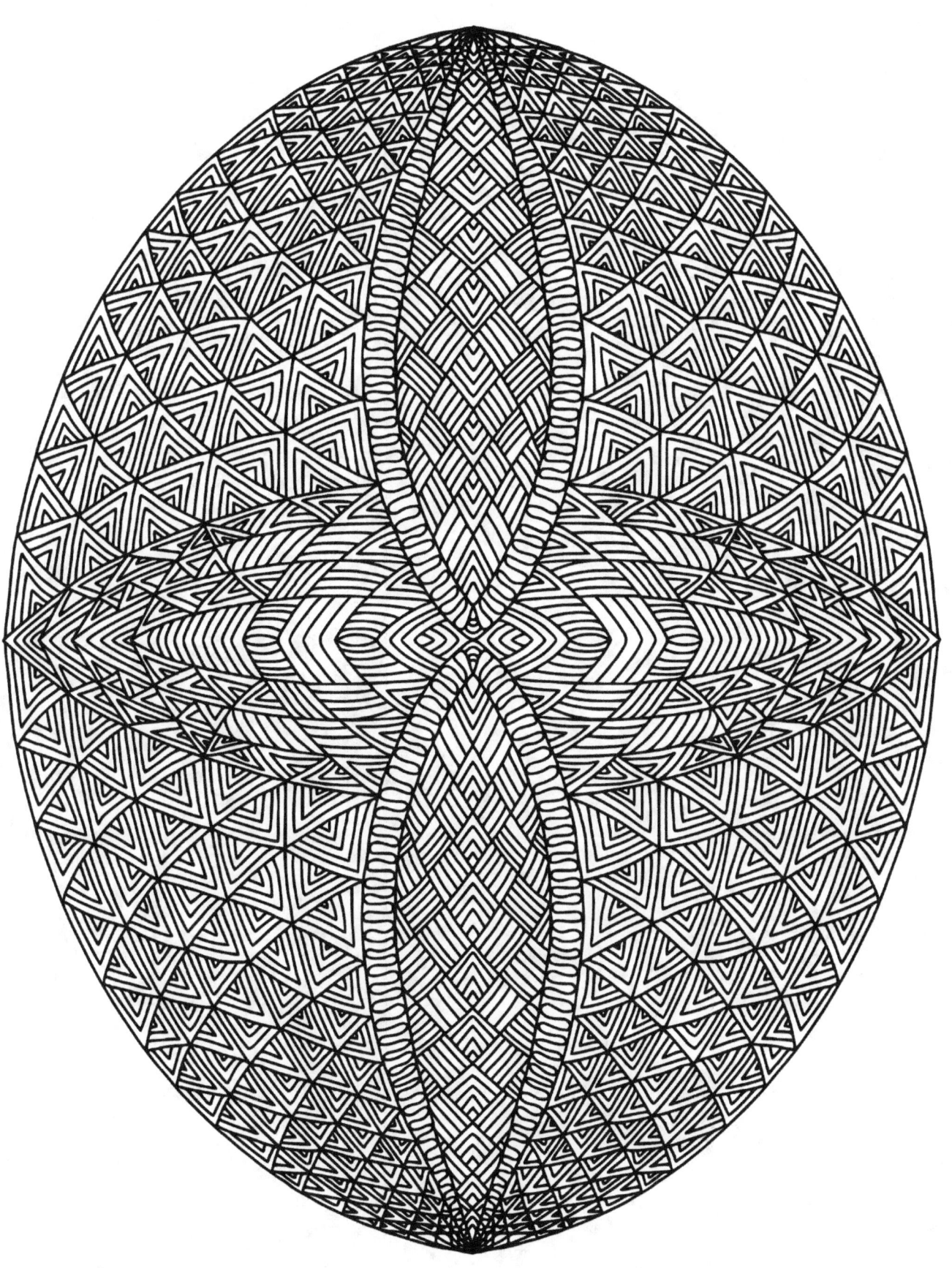

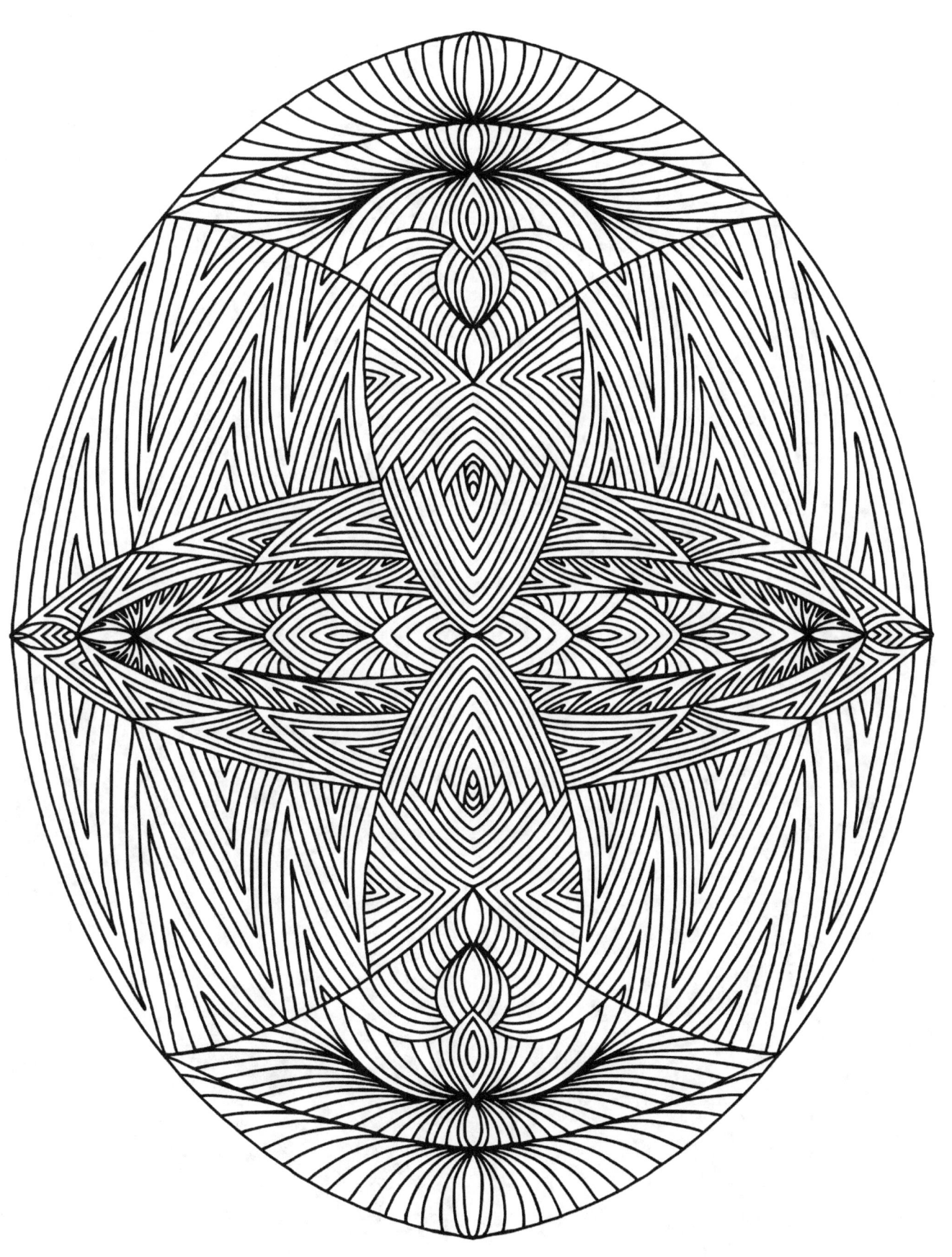

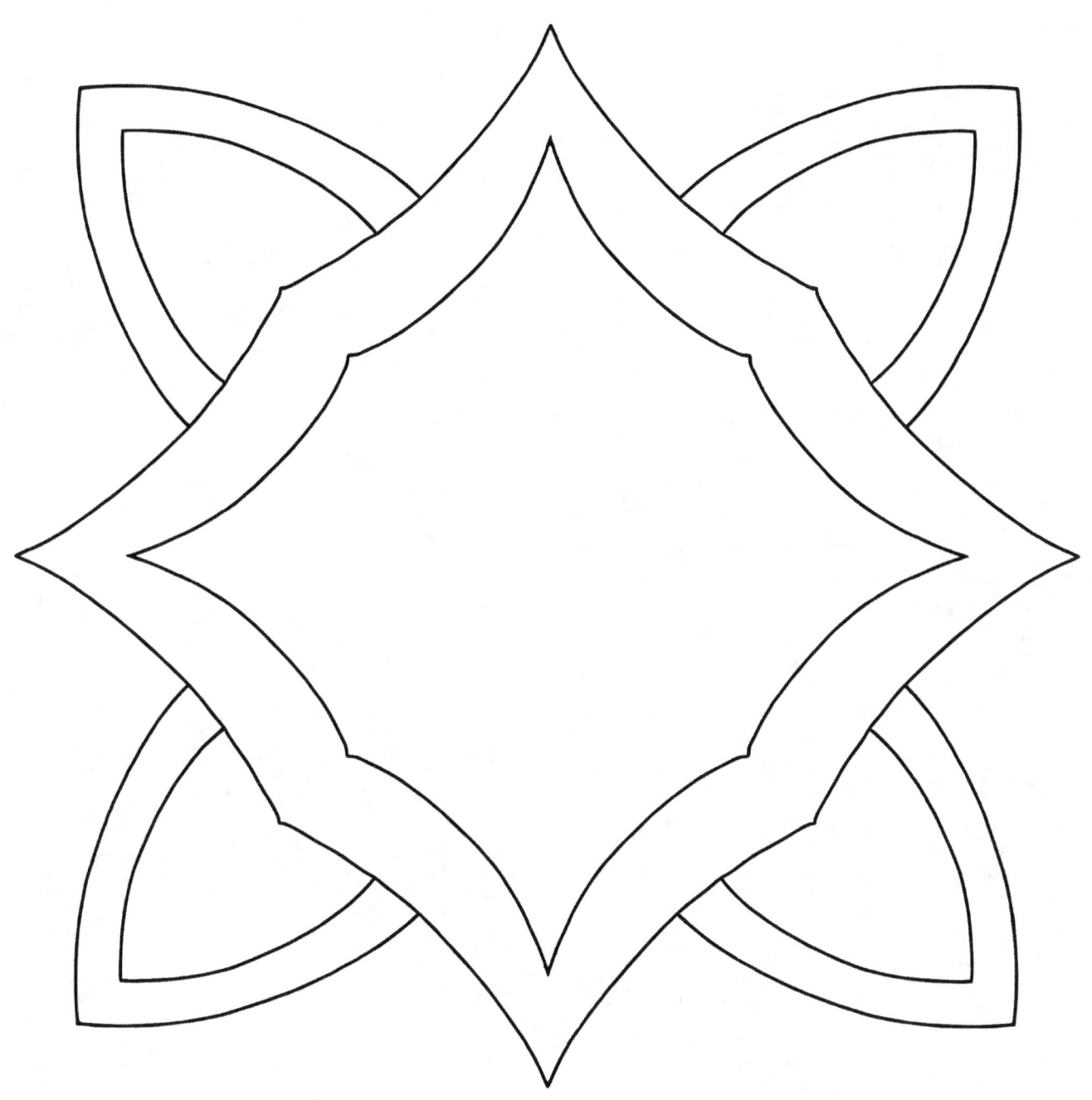

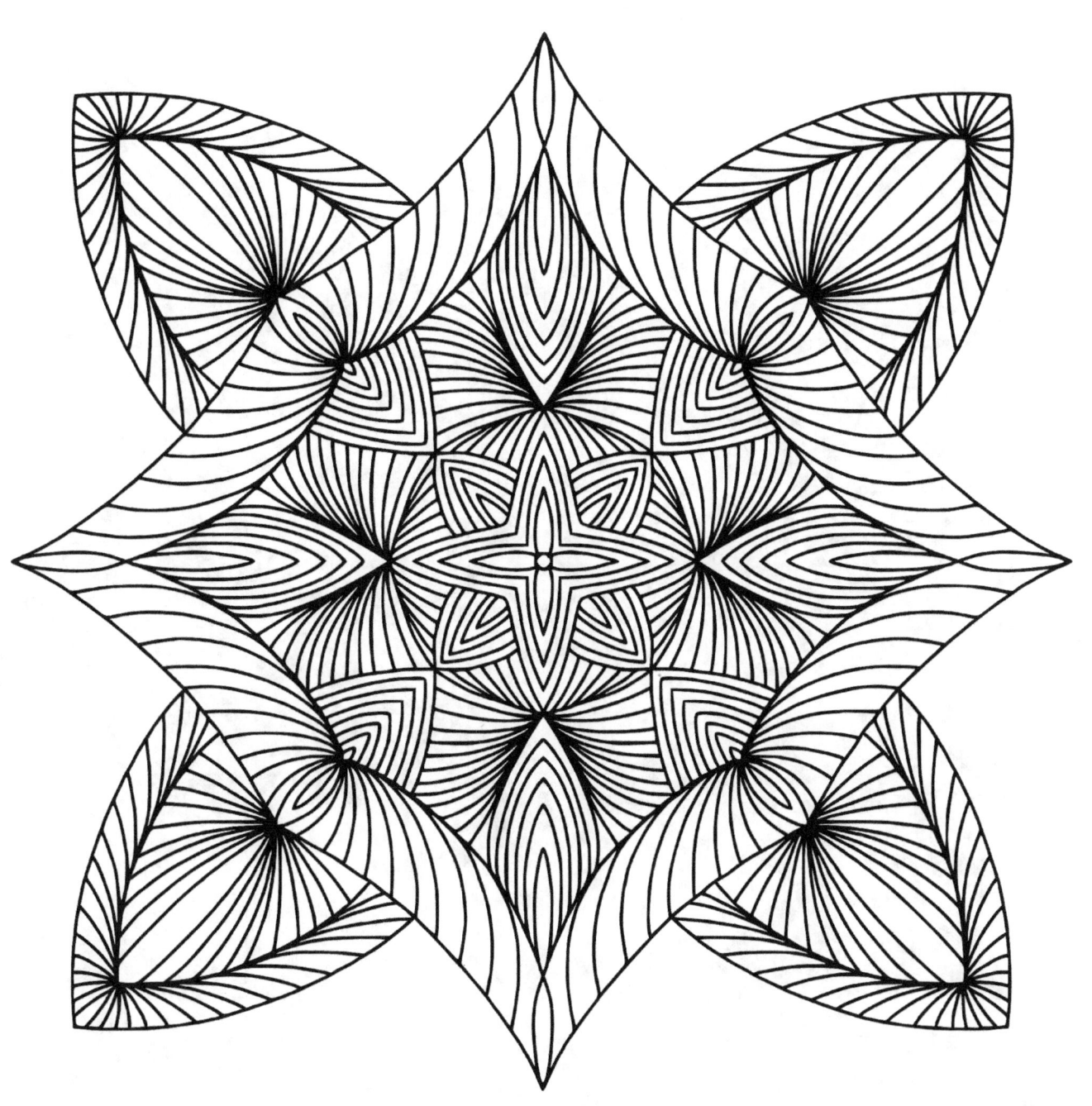

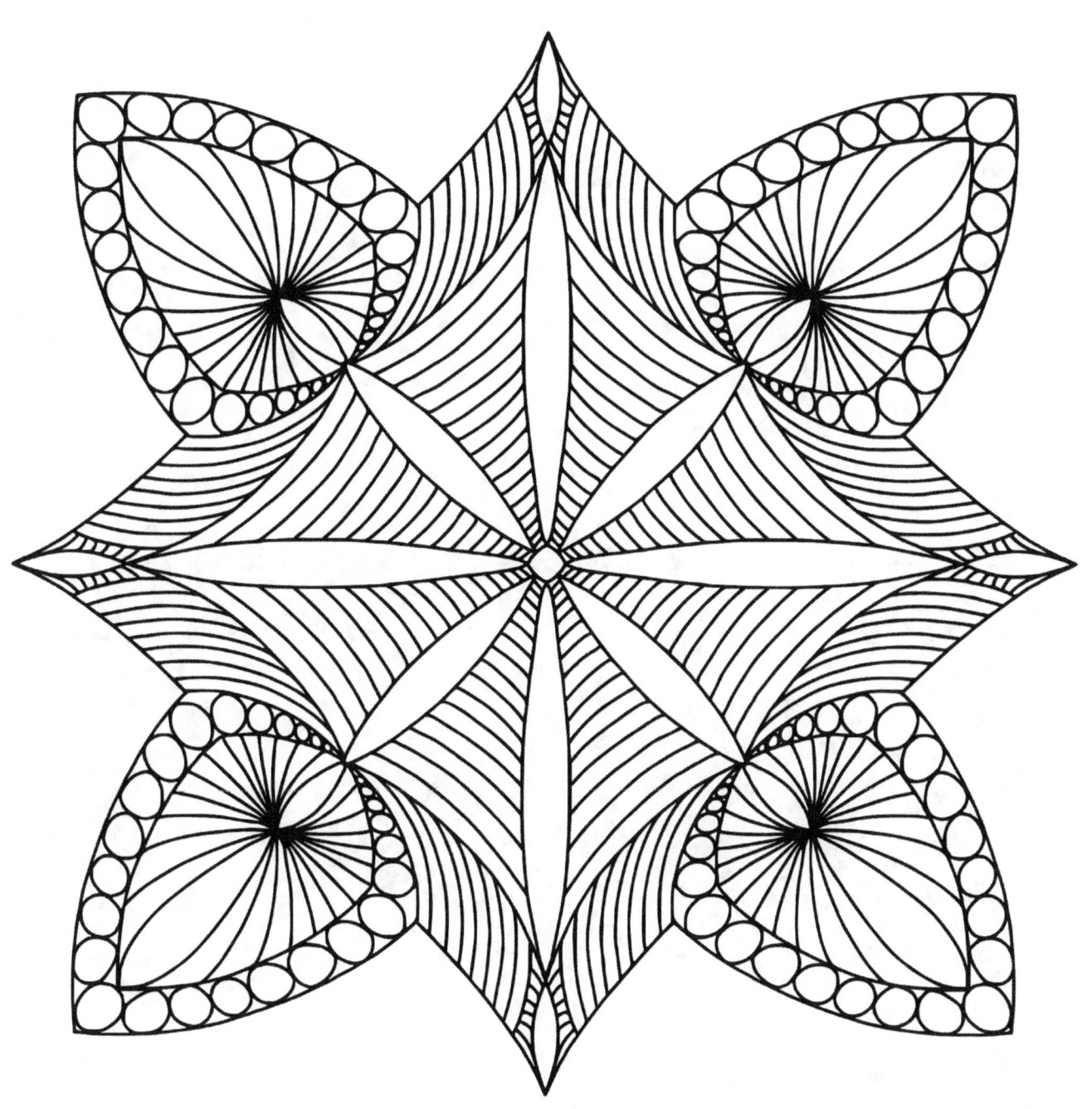

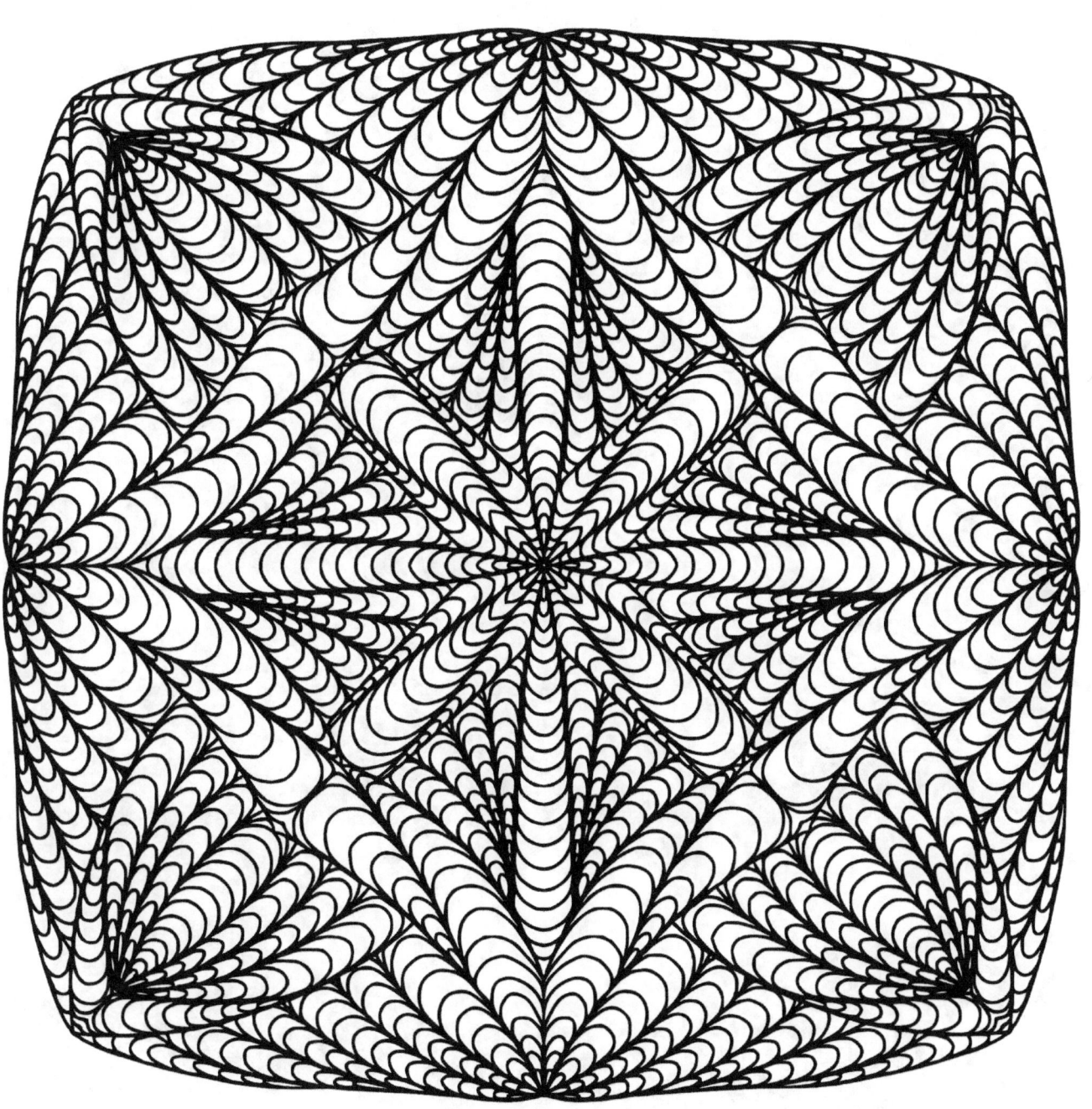

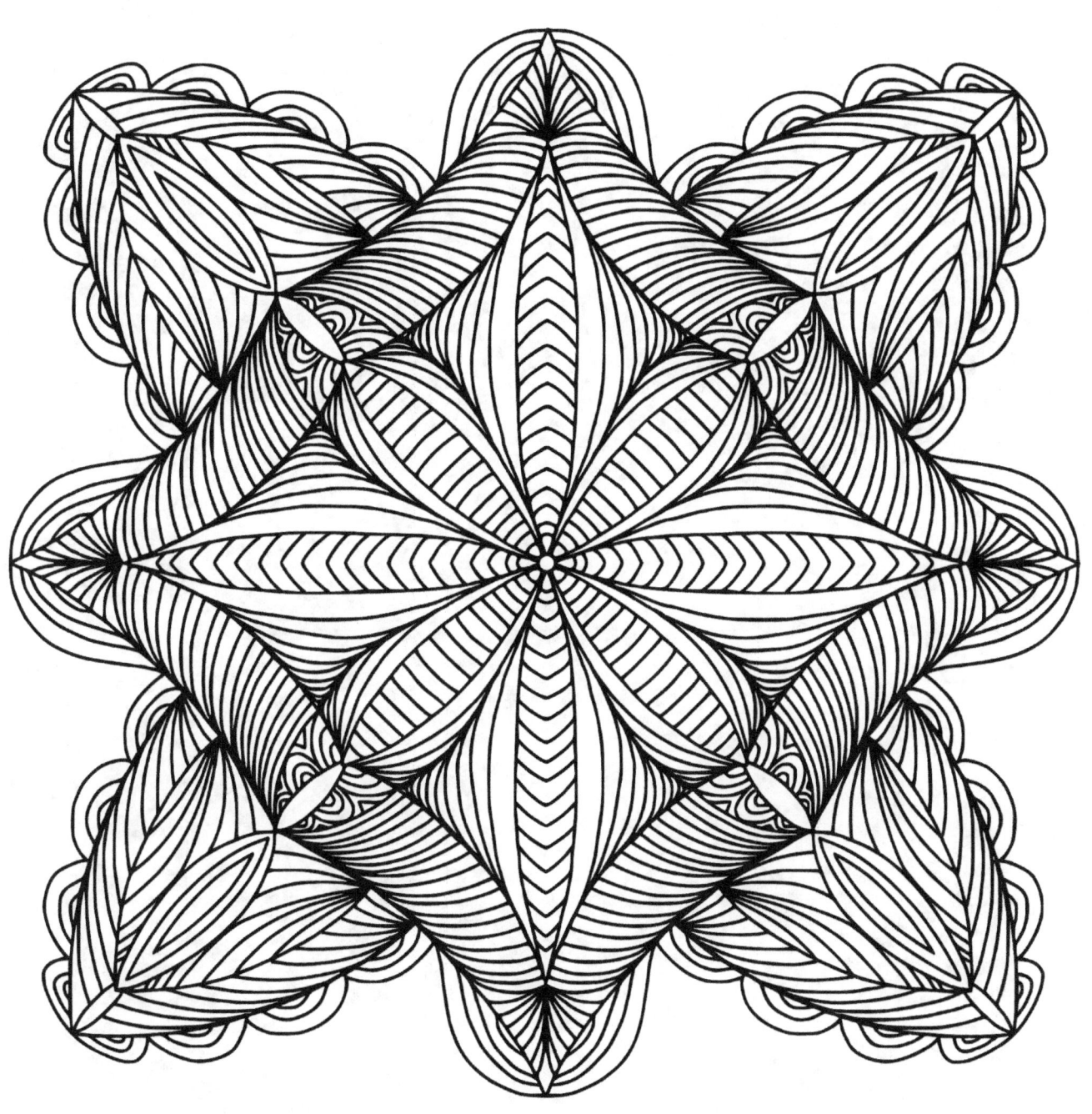

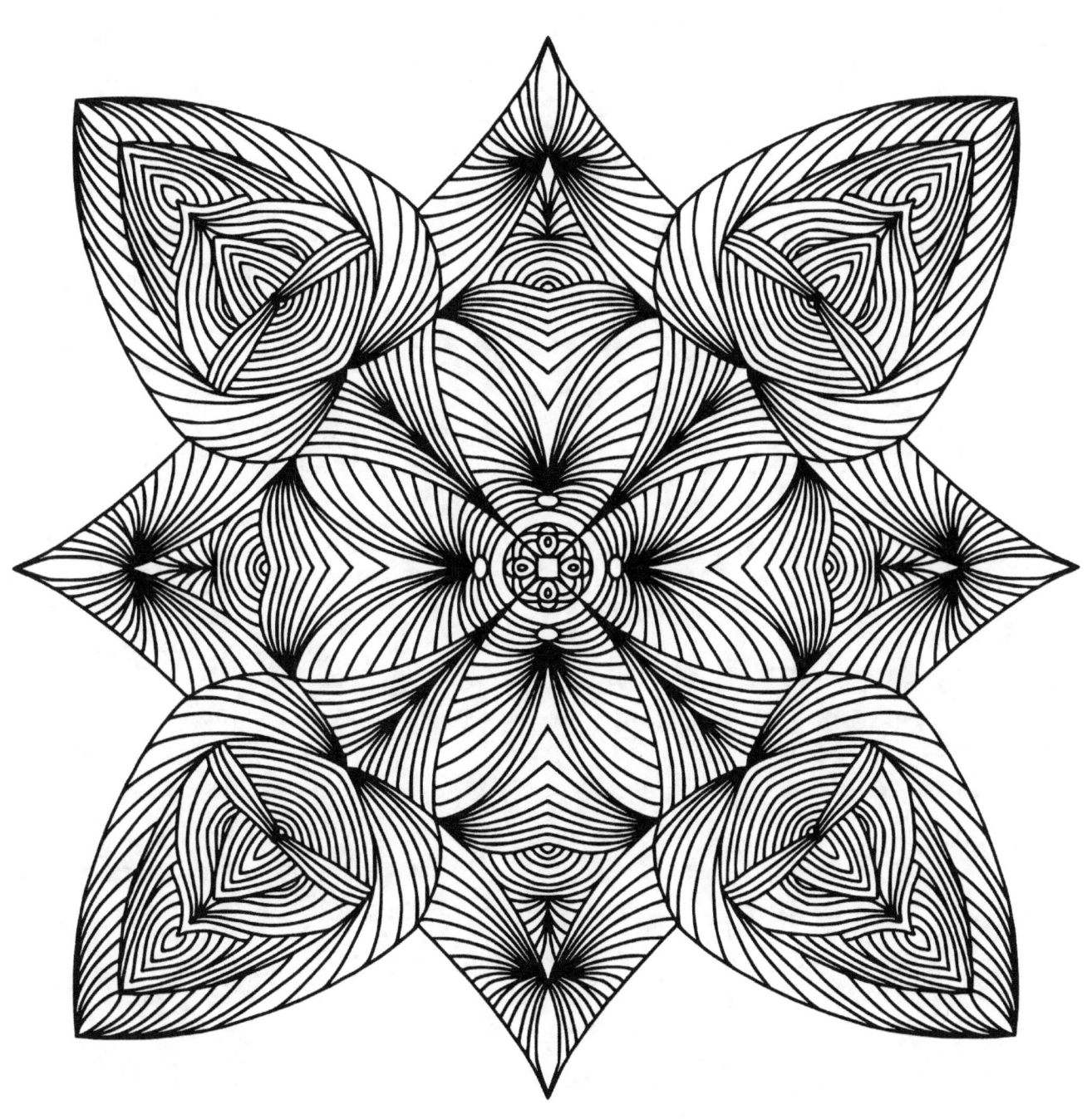

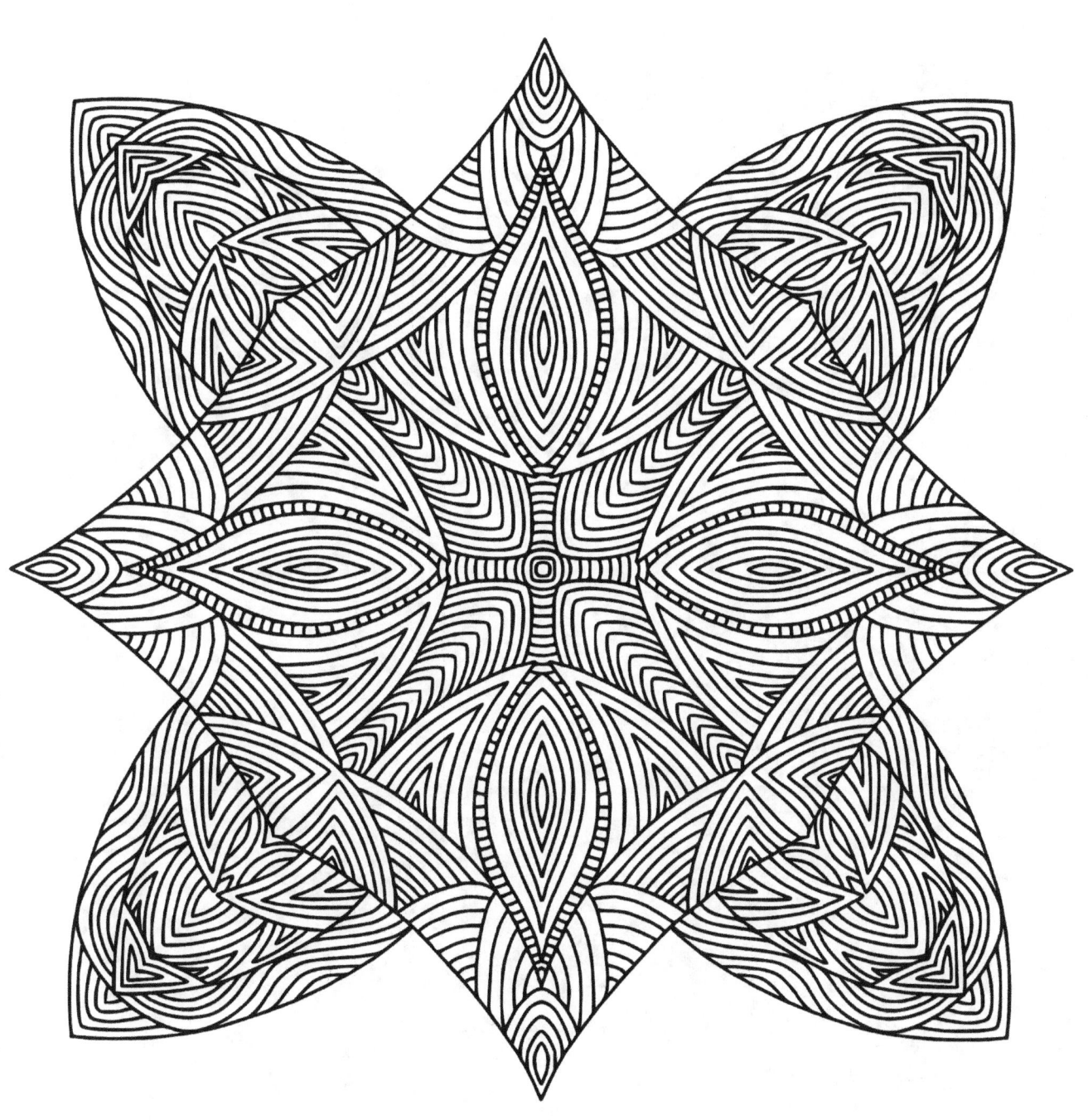

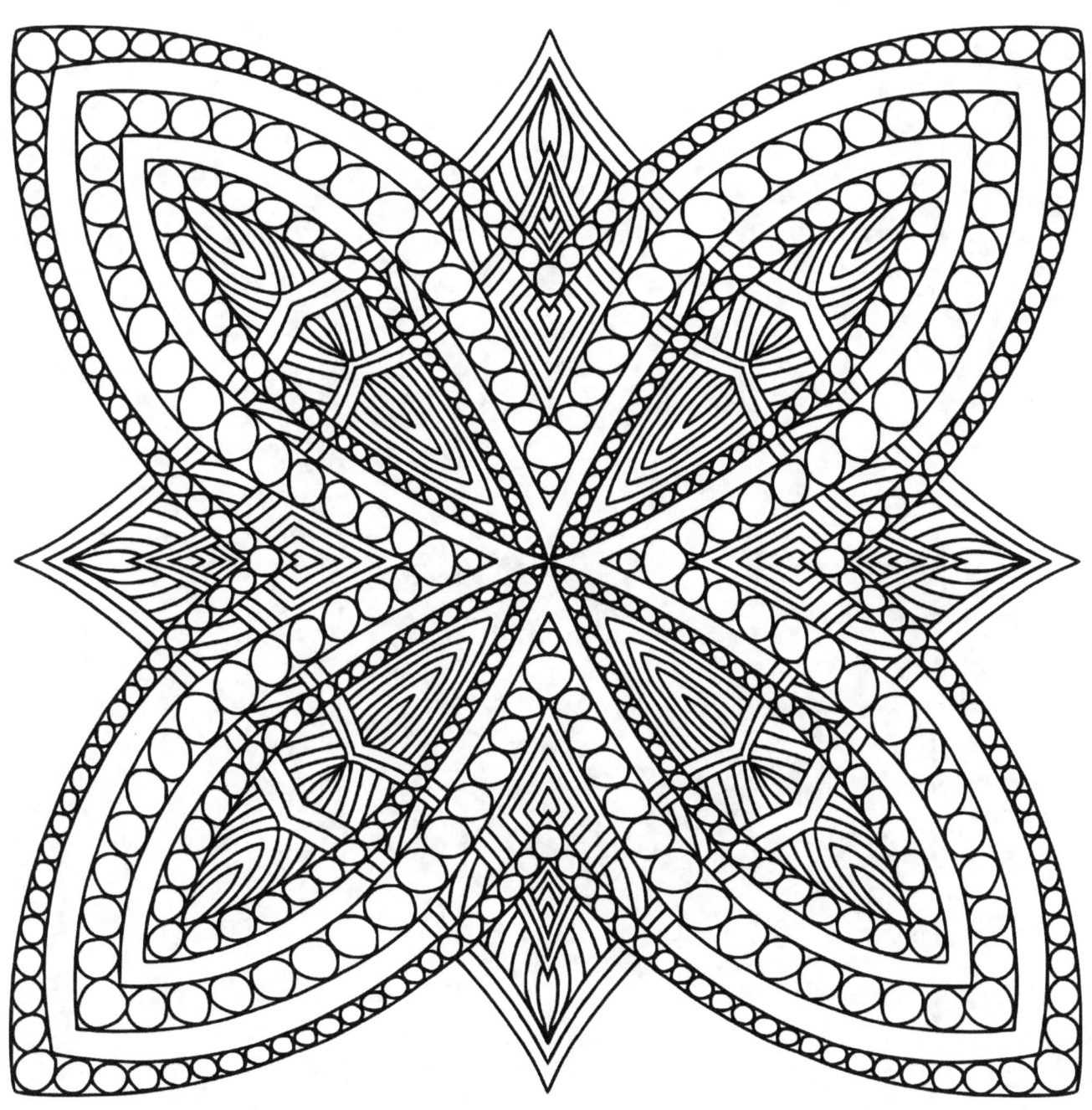

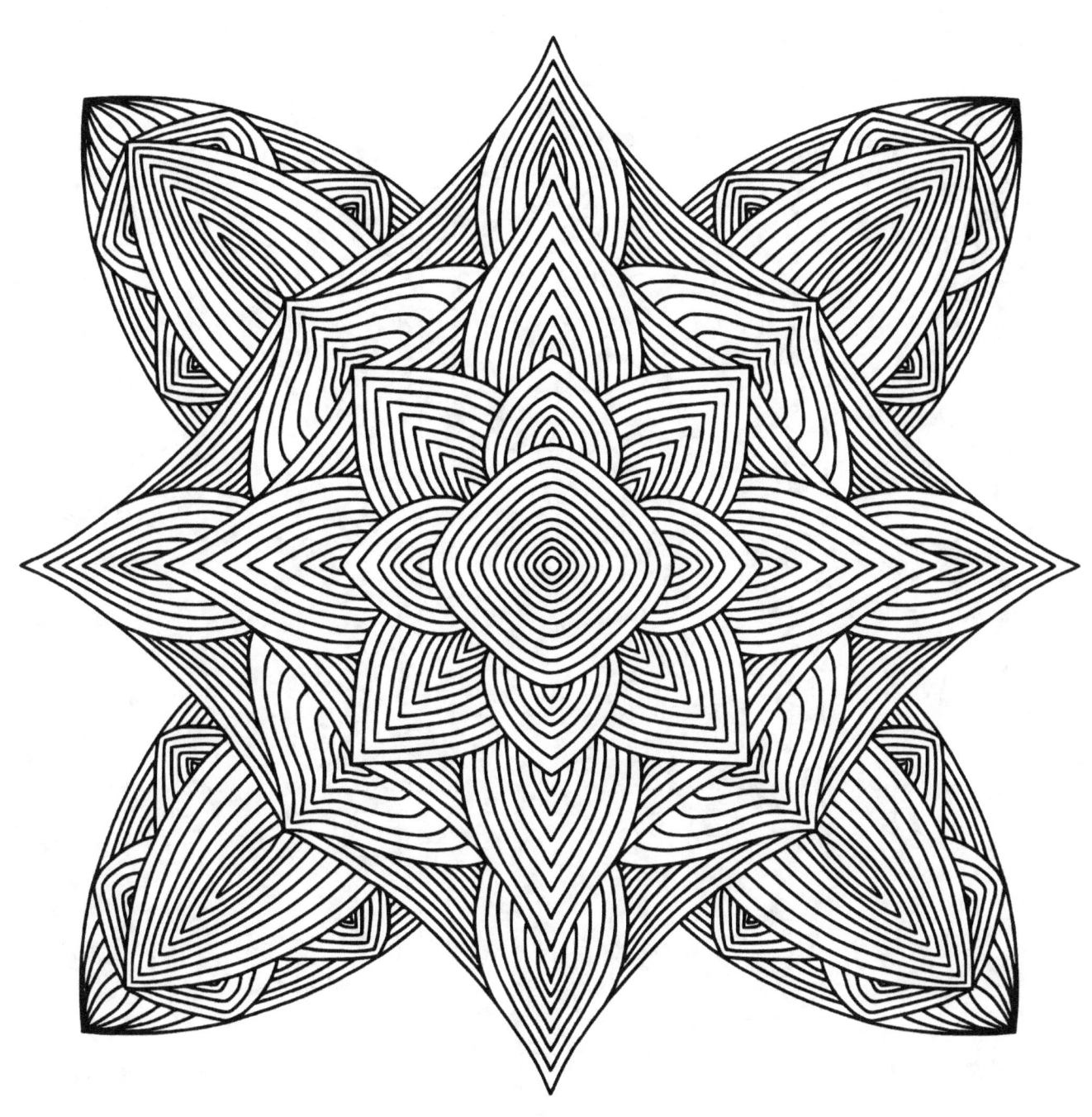

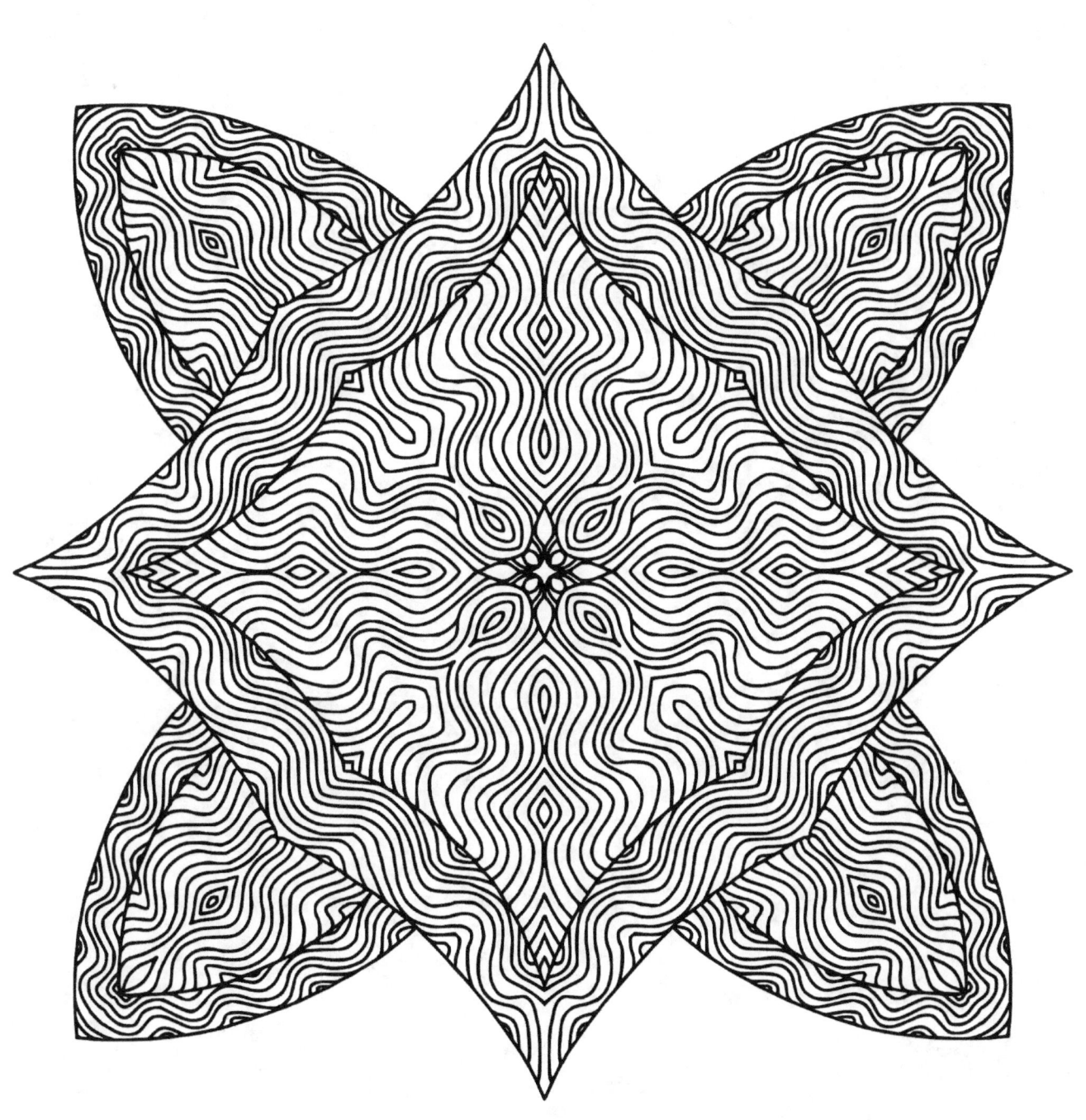

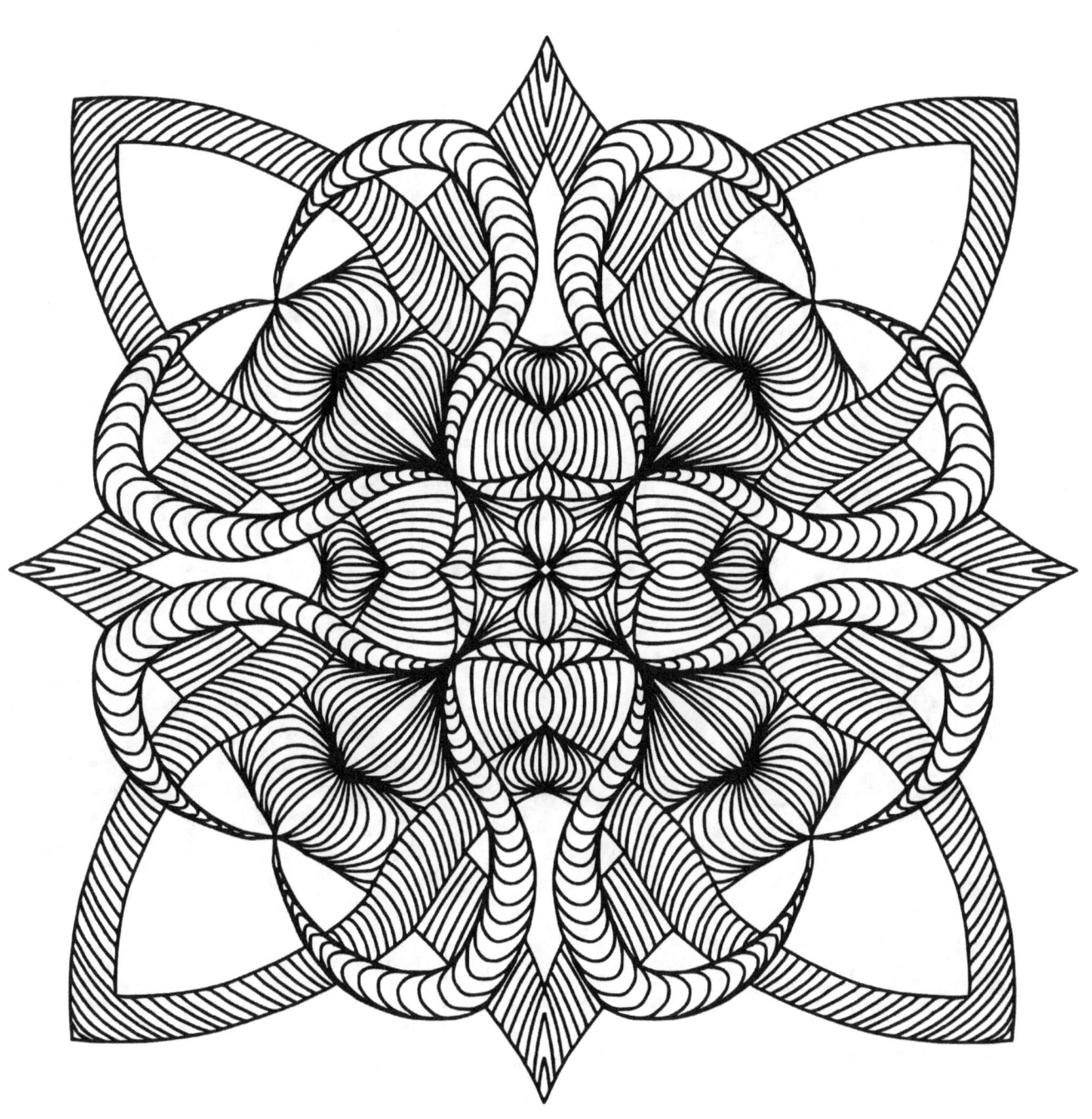

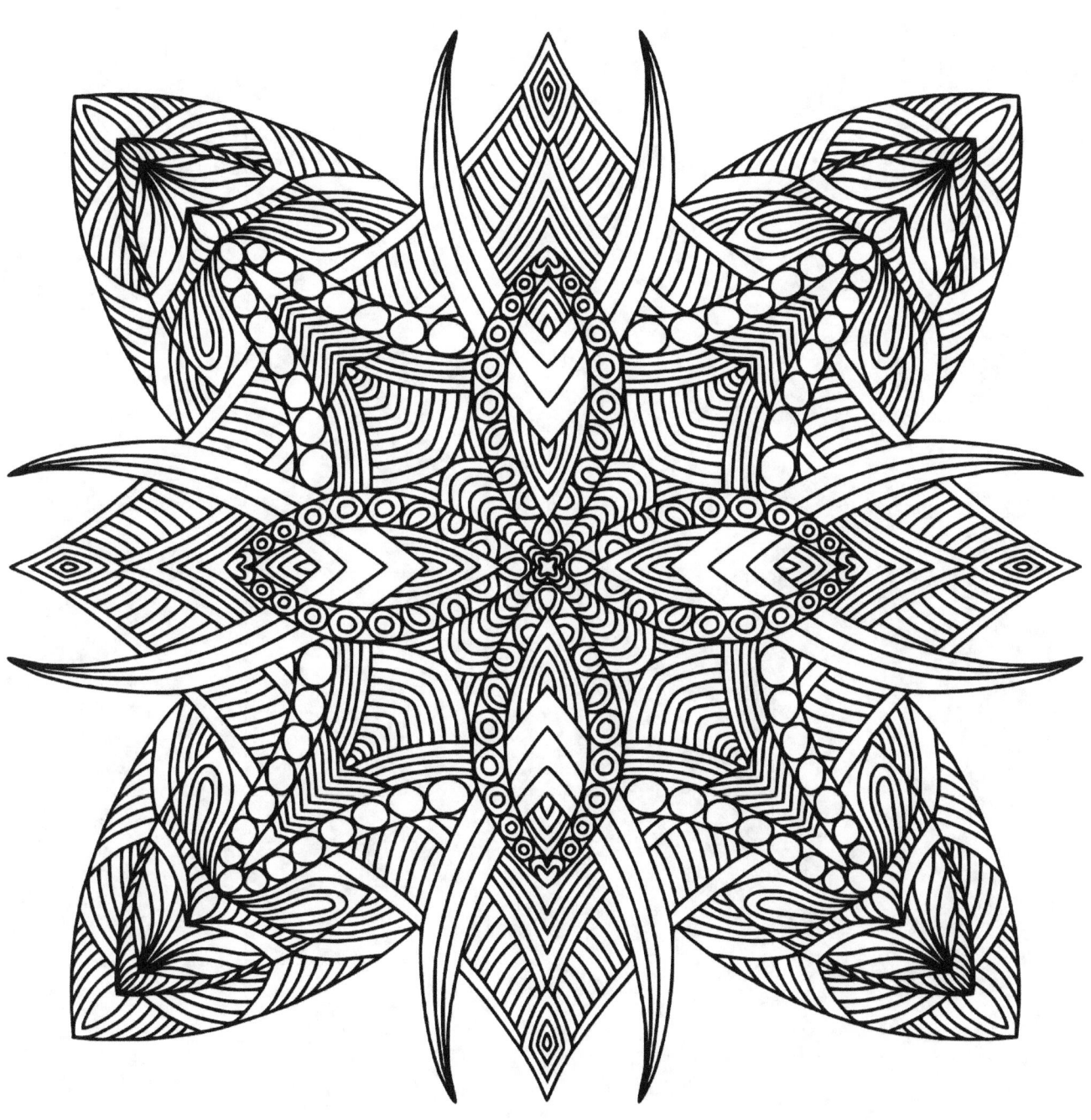

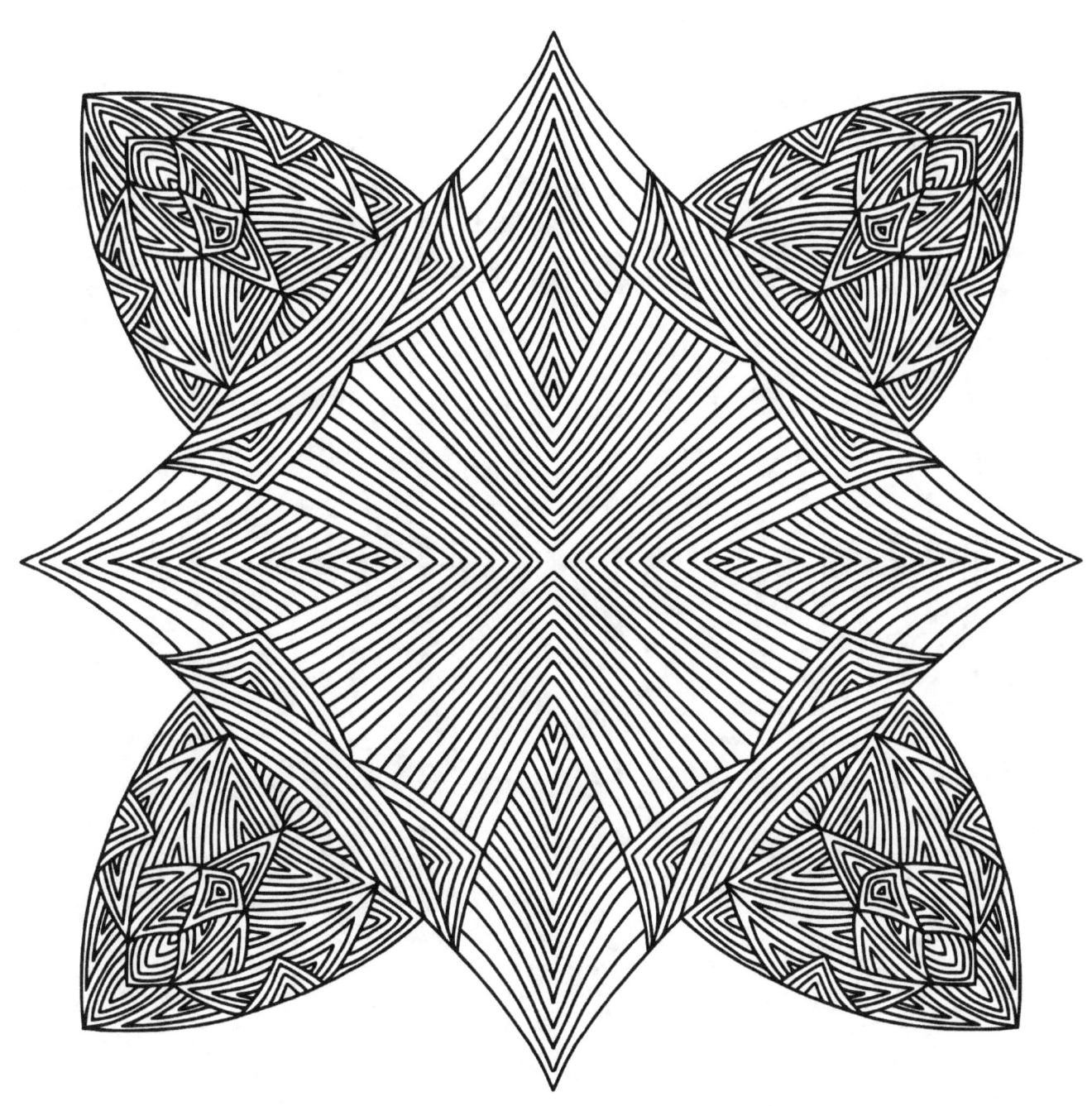

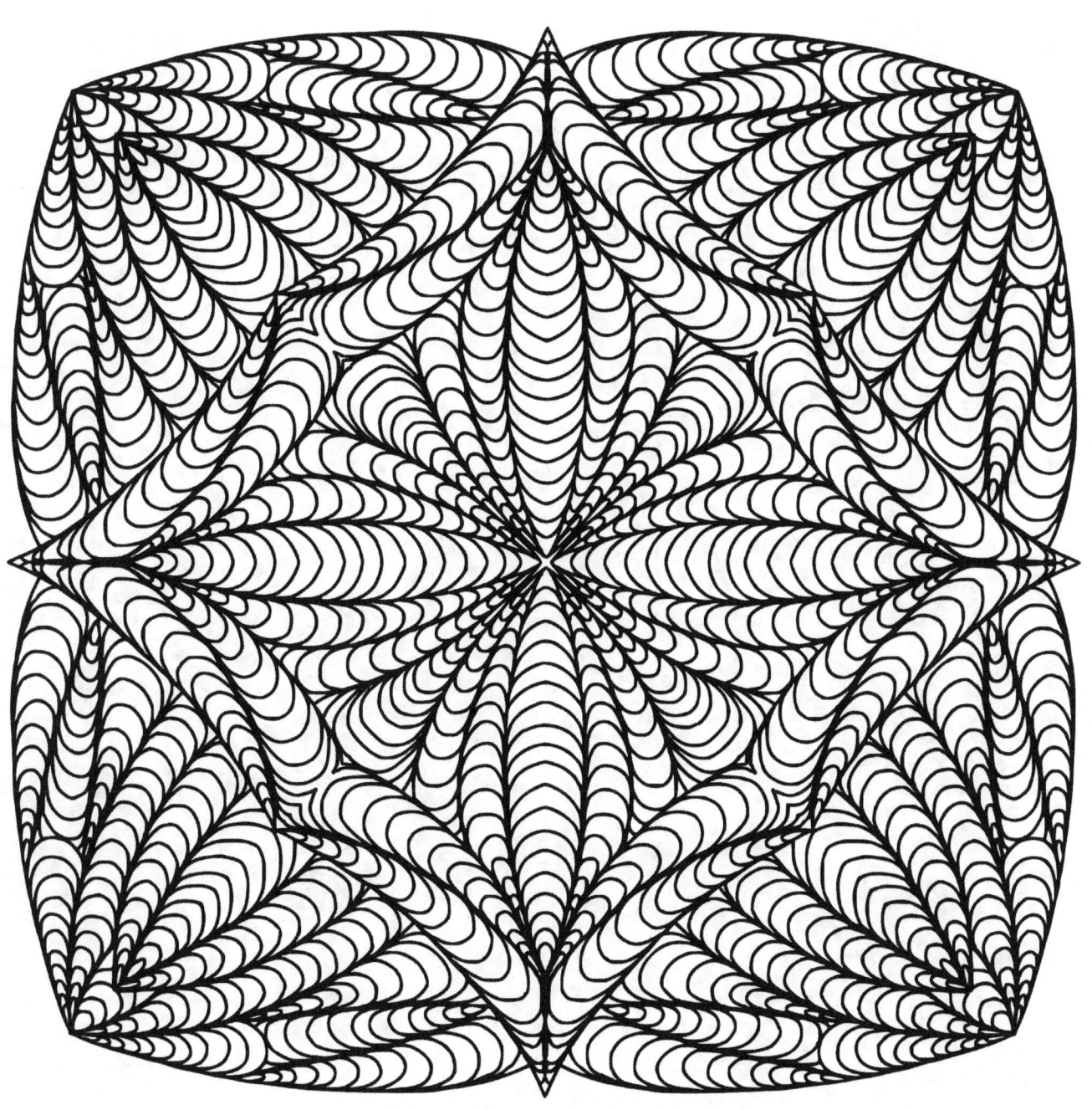

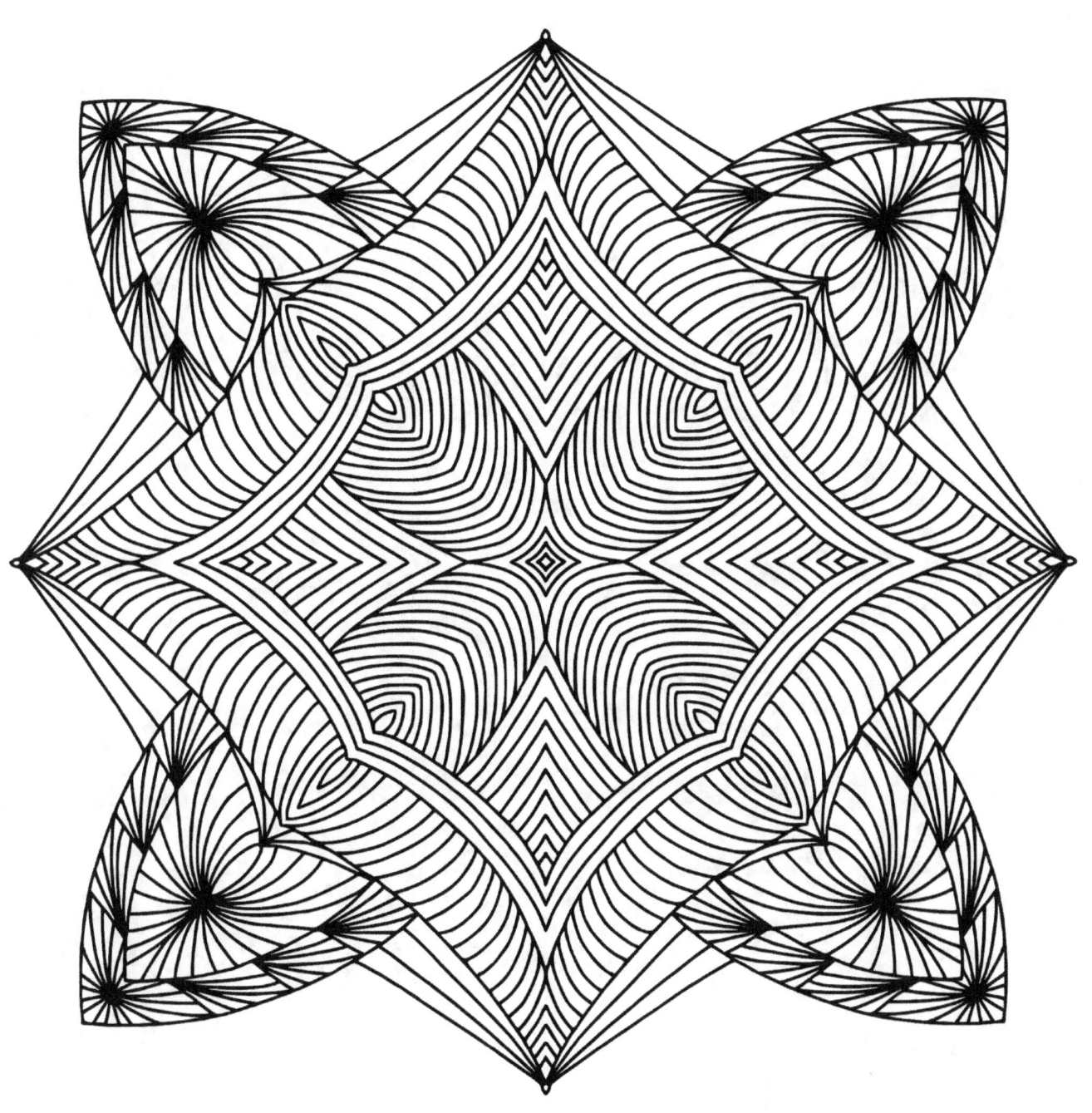

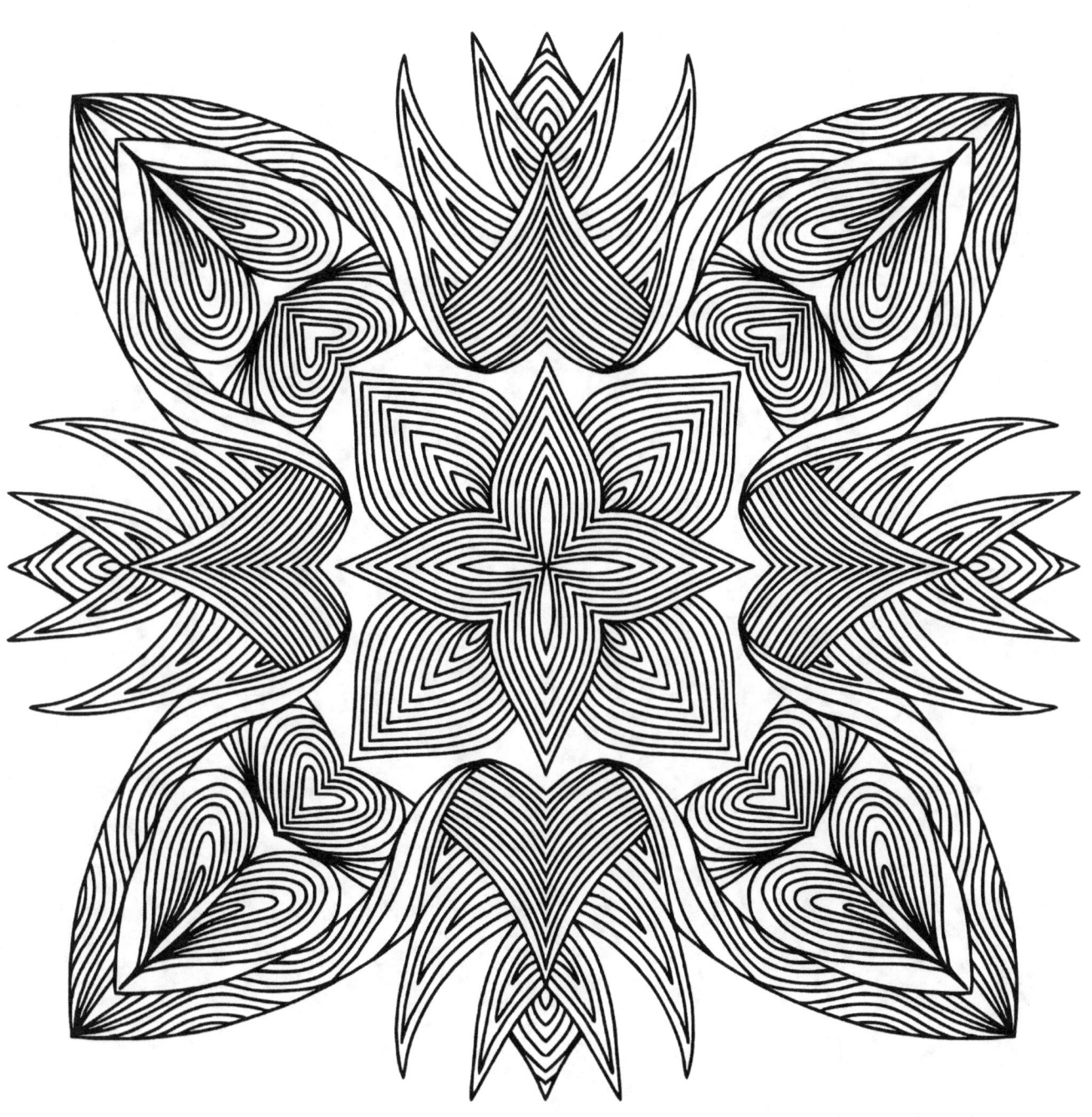

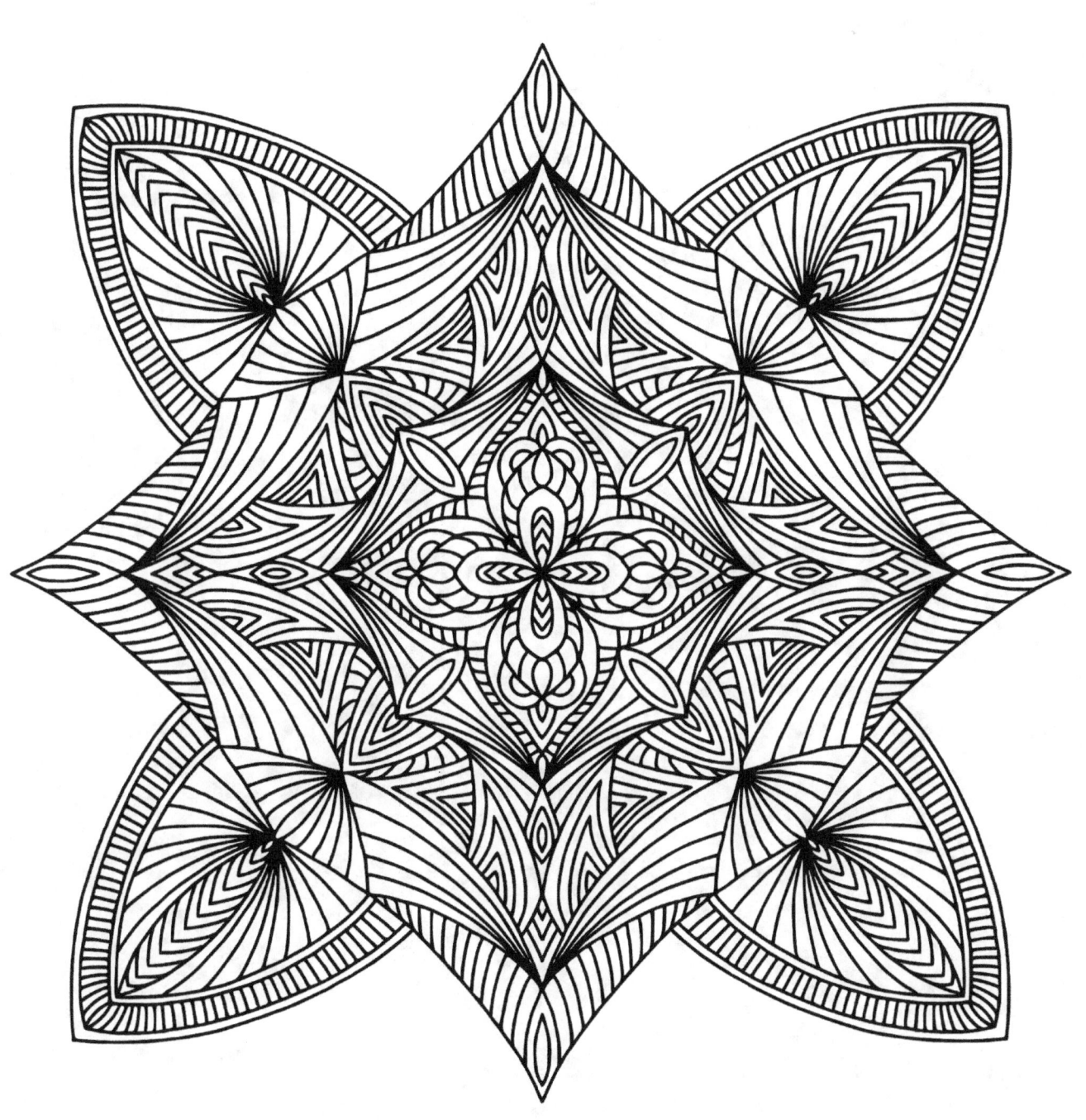

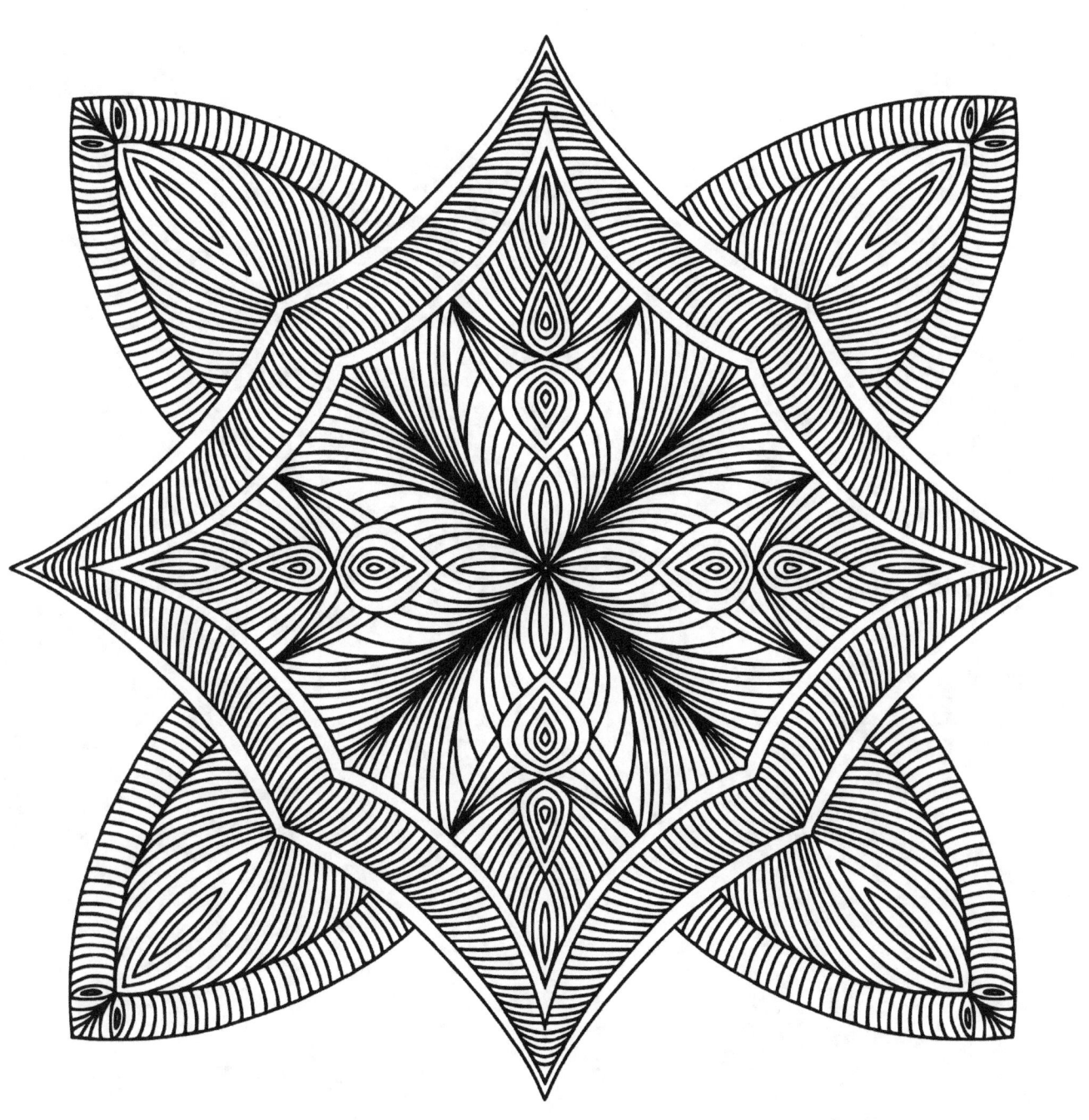

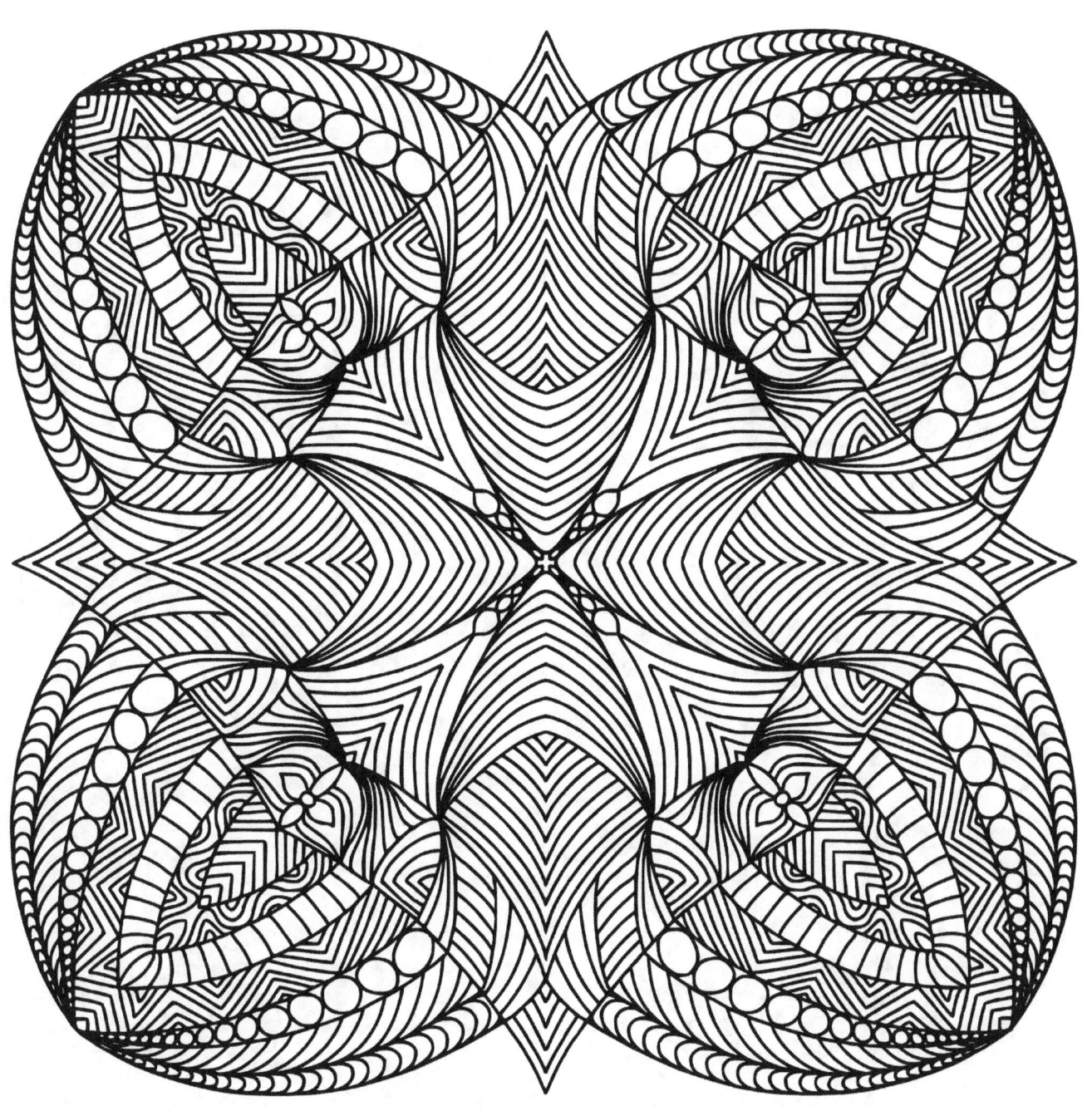

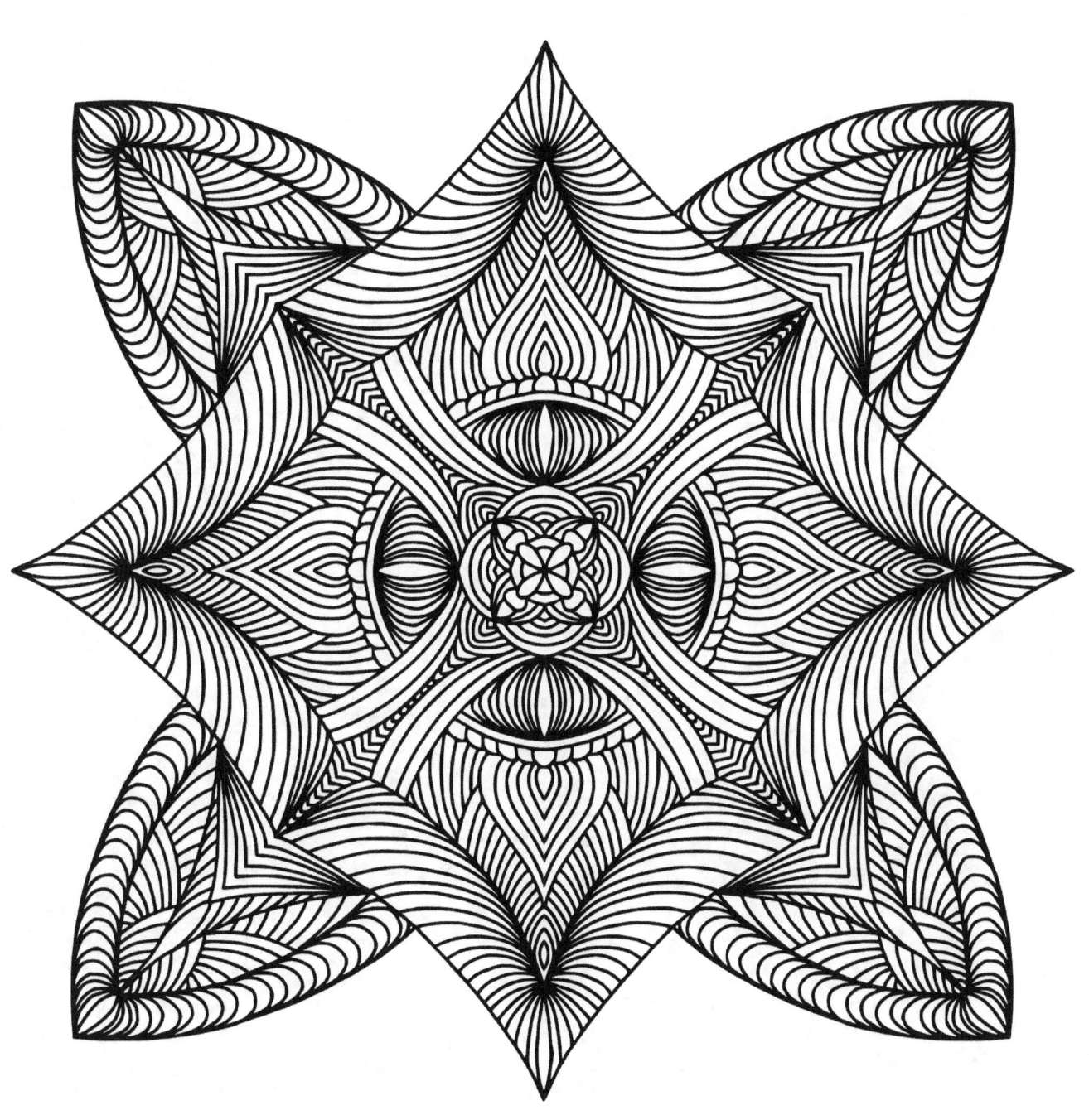

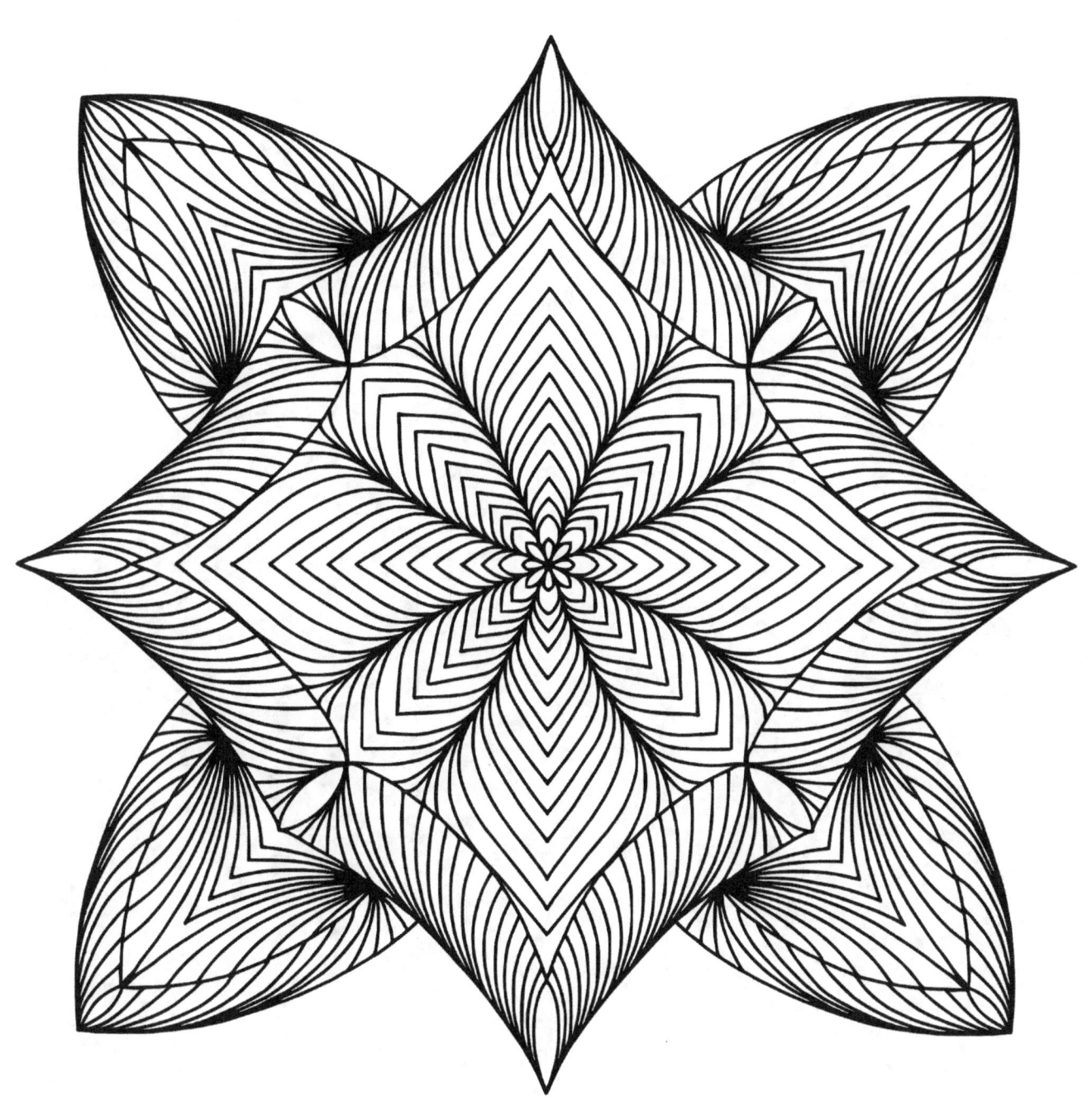

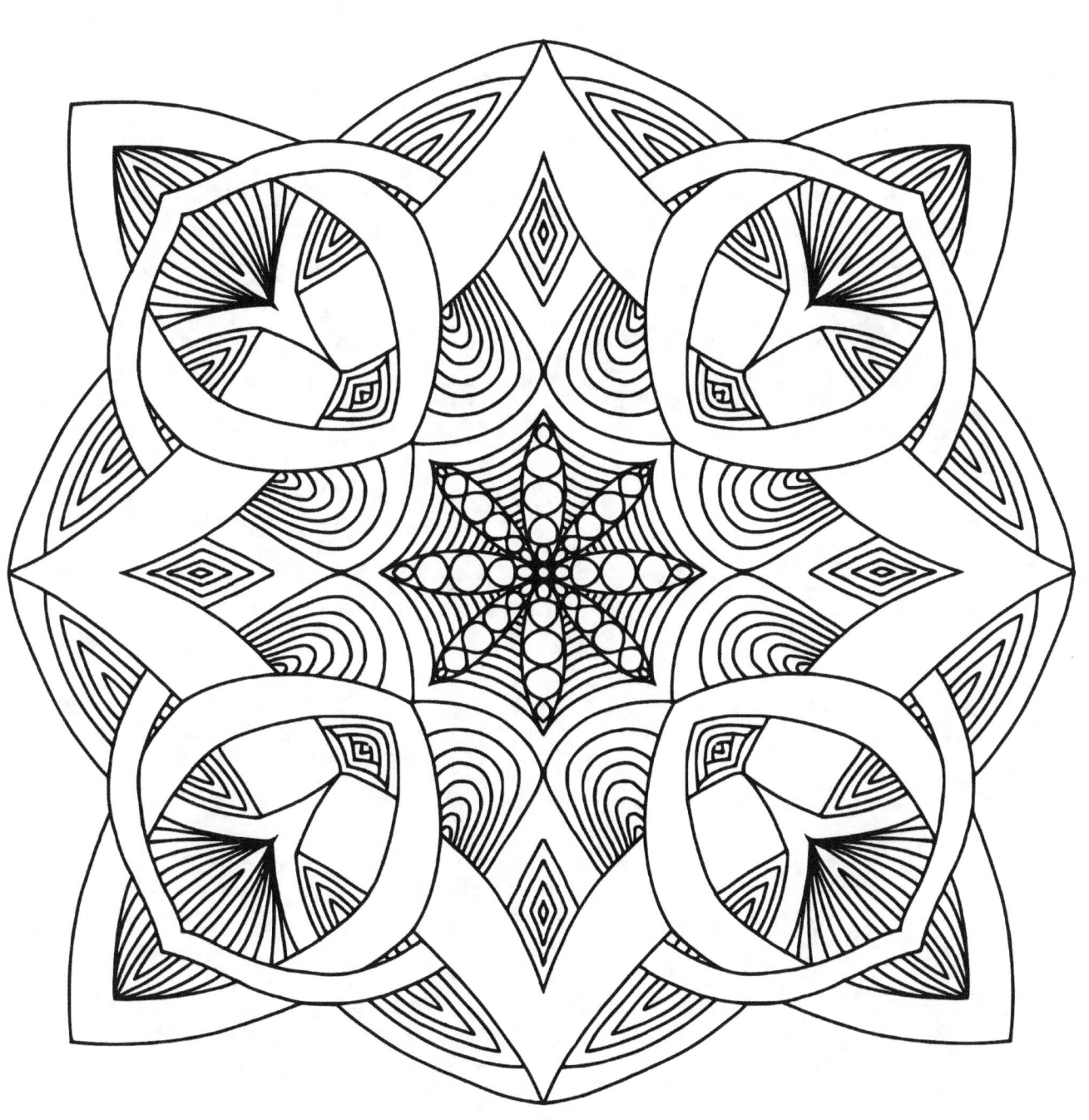

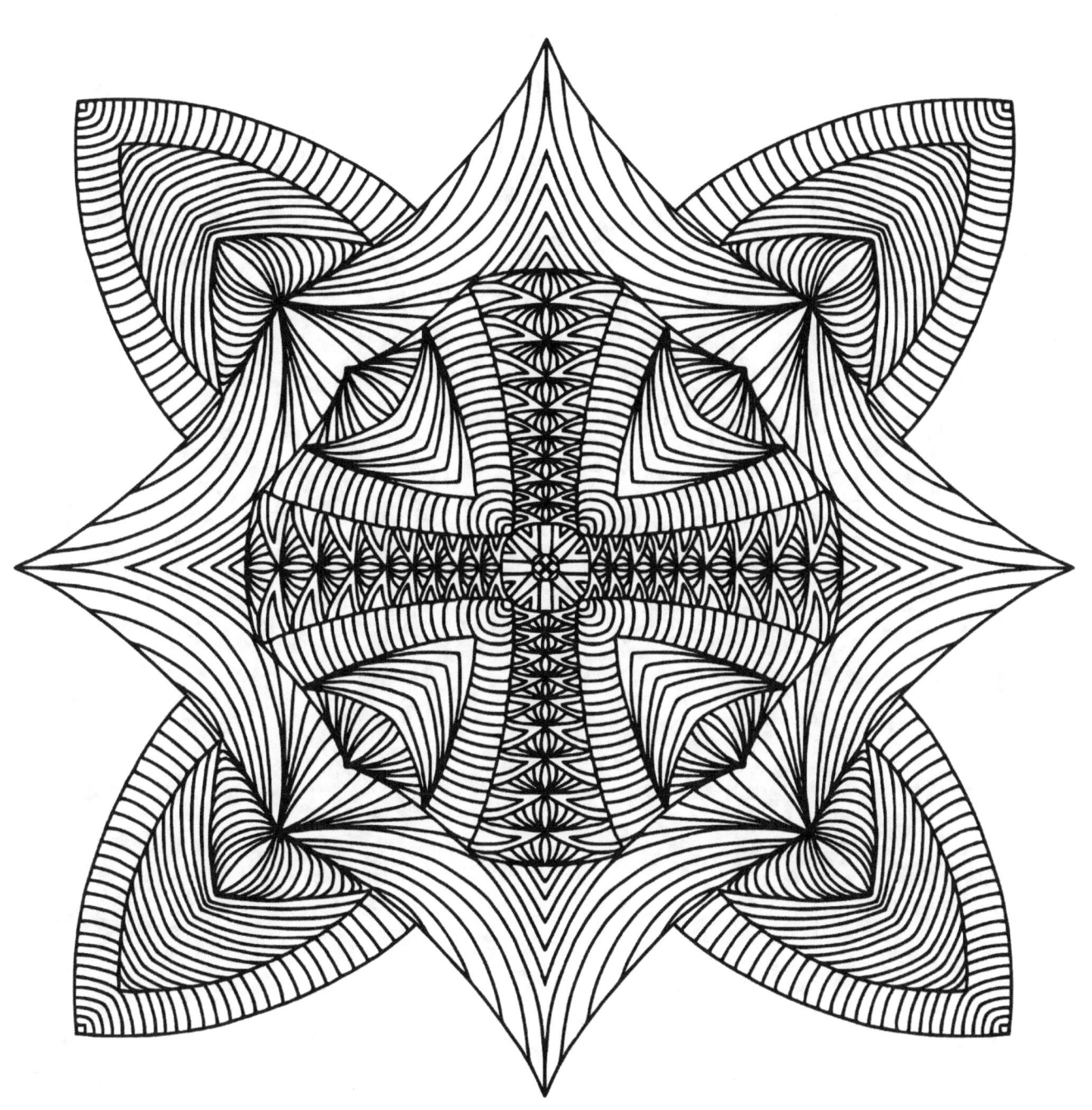

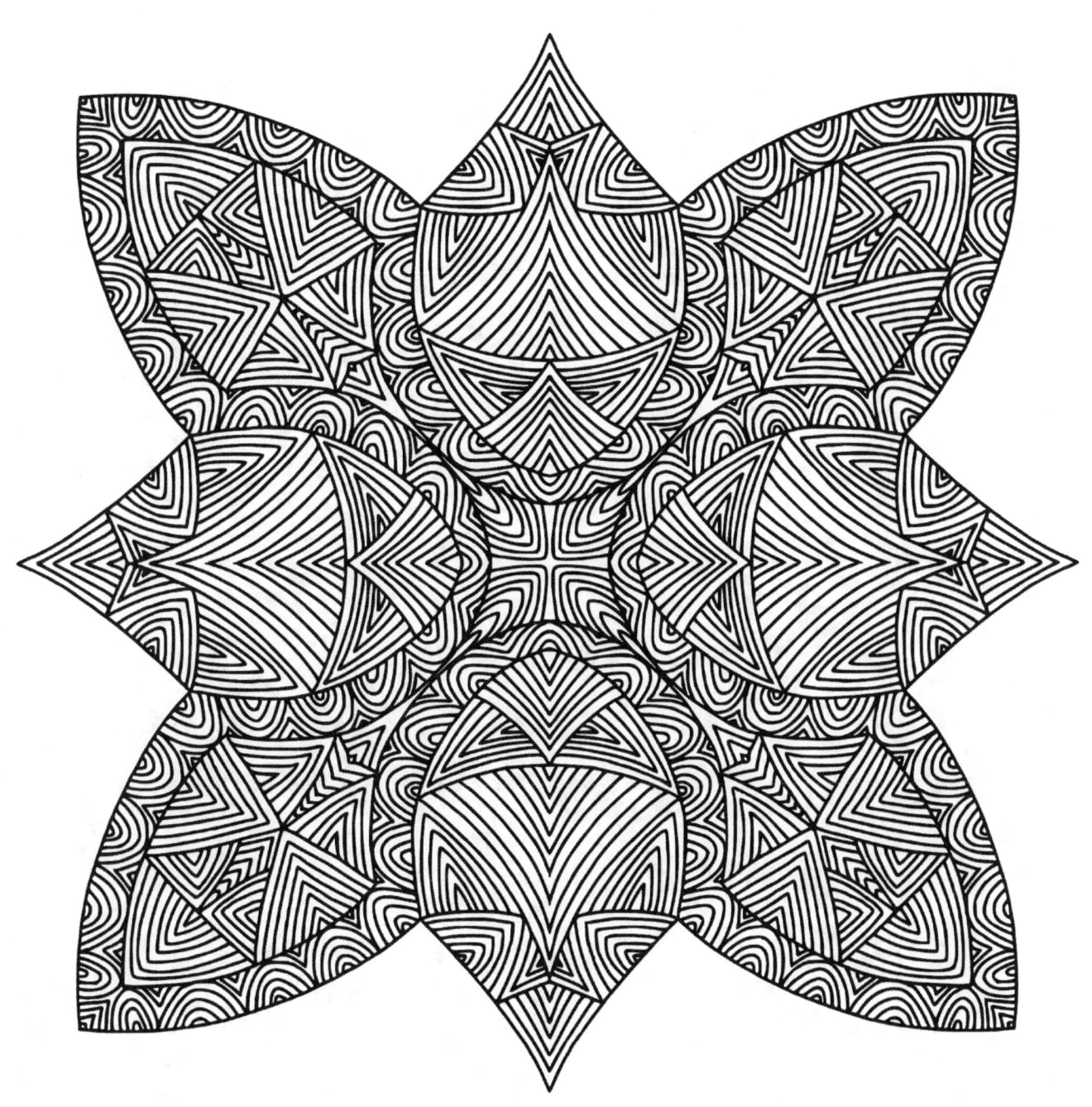

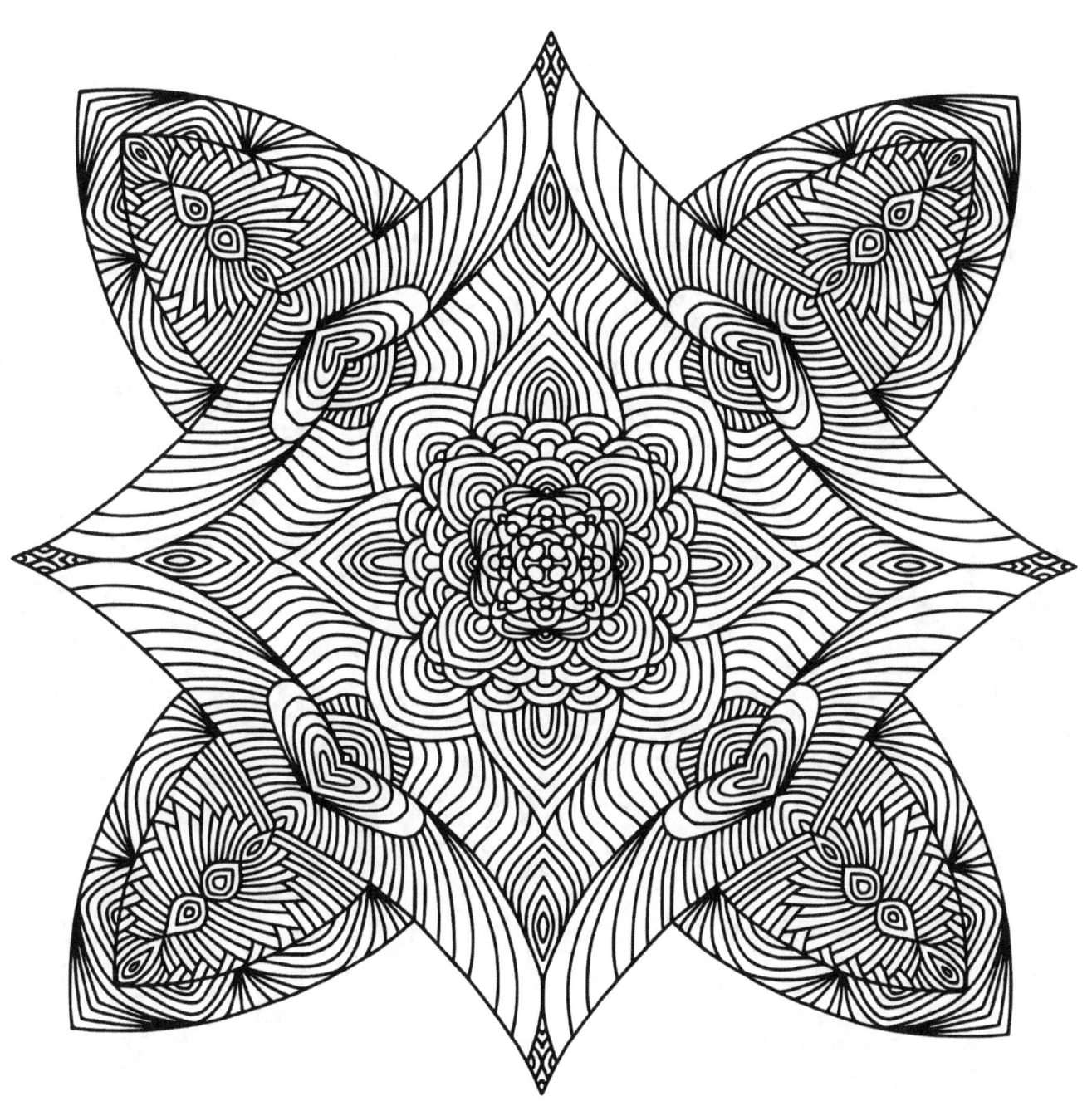

www.ingramcontent.com/pod-product-compliance
Lightning Source LLC
Chambersburg PA
CBHW082322220526
45470CB00008B/2383